Teaching to the Standards of Effective Practice

A Guide to Becoming a Successful Teacher

Robert Wandberg

Minnesota State University, Mankato

John Rohwer

Bethel College, St. Paul

Boston   New York   San Francisco
Mexico City   Montreal   Toronto   London   Madrid   Munich   Paris
Hong Kong   Singapore   Tokyo   Cape Town   Sydney

We dedicate this book to our families:

Our wives; Barb Wandberg and Marletta Rohwer
Our children; Heather and David, Brant and Jared

Your support for our work has made a significant difference

Executive Editor and Publisher: Stephen D. Dragin
Editorial Assistant: Barbara Strickland
Marketing Manager: Tara Whorf
Production Editor: Anna Socrates
Editorial Production Service: Chestnut Hill Enterprises, Inc.
Composition Buyer: Linda Cox
Manufacturing Buyer: Andrew Turso
Cover Administrator: Kristina Mose-Libon
Electronic Composition: Publishers' Design and Production Services, Inc.

For related titles and support materials, visit our online catalog at www.ablongman.com.

Between the time Website information is gathered and then published, it is not unusual for some sites to have closed. Also, the transcription of URLs can result in unintended typographical errors. The publisher would appreciate notification where these errors occur so that they may be corrected in subsequent editions.

Library of Congress Cataloging-in-Publication Data

Wandberg, Robert.
    Teaching to the standards of effective practice : a workbook to prepare and guide a successful teaching experience / Robert Wandberg, John Rohwer.
        p. cm.
    Includes bibliographical references and index.
    ISBN 0-205-34407-0
    1. Student teaching—Handbooks, manuals, etc. I. Rohwer, John. II. Title.

LB2157 .W36 2003
370'.71—dc21

2002026045

Printed in the United States of America
10 9 8 7 6 5 4 3 2 1   08 07 06 05 04 03 02

Contents

12   *Beyond Student Teaching*   249

Appendices   271

A   *Professional Organizations*   271

B   *State Certification Offices*   273

C   *Job Fair Record Form*   277

Foreword

Over the years, I have listened to stories of student teachers. The joys and frustrations shared by them reveal field experiences and clinical practices that vary from benign neglect, to regimentation that dismisses enjoyment, to meaningful collaboration with valued colleagues. Likewise, other experienced educators, have expressed similar feelings of hope or bewilderment through their involvement and work with student teachers.

I am more convinced than ever that pre-service practice in a classroom must be a consistent and concerted partnership. *Teaching to the Standards of Effective Practice* sets the agenda. Mentoring that occurs between a cooperating teacher or university supervisor and the student assigned as an apprentice is not a singular shot of advice. Induction is not synonymous with indoctrination. Nor should it be left to fate or a magic wand. Without thoughtful, intentional preparation and timely, genuine feedback, field experiences and clinical practice are, at best, sterile independent studies.

Teaching to the Standards of Effective Practice is about being able to effectively communicate the reality and mystique of education. Using the Interstate New Teacher Assessment and Support Consortium (INTASC) Standards as a basis to navigate the complexity of education provides common ground for the preparation of future teachers.

Negotiating personal and professional terrain during a period of intense change requires profound commitment and perseverance. Knowing what, when, where, how, and why is a decision-making process that is compounded by the diversity inherent in and among individuals, the demographics of a classroom, and the dynamics of the school in the community.

Learners, regardless of their age, construct meaning from their many experiences. Success in the teaching profession requires a strong foundation. Preparation to act with knowledge, insight, and skill in the education profession begins with a series of well-designed opportunities that can be replicated or generalized with automaticity in real situations. If the agreed-upon concepts and behaviors of the profession are worth knowing and practicing, then experienced educational veterans must be actively involved in guiding the novice learner.

Teaching to the Standards of Effective Practice exemplifies the notion that teaching is not for the underprepared. While true that precarious beginnings can have successful endings, auspicious first experiences—where the entry-level teacher is equipped with confidence as a result of knowledge and skill building using a network of support—are more desirable. The enthusiasm of a young teacher matched with the experience of a professional create an environment where mutual respect and trust precipitate the discovery of strengths and when necessary, the amelioration of weaknesses.

The authors and other expert commentators in *Teaching to the Standards of Effective Practice* consistently reinforce the INTASC Standards of the profession by creating a forum for dialogue and active participation. They utilize what they know to be useful in preparing young educators to be successful in their chosen vocation. These are seasoned educators who model best practice in using subject matter knowledge, understanding student diversity, designing instructional strategies, managing learning environments, communicating, planning instruction, assessing and evaluating, reflecting on the profession, collaborating, and building relationships.

Teaching to the Standards of Effective Practice affirms the notion that education should not be a mystery, left to chance, myth, or media perceptions.

The text sets a standard for excellence by aligning with standards that guide one to a clear understanding of why they do what they do. It creates a vision of expectations that leads the way in dispelling the idea that anyone can walk in the schoolhouse door ready to teach.

Roberta Brack Kaufman, Dean
College of Education
Concordia University
St. Paul, Minnesota

Preface

Using Teaching to the Standards of Effective Practice

"A caring teacher hands children their passport to the future."—*Jenlane Gee*

The purpose of *Teaching to the Standards of Effective Practice* is to provide students in teacher preparation programs with the wisdom and ultimately the confidence to complete a successful experience that leads to favorable and productive career options.

Together, the two authors have over 60 years of experience working as classroom teachers, cooperating teachers, and university supervisors of student teachers. Some of the challenges that teachers face are similar to challenges of years past; some are new and emerging challenges of the 21st century. *Teaching to the Standards of Effective Practice* focuses on many of those challenges by presenting information and activities designed to assist pre-service teachers in completing a successful student experience. The information is research based. The activities require action and reflection.

Teaching to the Standards of Effective Practice can serve as a valuable resource book prior to, during, and following the preparation for becoming a teacher.

Prior to student teaching, it can provide considerable preparatory insight into the dimensions and reality of teaching. The information and activities can diminish many of the questions and concerns students typically have about teaching.

During the actual student teaching experience, the activities and information found in here can equip the student teacher with the knowledge and skill that will empower sound decision making and problem solving in the areas of teaching and learning. This is an important component in the development of classroom confidence.

Following the student teaching experience, student teachers are often faced with many decisions and possible directions to consider. *Teaching to the Standards of Effective Practice* can provide information and activities that will increase the student's capacity to make well-informed decisions. Helpful hints regarding the job market, résumés, and interviews are just some of the important and timely topics.

It is our hope that pre-service teachers will complete their experience with a solid background and a sound understanding of the complexities of teaching and learning and that many of the mysteries of teaching will have disappeared.

Acknowledgments

The authors take pleasure in recognizing and offering a special thank you and appreciation to several individuals for their thoughtful insights, suggestions, and contributions this textbook:

Roberta Brack Kaufman, Dean at Concordia University's College of Education in St. Paul, Minnesota.

Chet Bradley, Region II Director at Cardinal Stritch University's College of Education in Madison, Wisconsin.

Clint E. Bruess, Ed.D., CHES, Dean Emeritus and Professor at University of Alabama Birmingham's School of Education and Department of Human Studies in Birmingham, Alabama.

Carol Cummings, Ph.D., Educational Consultant, Author, and Researcher at Seattle Pacific University in Seattle, Washington.

Charlotte Danielson, Lead Developer at Educational Testing Service in Princeton, New Jersey.

Diane Hoffbauer, Ed.D., Director of Curriculum and Instruction at North Slope Borough School District in Barrow, Alaska.

Susan J. Moore, Student Teaching Supervisor at Minnesota State University in Mankato, Minnesota.

Glenn Olson, Principal of Ipalook Elementary School in North Slope Borough School District, Barrow, Alaska.

Mary J. Otto, Student Teaching Supervisor at Minnesota State University in Mankato, Minnesota.

Tracy Pellett, Ed.D., Director of Clinical & Field Experiences for Minnesota State University's College of Education in Mankato, Minnesota.

Ann C. Slater, Ed.D., CHES, Lead Teacher/Strategies for Success at White Knoll High School in Lexington School District One, Lexington, South Carolina.

Jay B. Rasmussen, Ph.D., Professor of Education and Director of Graduate Programs in Education at Bethel College in St. Paul, Minnesota.

Kathleen M. Rourke, Ph.D., RN, CHES, Associate Dean at Indiana University of Pennsylvania's College of Health and Human Services in Indiana, Pennsylvania.

We also thank the following reviewers for their helpful insights: Roberta Brack Kaufman, Concordia University; David M. Moss, University of Connecticut; Kenneth A. Parker, University of Massachusetts; Karen S. Piepmeier, University of California—Santa Barbara; and Susan C. Scott, University of Central Oklahoma.

Introduction: Teaching to the Standards of Effective Practice

"Knowledge is never a substitute for experience."
—unknown

Entering Professional Practice

"The urge to quit is the signal that an opportunity to excel is at hand."—unknown

Your professional education preparation journey continues . . . to the new phase of professional practice—student teaching.

You are about to embark on an exciting and challenging phase of your professional preparation journey. During your student teaching experience, you will be crossing a very important bridge—the bridge connecting professional preparation with professional practice. This phase constitutes a major transition from the countless hours of professional education preparation coursework (lectures, notes, videos, quizzes, final exams, research projects, learning activities, demonstrations, and presentations) to professional practice. You are now going to the other side of the desk.

Currently, you are participating in one of nearly 1400 college and university teacher education programs in the United States. These institutions are graduating approximately 105,000 potential teachers every year.

You have completed the required and elective courses that were designed to provide you with the content, theory, philosophy, history, growth and development, psychology, foundation, methods, materials, and curriculum related to your chosen teaching field. Perhaps you have had some limited, or extensive, opportunities to observe and work with children or youth in educational settings as part of your professional preparation or other activities.

Student teaching is the time for you to demonstrate your teaching wisdom—the knowledge and skill you possess in a "real" educational setting, with "real" students. Now is the time to turn your professional and academic preparation into front-line action. With the caring and supportive guidance from cooperating teachers and university supervisors, your student teaching journey can be an exciting and successful experience. For the most part, it will not be easy. Some nights will be long as you construct lesson plans; some weekends will be short as you develop solid assessment and evaluation strategies and activities for your students. Good teaching requires effort. Hopefully, many of your other personal responsibilities can be reduced, minimized, or even eliminated during your student teaching experience. For example, it may not be the best idea to plan a wedding during your student teaching experience.

A Successful Journey

"Whether you think you can or think you can't— you are right."—Henry Ford

Successful journeys take planning and preparation . . . generally lots of planning and preparation. Most of you actually started this journey many years ago when you first started attending school. Many of you may have "played school." You began to understand the intent and purpose of the school. You began to

1

understand the intent and purpose of your teachers. As you look back at your schooling years, you remember many of your teachers—with perhaps different levels of admiration. You probably remember some of your teachers on the ends of the continuum—the ones that you liked, respected, and enjoyed and because of this, you may also have "learned" a lot in their classes. On the other end of the continuum, you may remember teachers that you classified as mean, unfair, or biased toward some students. (See Activity 0:1, A Memory from the Past.)

A quote from Benjamin Mays can offer some guidance: "It must be borne in mind that the tragedy of life doesn't lie in not reaching your goal. The tragedy lies in having no goal to reach. It isn't a calamity to die with dreams unfulfilled, but it is a calamity not to dream. It is not a disaster to be unable to capture your ideal, but it is a disaster to have no ideal to capture. It's not a disgrace not to reach the stars, but it is a disgrace to have no stars to reach for. Not failure, but low aim is sin."

Textbook Organization

"They say you're born to teach, and it must have been like that for me because I know education is the field where I belong. It's not just the love of children, but it's hope for the future."—*Sandra Fernandez*

Teaching to the Standards of Effective Practice is organized around a professional framework—the ten INTASC Standards. These ten standards developed by the Interstate New Teacher Assessment and Support Consortium (INTASC) identify and reflect the knowledge and skill necessary for beginning teachers. The ten INTASC Standards were developed in cooperation with state agencies, colleges, universities, and national organizations.

The blending of the necessary knowledge and skill required for successful and effective teaching is complex. Because of this intricate network of knowledge and skill, an organizing framework is helpful to both beginning and experienced teachers. As you will see in this book, the INTASC Standards break down the essential elements of teaching and learning into manageable, understandable components.

Have you ever been taught how to perform an overhand tennis serve? Or some other complex skill? Many times, the teacher will break the skill down into important parts, concentrating on one part at a time.

Eventually, the parts are combined. Likewise with teaching and learning. Having a framework containing the essential parts is crucial; but having to learn them all at one time—as with an overhand tennis serve—can be overwhelming. As you become more experienced, comfortable, and confident with each part, you will be able to combine the parts into an effective teaching and learning repertoire.

Chapter | INTASC Standards Alignment

Chapter 1 | Standard #1: Subject Matter. The teacher understands the central concepts, tools of inquiry, and structure of the discipline and is able to create learning experiences that make these aspects of subject matter meaningful to students.

Chapter 2 | Standard #2: Student Learning. The teacher understands how children learn and develop, and can provide learning opportunities that support their intellectual, social, and personal development.

Chapter 3 | Standard #3: Diverse Learners. The teacher understands how students differ in their approaches to learning and creates instructional opportunities that are adapted to diverse learners.

Chapter 4 | Standard #4: Instructional Strategies. The teacher understands and uses a variety of instructional strategies to encourage students' development of critical thinking, problem solving, and performance skills.

Chapter 5 | Standard #5: Learning Environment. The teacher uses an understanding of individual and group motivation and behavior to create a learning environment that encourages positive social interaction, active engagement in learning, and self-motivation.

Chapter 6 | Standard #6: Communication. The teacher uses knowledge of effective verbal, nonverbal, and media communication techniques to foster active inquiry, collaboration, and supportive interaction in the classroom.

Chapter 7 | Standard #7: Planning Instruction. The teacher plans instruction based upon knowledge of subject matter, students, the community, and curriculum goals.

Chapter 8 | Standard #8: Assessment and Evaluation. The teacher understands and uses formal and informal assessment strategies to evaluate and ensure the continuous intellectual, social, and physical development of the learner.

Chapter 9 | Standard #9: Reflection and Professional Development. The teacher is a reflective practitioner who continually evaluates the effects of his/her choices and actions on others (students, parents, and other professionals in the learning community) and who actively seeks out opportunities to grow professionally.

Chapter 10 | Standard #10: Collaboration, Ethics, and Relationships. The teacher fosters relationships with school colleagues, parents, and agencies in the larger community to support students' learning and well-being.

Chapter 11 | Documentation and Evidence. During the student teaching experience, student teachers are frequently required to demonstrate, or document, their competence in a variety of ways. The purpose of this chapter is to provide several samples of Evidence Forms. These Evidence Forms may be used to assess, evaluate, and "prove" your teaching and learning progress and competence.

Chapter 12 | Beyond Student Teaching. This chapter contains considerable information to help make the steps following student teaching more successful and rewarding. Suggestions on recommendations, resumes/cover letters, interviews, resources (national/international), opportunities, activities/timelines for job search, Internet resources for job search, internet teaching resources, licensure, portfolios, career fairs, and optional paths to traditional teaching.

Another Framework

In addition to the ten INTASC Standards, there are several other frameworks for describing and defining teacher competence. One of the more popular models is the nationally recognized framework for teaching presented by Charlotte Danielson (*Enhancing Professional Practice: A Framework for Teaching* ASCD, 1996). Danielson's four domains are:

Domain 1: Planning and Preparation
Domain 2: The Classroom Environment
Domain 3: Instruction
Domain 4: Professional Responsibilities

Each of Danielson's four domains is subdivided into five or six components.

To illustrate the connection and alignment, Danielson clusters the ten INTASC Standards into her four domains in this way:

INTASC Standards	Danielson's Domain(s)
1. Subject Matter	Domains 1, 3
2. Student Learning	Domains 1, 3
3. Diverse Learners	Domains 1, 2, 3
4. Instructional Strategies	Domains 1, 3
5. Learning Environment	Domains 1, 2, 3
6. Communication	Domains 2, 3
7. Planning Instruction	Domains 1, 3
8. Assessment and Evaluation	Domains 1, 3, 4
9. Reflection and Professional Development	Domain 4
10. Collaboration, Ethics, and Relationships	Domains 1, 4

Special Features

Teaching to the Standards of Effective Practice contains many special features designed to support and guide a successful student teaching experience. They are:

Performance Indicators. Performance indicators are provided for each of the INTASC Standards. Performance indicators are a series of specific concepts and skills teachers should know and be able to do. They are intended to help teachers focus on the skills most essential to the development of an effective teacher. In other words, they are descriptors of effective teaching and learning practices.

Opening Vignette. Opening vignettes are brief stories designed to illustrate "real-life" teaching/learning situations in the context of the INTASC Standard.

Self-Assessment. Each chapter has a self-assessment feature. Self-assessments are useful ways to gather information on the degree to which you are, or are not, connected to the corresponding INTASC Standard. The self-assessment can provide you and your teachers with information that may help them determine or predict teaching and learning success and ability. Self-assessments may reveal your knowledge and skill strengths as well as your limitations. They may assist you in setting learning goals during, and beyond, your student teaching experience. You can learn a lot about your teaching and learning from self-assessments. The key to remember with self-assessments is that *you* interpret the information.

Supporting Activities.   Each chapter contains several supporting activities associated with the corresponding INTASC Standard. Supporting activities may involve observation, speaking, writing, predicting, valuing, listening, assessing, evaluating, or combinations of these. Some of the supporting activities are designed to be completed in teams of two or more, while others are individual.

Featured Commentary.   Featured commentaries are provided by guest authors. Each featured commentary is written by an individual with extensive knowledge and skill in the education field. The authors are considered by their colleagues and peers to be experts in the professional preparation of teaching and learning. The purpose of the featured commentary is threefold: First, for you, the reader, to gain professional educational insight from an expert in the field. Second, to better understand and connect the essence of the specific INTASC Standard to the real world of teaching and learning. And finally, it is intended to provide and reinforce the importance and significance of the specific INTASC Standard.

Case Study.   Case studies are an excellent means to further connect professional preparation to professional practice. Each case study illustrates a real-life teaching/learning situation faced by student teachers. Case studies help to convey a common or unique student teaching related issue, problem, or situation. They may involve students, parents, school administrators, cooperating teachers, university supervisors, or other individuals associated with the school program. Case studies allow you to play "what if" with the possible solutions and examine possible outcomes and consequences. Each case study is followed by a series of questions to provoke reflection. The exploration of case studies can lead to reinforced confidence in the student teaching experience.

Student-to-Student Tips.   For the most part, all K–12 public school teachers have gone through a student teaching experience. Many have served as cooperating teachers. Most university supervisors have themselves experienced student teaching firsthand and have continued on to classroom teaching. Thousands of individuals, from colleges and universities across the country, complete their professional preparation through student teaching every year. Each chapter contains hints, insights, and advice from those who have, or continue to be, involved in the student teaching experience. The wisdom in this section comes primarily from current and former student teachers. The underlying theme and purpose of this section is sharing thoughts that will make student teaching a positive, successful journey.

Quotes.   "A short saying often contains much wisdom."—*Sophocles* (450 B.C.E.) Need we say more?

Bibliography.   Each chapter concludes with a bibliography.

Appendices.   The final section of the textbook contains the appendices. Each appendix contains several types of resources. Ask classroom teachers what they want or need to enhance their teaching. One of the most common answers is—resources! Teachers are typically always on the "look out" for resources connected to their teaching responsibility. Resources come in many formats. They may be electronic such as in the case of the Internet or software. They may be through magazines, TV, or newspapers. Resources may be textbooks, reference books, and fiction and non-fiction readings. Videos, photographs, slides, movies, and music frequently enhance a teaching lesson. An often overlooked teaching resource is the human resource—individuals in the school and community willing to share their time, expertise, and stories. In other words, resources come in many varieties.

Foundation

"If I had one piece of advice for first-year teachers, I'd tell them to give themselves credit for what they do right and to remember that inspiring in students an excitement about learning is no small thing."
—*Julie Olin Schulz*

Student Teaching: Your First Days

The days and hours leading up to your first days as a student teacher can cause anxiety. This is quite normal. Most student teachers have the "butterflies" as they prepare for those first days. Having a goal, a plan, and a mission for those first days will provide direction and may help to relieve some of your apprehension. Activity 0.2, "Your First Days of Student Teaching," provides several common actions and questions designed to help you get to know your school better.

In addition to the items in Activity 0.2, your university supervisor may require additional information.

Week One

"The map of progress has no straight roads."
—unknown

For many reasons, all student teachers do not move from classroom observer to classroom teacher at the same rate. For example, universities may have different entry procedures and requirements or the cooperating teacher may select the most conducive time based on student learning or the comfort of the student teacher. Here are some general guidelines:

- Observe, ask questions, explore resources, and assist in classroom management.
- Learn the names of students.
- If appropriate, teach or co-teach a selected mini-lesson.
- Plan for some limited teaching responsibility of one class/section next week

See Activity 0.5, "Bridging Gaps," for additional information.

Student Absences

One of the major teaching challenges is how to appropriately and effectively deal with student absences—especially those that are excessive. There are three inevitable situations in teaching, whether you are a student teacher or certified teacher, that require constant attention and planning.

- Some students were absent yesterday.
- Some students are absent today.
- Some students will be absent tomorrow.

Consistently, without failure, preparing for these three inevitable situations is a vital component of efficient and effective planning and preparation.

Parents of younger students tend to write more notes to their teachers than the parents of older students. Often a parent will write absence excuses for their children. On a lighter side, not all excuses a teacher receives from parents are written free of grammatical errors or misinterpretation. One desirable quality of a teacher is that he/she have a good sense of humor. Humorous situations occur regularly throughout teaching and learning situations. Enjoy them! Activity 0.3, "Student Excuses from Parents," will help you see one way this humor may exist.

What Drives Teachers Wacky?

Are you prepared to face some common student statements during class? A survey of teachers revealed twelve common statements by students that tend to "drive teachers wacky." How can you, in your lesson planning, prepare a lesson that will minimize the frequency of these common student statements?

1. "Can we write on both sides of the paper?"
2. "I didn't hear that question."
3. "Are the test papers graded yet?"
4. "Do we have to write this in ink?"
5. "I had my paper all written but I left it at home."
6. "Did you say our notebooks were due today?"
7. "I can't find that place."
8. "I lost my book."
9. "Do I have to get up in front of the class?"
10. "I didn't get that far."
11. "I couldn't get the book."
12. "What are we going to do next?"

By the way, these twelve student statements were the Teachers' Top Concerns in 1920—from the 1920 Winona High School (Minnesota) yearbook. Most veteran teachers will confirm that these statements still frequently exist in today's classrooms.

Teachers' Code of Ethics

Do you know the code of ethics for your profession? Many professional organizations have a statement of ethics that guide the behavior of those in that profession. Medical doctors have the Hippocratic Oath. Psychiatrists, counselors, lawyers, religious leaders, and educators, among others, also have a code of ethics. The National Education Association (NEA), in 1975, adopted a code of ethics for teachers. The code of ethics helps to define moral, appropriate behavior. Teachers are required to make countless decisions every day. The code of ethics will aid and support you in making your decisions. The code of ethics will help you in much the same way a compass helps a person lost in the forest. For a better understanding of the NEA Code of Ethics of the Education Profession, see Activity 0.4, "Code of Ethics of the Education Profession."

Special Education Language

Suppose you were in a foreign country and didn't understand the local language. It would be difficult to enter in a conversation. Likewise, it can seem as if you are in a foreign country listening to veteran teachers talk about teaching, learning, students, and programs. Many professions have a specialized language. Education is no exception—especially as it relates to the specific area of special education. In 1975 Congress enacted a new law called the Education of All Handicapped Children Act of 1975. This law became better known as Public Law 94-142. This law is now called Individuals with Disabilities Education Act (IDEA). Under IDEA, federal money is provided to state and local educational agencies to help them educate students from birth to age 21. One component of IDEA states that students with disabilities have the right to inclusion in programs and buildings with peers who do not have disabilities. For this reason, depending on your specific student teaching assignment, your classes may include students with a wide range of disabilities and abilities. Regardless, as an education professional it is important to learn and understand some of the basic acronyms associated with special education. Speak with special education staff to learn and understand the commonly used terms.

Bridging the Gap

The ideal cooperating teacher has many professional characteristics. He/she is a committed teacher with a strong teaching knowledge and ability in the subject area(s). And, he/she can create a positive learning environment and working relationship with the student teacher.

However, even in the best situations, gaps sometimes exist between student teacher and cooperating teacher. As a younger student teacher, you may have a far better understanding of the student's culture—music, movies, TV, fashion, behavior, and slang. There may be a significant age difference between student teacher and cooperating teacher. In some cases, the student teacher may be several years older than the cooperating teacher.

Activity 0.5, "Bridging Gaps," will help you identify possible gaps early in the student teaching experience, which in turn could foster a positive experience

for both student and cooperating teacher. The key is to use these gaps as assets rather than barriers.

Teacher or Friend?

Many student teachers are not much older than the students they are assigned to teach. This is especially true for high school student teachers. Age proximity can add an entirely new dimension to student teaching. The authors of this textbook have supervised many student teachers who have had students who became infatuated with the student teacher. High school students have asked their student teachers for a date. When this fascination is exhibited in a student's behavior, it may create additional pressures and challenges on the student teacher.

Most student teachers (and veteran teachers) want to be liked by their students. Veteran teachers (in all but a few rare instances) have the experience and wisdom to easily deal with infatuated students in a professional manner.

Student teachers, however, often lack the experience and confidence to effectively deal with infatuated or overly affectionate students. There is just one rule for the student teacher to remember and follow: Never, never, never have any friendship with any student that goes beyond an ethical, educational, and professional relationship. Challenge yourself by completing Activity 0.6, "What Would I Do or Say?"

And one final, but important question to consider . . . what would you do if your cooperating teacher asked you out?

Another area that is sometimes difficult for a student teacher is the concern about proper and appropriate attire. A usually safe rule is to dress slightly above the "middle attire" in the department or team in which you are teaching. Generally, attire appropriateness is different from department to department. Art, industrial technology, and physical education teachers may have very different "dress expectations" than teachers in other disciplines. A teacher's attire may have a significant effect, positively or negatively, on students and staff.

Body piercings among student teachers have caused concern for some veteran teachers, administrators, students, and students' parents. In one instance an elementary student teacher, while reaching for a projection screen, inadvertently displayed her pierced navel to the students. The next morning several of the students' parents had called the school administration to express their concern about the incident. Many parents were outraged that this "display" occurred and demanded all sorts of consequences for the student teacher. Consequently, it was very upsetting to the student teacher and for several days distracted her from her primary teaching assignment. From the authors' experience, body piercings (other than in the ear) among student teachers have been viewed primarily as negative by cooperating teachers and administrators.

In another situation, shortly after a young female elementary student teacher arrived, many of the female students had a hair style exactly like the student teacher. Was this positive or negative?

A teacher's appearance can be of great concern for the students' parents. This is especially true if it goes against their picture of a "role model." Parents are generally not afraid to call the school and report what they deem to be "out of order."

The whole point about attire and other characteristics is the basic fact that it's usually the older, more experienced, and sometimes more conservative administrators and teachers on the interview teams. Considerations for securing the most "qualified" teacher for a position opening may involve looking for the person who represents the values of the school and community. Bottom line: Your appearance may be worth more than you think!

Activity 0.1 A Memory from the Past

Context When individuals are asked about the people who have had a major, positive influence on their lives, former teachers are often among those mentioned.

Purpose To deepen your understanding of teacher traits, attributes, and characteristics that enhance teaching and learning.

Directions

- Think about your elementary, middle, and high school teachers. Focus on one that conjures some very positive, favorable "teaching and learning" memories. What subjects/content did this person teach? Could it be in the same area you are student teaching?

- Draw a sketch of the teacher as you remember him or her. What did the teacher look like? Tall or short? Thin or not so thin? Long or short hair? What other features can you remember about this teacher? Perhaps you can you remember his/her name. If yes, put in under the sketch. Spelling doesn't count on this one.

- List the attributes and qualities of this person that made a such a positive, favorable memory on the right side of your sketch.

_____

_____

_____

_____

_____

_____

_____

_____

_____

_____

_____

_____

Do you see this teacher as a role model for you? Why or why not?

_____

_____

_____

_____

_____

_____

Activity 0.2   Your First Days of Student Teaching

Context   The days and hours leading up to your first days as a student teacher can cause great anxiety. This is quite normal.

Purpose   Having a goal for those first days will provide direction and may help to relieve the some of your apprehension.

Directions   Put an X in front of the actions/questions you have satisfied. Label the items that are not applicable with an N. Don't overwhelm your cooperating teacher with all of these questions at once. Search out other school staff to help you find these answers.

Meet/Greet People

_____ Principal

_____ Assistant Principal(s)

_____ Dean of Students

_____ Counselors (especially those who are assigned to your students)

_____ Department Chair

_____ Team Leader

_____ Psychologist

_____ Social Worker

_____ Police Liaison Officer

_____ Media Director

_____ Speech/Language Director

_____ Nurse

_____ Special Education Leader

_____ Department Colleagues

_____ Secretarial Staff

_____ Custodial Staff

_____ Other student teachers in the building

Visit

_____ Media Center: What services do they offer?

_____ AV Department: What services do they offer?

_____ Production: What services do they offer?

_____ What is the procedure for duplicating materials?

_____ How far in advance do I need to plan in order to get the materials I need?

_____ Computer Lab: What services do they offer? How far in advance do I need to sign up?

Classroom Procedures/Schedules

_____ Where are the course and district curriculum guides?

_____ Where do I get a course textbook? Is a teacher's edition available?

_____ Where do I get a school handbook?

_____ Where are the classroom seating charts?

_____ What is the attendance policy and procedure?

_____ What is the daily class time schedule?

_____ How are students dismissed from class when they become ill?

_____ What should be done if a student is out of control during the class or in the hall?

_____ What classroom supplies/materials do I need to provide?

Special Meetings

_____ When are parent conferences? How are the conferences scheduled?

_____ What materials do I save to share with parents?

_____ What topics should I cover in the conference?

_____ When are staff meetings?

_____ When are cooperating teacher and student teacher meetings?

_____ When are "special schedule" days?

Miscellaneous

_____ What do I do when a parent comes to seek or share information during instructional time?

_____ What is my responsibility for monitoring students before and after school, between classes, in the lunchroom, or study hall?

_____ What is the school security policy for dismissing students?

_____ How do I report suspicious persons or suspicious behaviors including a suspected weapon or illegal substance?

_____ What are the procedures for reporting suspected child abuse?

_____ What is the procedure for a fire or severe weather?

_____ How should I address administrators and other staff?

_____ How should students address me and other school staff?

_____ Is there a teacher dress code? How should I dress?

_____ What are my required school arrival and departure times?

_____ What is the class grading policy? Is there a school grading policy?

_____ What do I do if a student/colleague is injured or becomes ill during class?

_____ What time can I get into the building? How late can I stay? Can I get into the building during the weekend?

_____ How do I use the telephone, voice mail, and e-mail systems?

_____ Do I need a parking permit? How do I get one?

_____ How do I get a classroom key?

_____ Where do I eat lunch? How much does it cost?

_____ Where are the staff rest rooms?

_____ Where can I keep my personal and instructional materials?

_____ What do I do if I'm ill or late?

_____ What do I do if I become ill during class?

_____ How do I summon help if I need assistance during class?

_____ What are the cooperating teacher's expectations of me?

Activity 0.3   Student Excuses from Parents

Context   Parents of younger students tend to write more notes to their teachers than the parents of older students. Often a parent will write absence excuses for their children. Not all excuses a teacher receives from parents are written free of grammatical errors or misinterpretation.

Purpose   To better understand that humor exists throughout teaching and learning situations.

Directions   Find and correct the errors in these written excuses for students from their parents.

1. Please excuse Chris from school last Friday. He had an acre in his side.

2. Please excuse John for being absent January 28, 29, 30, 31, 32, 33.

3. Jim was absent yesterday because he had a stomach.

4. Mary could not go to school yesterday because she was bothered by very close veins.

5. Please excuse Gloria last week. She was sick and under the Doctor.

6. My son George is under the Doctor's care and should not take P.E. . . . please execute him.

7. Lillie was absent from school yesterday because she had a gang over.

8. Please excuse Roland from P.E. for a few days. Yesterday he fell out of a tree and misplaced his hip.

9. Please excuse Joey Tuesday. He had loose vowels.

10. Please excuse Joyce from jim today. She is administrating.

11. My daughter couldn't come to school on Monday because she was tired. She spent the weekend in bed with some marines.

12. Ralph was absent yesterday because of a sour trout.

13. Please excuse Wayne for being out yesterday, because he had the fuel.

14. Please excuse Sandra from school on Wednesday. She was in bed with gramps.

15. Julie was absent this morning because she missed her bust.

16. Please excuse Sarah for being absent. She was sick and I had her shot.

Activity 0.4   Code of Ethics of the Education Profession

Context   Many professions have a code of ethics. The code of ethics may describe the philosophy, code of conduct, and/or the professional principles. The National Education Association (NEA), in 1975, adopted a code of ethics for teachers. The NEA Code of Ethics of the Education Profession has three sections: (1) Preamble, (2) Principle I: Commitment to the Student, and (3) Principle II: Commitment to the Profession.

Purpose   An understanding the elements of the Code of Ethics of the Education Profession will serve as a guide for your teaching and learning choices and actions.

Directions   Read the Preamble to Code of Ethics of the Education Profession, Principle I: Commitment to the Student, and Principle II: Commitment to the Profession. Then read the 16 statements. If the statement corresponds to Principle I: Commitment to the Student, put the letter "S" on the line preceding the statement. If the statement corresponds to Principle II: Commitment to the Profession, put the letter "P" on the line preceding the statement.

Preamble

The educator, believing in the worth and dignity of each human being, recognizes the supreme importance of the pursuit of truth, devotion to excellence, and the nurture of the democratic principles. Essential to these goals is the protection of freedom to learn and to teach and the guarantee of equal educational opportunity for all. The educator accepts the responsibility to adhere to the highest ethical standards. The educator recognizes the magnitude of the responsibility inherent in the teaching process. The desire for the respect and confidence of one's colleagues, of students, of parents, and of the members of the community provides the incentive to attain and maintain the highest possible degree of ethical conduct. The Code of Ethics of the Education Profession indicates the aspiration of all educators and provides standards by which to judge conduct.

The remedies specified by the NEA and/or its affiliates for the violation of any provision of this Code shall be exclusive and no such provision shall be enforceable in any form other than the one specifically designated by the NEA or its affiliates.

Principle I • Commitment to the Student.   The educator strives to help each student realize his or her potential as a worthy and effective member of society. The educator therefore works to stimulate the spirit of inquiry, the acquisition of knowledge and understanding, and the thoughtful formulation of worthy goals. *In fulfillment of the obligation to the student, the educator. . . .*

Principle II • Commitment to the Profession.   The education profession is vested by the public with a trust and responsibility requiring the highest ideals of professional service. In the belief that the quality of the services of the education profession directly influences the nation and its citizens, the educator shall exert every effort to raise professional standards, to promote a climate that encourages the exercise of professional judgment, to achieve conditions that attract persons worthy of the trust to careers in education, and to assist in preventing the practice of the profession by unqualified persons. *In fulfillment of the obligation to the profession, the educator. . . .*

Statements

1. _____ Shall not misrepresent his/her professional qualifications.

2. _____ Shall not unreasonably restrain the student from independent action in the pursuit of learning.

3. _____ Shall not unreasonably deny the student's access to varying points of view.

4. _____ Shall not accept any gratuity, gift, or favor that might impair or appear to influence professional decisions or action.

5. _____ Shall not deliberately suppress or distort subject matter relevant to the student's progress.

6. _____ Shall not intentionally expose the student to embarrassment or disparagement.

7. _____ Shall not on the basis of race, color, creed, sex, national origin, marital status, political or religious beliefs, family, social or cultural background, or sexual orientation, unfairly:

   a. Exclude any student from participation in any program
   b. Deny benefits to any student
   c. Grant any advantage to any student

8. _____ Shall not disclose information about students obtained in the course of professional service unless disclosure serves a compelling professional purpose or is required by law.

9. _____ Shall not in an application for a professional position deliberately make a false statement or fail to disclose a material fact related to competency and qualifications.

10. _____ Shall not assist any entry into the profession of a person known to be unqualified in respect to character, education, or other relevant attribute.

11. _____ Shall not knowingly make a false statement concerning the qualifications of a candidate for a professional position.

12. _____ Shall not assist a non-educator in the unauthorized practice of teaching.

13. _____ Shall not disclose information about colleagues obtained in the course of professional service unless disclosure serves a compelling professional purpose or is required by law.

14. _____ Shall not knowingly make false or malicious statements about a colleague.

15. _____ Shall make reasonable effort to protect the student from conditions harmful to learning or to health and safety.

16. _____ Shall not use professional relationships with students for private advantage.

Activity 0.5   Bridging Gaps

Context   Often there are several differences between student teachers and cooperating teachers. The two most obvious differences are age and teaching experience. Bridging these gaps early in the student teaching experience can create a more positive experience for both student and cooperating teacher.

Purpose   The goal of this activity is to better understand differences and then use those differences as assets, rather than barriers, to a successful experience.

Directions   Listed below are twelve comments made by student teachers before, during, and following their experiences. Put the letters *MI* on the line in front of the six comments that you feel are the "most important" messages for you to give to your cooperating teacher. You may add others.

_____ Be straightforward with comments—positive and/or negative. Don't make me guess at the intent and meaning.

_____ Be straightforward with expectations—time, place, format, length, date—e.g. "When do you want this?" and "When do I take over?"

_____ Please understand, as a young adult student teacher, I have a pretty good understanding of the student's culture—music, movies, TV, fashion, behavior, and slang.

_____ I need to balance teaching and living and therefore need time to relax and be with family and friends.

_____ Please treat me as a professional student teacher. It has a great impact on my self-esteem, confidence, and also how the students perceive me.

_____ I want, expect, and appreciate your help. (e.g., lesson planning and classroom management). I may have only had the opportunity to practice lessons "on" my college classmates—who typically did not pass notes or have interrupting chatter during my lesson.

_____ Help me find, and not cross the line, between being a teacher and friend.

_____ Help me understand the non-classroom part of teaching—e.g., workshops, faculty meetings, parent conferences, special education meetings, seminars, budget discussions, student assemblies, and scheduling conversations.

_____ Technology is an important part of teaching and learning. Let's share our expertise.

_____ I trust your experience. If you really know something won't work—tell me!

_____ Understand that I will make mistakes; I'm here to learn.

_____ Help me find the help I need. You don't have to do it for me. Give me some directions and options.

_____ _____

_____ _____

_____ _____

_____ _____

_____ _____

Activity 0.6 What Would I Do or Say?

Context Student teachers often find themselves facing a student question or situation that is totally unexpected and consequently catches them completely off guard. These moments can really fluster you! Or even worse, they can cause embarrassment, stress, anxiety, worry, and frustration.

Purpose The goal of this activity is to better understand, predict, and prepare for personal and challenging student questions and situations. These questions and situations usually arise when you least expect them, sometimes during class and sometimes outside of class.

Directions Listed below are 40 questions or situations experienced, and voiced, by real student teachers. Describe, and practice, how you would respond to each.

What would you say or do if . . .

1. a student invites you to his/her home for dinner?

_____

_____

2. a local member of the clergy asks to come to your class as a guest speaker?

_____

_____

3. the president of the student body toilet-papers your house?

_____

_____

4. a student deliberately destroys your personal property?

_____

_____

5. a student makes fun of another student while giving a report?

_____

_____

6. a fellow teacher approaches you after a faculty meeting to admonish you about your personal appearance?

_____

_____

7. a student asks for a ride home after school one evening?

_____

_____

8. your cooperating teacher becomes ill and will be hospitalized for four weeks?

_____

_____

9. a member of a group called the "Christian Coalition" asks to distribute literature to your class?

_____

_____

10. you—a student teacher—have been asked to be part of a homecoming skit at the coronation ceremony?

_____

_____

11. two girls get into a fight in your class?

_____

_____

12. a police officer comes to your room with an arrest warrant for one of your students?

_____

_____

13. two boys get into a fight in your class?

_____

_____

14. at a faculty meeting, your building principal calls on you to state your views regarding graduation standards in your field?

_____

_____

15. after a class period you find a container of illegal drugs under the chair of a student who is a "known troublemaker"?

_____

_____

16. an EBD student begins swearing after you hand him back a test which has a failing grade on it?

_____

_____

17. a fellow teacher offers to take one or two of your students on a weekend field trip?

_____

_____

18. a parent demands to see how his child's grades compare to the rest of the class members?

_____

_____

19. a student refuses to comply with your classroom rules?

_____

_____

20. a coach comes to your class during a unit test, and wants to have a team member speak with a university representative?

_____

_____

21. a parent meets with you and the principal to complain that your class is too demanding?

_____

_____

22. three of your better students have four identical wrong answers on a test?

_____

_____

23. a counselor brings a new student to your class who speaks no English, yet is now enrolled as your student?

_____

_____

24. a student hands in an essay that brags about illegal activities?

_____

_____

25. you are at a local restaurant and observe the captain of a sports team using tobacco and alcohol?

_____

_____

26. you hear that a fellow teacher criticizes your teaching in front of his class?

_____

_____

27. your principal informs you that a sexual harassment complaint has been filed against you?

_____

_____

28. in the middle of your unit test, the fire alarm sounds?

_____

_____

29. a student confides in you that she feels she is being treated unfairly by another teacher?

_____

_____

30. a student comes into your classroom and tells you about her life as an abused child?

_____

_____

31. the building principal informs you that your cooperating teacher is ill today and that they are unable to get a substitute?

_____

_____

32. a student asks you to go a movie?

_____

_____

33. a student is spreading rumors about your sexual activity?

_____

_____

34. several students ask why they can't have their regular (cooperating) teacher back?

_____

_____

35. your cooperating teacher asks you to go to dinner and a movie?

_____

_____

36. a student asks about your sexual preference?

_____

_____

37. a student asks if you had sex during high school?

_____

_____

38. a student wants to come in after school and get some "hints" on tomorrow's big test?

_____

_____

39. a student, during a test, has some of the test answers written on his/her hand?

_____

_____

40. a parent asks you how you balance student effort and student achievement when determining student grades?

_____

_____

1
Subject Matter

"Teaching, like learning, is an active constructive process where teachers attempt to make learning sensible and students attempt to make sense of learning."
—*Dole, Duffy, Roehler, and Pearson*

Standard #1 The teacher understands the central concepts, tools of inquiry, and structures of the discipline(s), and can create learning experiences that make these aspects of subject matter meaningful for students.

Performance Indicators: *The teacher . . .*

- Understands the subject matter and understands that the subject is linked to other disciplines and can be applied to work-integrated settings. The teacher's repertoire of teaching skills includes a variety of means to assist student acquisition of new knowledge and skills using that knowledge.

- Consistently plans and implements meaningful learning experiences for students.

Vignette During the junior high smoking unit, students were given information on peer pressure and the different types of peer pressure. They were also given information on several ways to say "no." All this information was discussed over a number of days. In groups, students had to utilize information given to them, and create a role-play situation. Several students were given the task of applying the pressure strategies that encourage smoking while others were to demonstrate ways in saying "no" to the class. Following the activity, one student raises her hand and asks David, her student teacher, "Why is it that my brother, who knows how to say no, decides to smoke anyway?" David does not know how to answer the question and looks in the direction of his cooperating teacher for help in answering the question.

Fundamental Principles

At the turn of the 20th century, John Dewey wrote about the dilemma in the preparation of teachers: the controversy between subject matter and methodology. At the turn of the 21st century, this debate continues to be argued. In fact the same questions are being asked: On the one hand, to what extent does teaching and learning to teach depend on the development of theoretical knowledge and knowledge of subject matter (Lowenberg 2000)? On the other hand, to what extent does it rely on the development of pedagogical method? Some educators will argue that teachers should be experts in their content-specific disciplines while others suggest that what matters is caring for students and having the skills to work effectively with them. Dewey ([1904] 1964) wrote, "Scholastic knowledge is sometimes regarded as if it were something assumed, method becomes an external attachment to knowledge of subject matter" (160). Clearly, the answer must be that it depends on both.

How can teachers teach what they do not know? This question captures the essence of why content knowledge is important in teaching. Danielson (1996) claims that regardless of teachers' instructional techniques, they must have sufficient command of a subject to guide student learning. Teachers must understand the content to be learned, the structure of the discipline of which that content is a part, and the methods of inquiry unique to that discipline. Although necessary for good teaching, subject knowledge is not enough. Teachers must also use pedagogical techniques particular to the different disciplines to help convey information and teach skills. Shulman's work (1987) supports this notion and states, "We expect teachers to understand what they teach and to understand it in several ways. They should understand how a given idea relates to other ideas within the same subject area and to ideas in other subjects as well"(14).

Herein lies a fundamental difficulty in learning to teach. Although some teachers have important understandings of the content, they often do not know how to create the learning experiences that make the subject matter meaningful for students. In spite of the commitment to teach all students, some teachers are unable to represent ideas in multiple ways, connect content to contexts effectively, and think about things in ways other than their own. For example, in their study of a middle school teacher's attempt to teach the concept of rate, Thompson and Thompson (1994) highlight the crucial role played by language. They vividly describe the situation of one teacher who, although he understood the concept of rate himself, was restricted in his capacity to express or discuss the ideas in everyday language. Satisfied with computational language for his own purposes, when this did not help students understand, he was not able to find other means of expressing key ideas. In addition, teachers may not be able to evaluate the content of their textbooks and adapt them effectively, or they may omit topics central to students' experiences. They may substitute student interest for content integrity in making choices about subject matter. Knowing subject matter and translating that knowledge to the lives of students is key to learning. Students learn more when they can understand how facts, concepts, and principles are interrelated (Smith 1985; Van Patten, Chao, and Reigeluth 1986).

Here we see three schools of thought: behaviorism, social learning, and cognitivism. Behaviorism is based on the belief that human behavior is determined by forces in the environment that are beyond our control rather than by the exercise of free will. Behaviorism stands in stark contrast to cognitivism, a philosophical orientation based on the belief that people actively construct their knowledge of the world through experiences and interaction rather than through behavioral conditioning. Behaviorism relies on knowledge derived from the physical world. Learning is based on the associations among stimulus, response, and reinforcement. The consequences of a behavior can come as either reinforcement or punishment. Individuals can learn from both. Reinforcement and punishment can be either positive or

negative. The terms positive and negative in this context do not mean good and bad; rather, positive means adding something (effects of the stimulus) to a situation, whereas, negative means taking something away (removal or reduction of the effects of the stimulus) from the situation. So, when students are not learning, for example, the behaviorists think there must be something wrong with the educational program. The way to solve the problem is to break down the program into its component parts and to fix the pieces that are broken, or to scrap the program altogether and try a new one. The challenge, then, is to engineer environments that produce desired results (McNergney and Herbert 2001; Arends, Winitzky, and Tannenbaum 2001).

The educational applications of behaviorism to enhance achievement and to improve conduct are many and varied. Schools use programmed instruction, both computer-based and print materials, to teach mathematics, reading, and other subject matter. These curricula are organized into discrete, sequentially ordered units of study, accompanied by unit tests, opportunities for feedback on performance, and chances to practice skills (McNergney and Herbert 2001).

The social learning theory views learning as a social process influenced by interactions with other people. In this theory, physical and social environments are influential in reinforcing and shaping the beliefs that determine behavior. A change in any of the three components—behavior, physical environment, or social environment—influences the other two. Self-efficacy, an essential component of the theory, is the person's belief that he or she is capable of performing the new behavior in the proposed situation. It means the individual knows what the behavior is and how to do it and depends on cognitive processes. It influences how much effort an individual applies to a task and what levels of performance he or she attains.

The environment is considered critical, as well, in social learning theory because the environment provides models for behavior. According to social learning theory, expectations may be learned by observing others in similar situations (also called observational learning). It takes place without any real reward for the learner, although he or she observes outcomes of others' behaviors. Observational learning sometimes can be a shortcut to learning, because the learner uncovers rules for behavior without the trial-and-error attempts of personal experience. It is the basis for modeling. By purposefully observing others, the student may determine whether a certain behavior or response is socially acceptable or reinforcing and base his or her decision to adopt that behavior on that information. In this way, behavior may be established rather than changed.

For many years, teachers followed the notion that knowledge was something to be transmitted to students, and so they relied on teaching methods that treated students as passive learners. Education meant transferring knowledge and skills from the expert teacher to the naïve student. Researchers (Anderson and Smith 1987; Stykes and Bird 1992) claim that this early view of teaching infused knowledge into a vacuum. Dewey (1938) and Piaget (1948), however, both believed that children actively construct their knowledge of the world. Piaget (1948) proposed that students cannot be "given" information which they cannot immediately understand and use. Instead, they must "construct" their own knowledge. They build their knowledge through experience. Experiences enable them to create mental models which change, enlarge, and become more sophisticated over time. Therefore, two key Piagetian principles for teaching and learning are: (a) learning is an active process and (b) learning should be authentic and "real." So, while information is important, it's introduced as an aid to problem solving and functions as a tool rather than an isolated arbitrary fact. In addition, meaning is constructed as students interact in meaningful ways with the world around them. In other words, less emphasis is placed on isolated "skill" exercises that try to teach something like long division or end-of-sentence punctuation. Students still learn these functions, but they are more likely to learn them if they are engaged in meaningful activities (such as conducting a community-based survey, writing and editing a class newspaper, or producing and directing a news spot to be aired on closed-circuit school monitors). Whole activities, as opposed to isolated skill exercises, authentic activities that are inherently interesting and meaningful to the student, and real activities that result in something other than a grade on a test or a "Great, you did well" from the worksheet assignment or project, are the emphasis. Learning is an active, not an absorptive process.

Alternatives to the behaviorist and social learning outlooks take a variety of forms, loosely called cognitivism (from *cognition*, the process of thinking and knowing). On the basis of research on thinking, cognitive psychologists assert that people are not passively conditioned by the environment but rather are active learners. Knowledge is acquired by active engagement in the learning process of the student.

Educators who favor teaching models based on cognitivism often choose student-centered learning experiences. They assist students by teaching them study skills, thinking skills, and problem-solving skills. In education, the movement to modify curriculum and instruction to reflect the cognitivist outlook is called constructivism. The basic idea of constructivism is that knowledge must be constructed by the learner; it cannot be provided by the teacher. The implications of constructivism relative to learning and teaching are that students are responsible for their own learning and the teacher is responsible for creating an appropriate learning environment (McNergney and Herbert 2001; Reynolds 1992; Heuwinkel 1996).

The constructivist view of education advocates that teachers should (Brooks and Brooks 1993):

- Encourage and accept student autonomy and initiative
- Use primary sources along with interactive materials
- Allow student responses to drive lessons and alter content
- Inquire about students' understanding of concepts before sharing their own understandings
- Encourage students to engage in dialogue, both with the teacher and with one another
- Encourage student inquiry by asking thoughtful, open-ended questions and encouraging students to ask questions of each other
- Seek elaboration of students' initial responses
- Engage students in experiences that might create/ result in contradictions and then encourage discussion
- Allow wait time after posing questions
- Provide time for students to construct relationships ·
- Nurture students' natural curiosity through frequent use of discovery, problem solving, and investigation

In the constructivist classroom, knowledge is directly experienced, acted upon, tested, or revised by the learner (Papert and Harel 1991). The constructivist classroom presents the learner with opportunities to build on prior knowledge and understanding to construct new knowledge and understanding from authentic experience. Students are allowed to confront problems full of meaning because of their real-life context. In solving these problems, students are encouraged to explore possibilities, invent alternative solutions, collaborate with other students, try out ideas and hypotheses, revise their thinking, and finally, present the best solution they can derive. To do so involves the incorporation of developmentally appropriate techniques (Bredekamp and Copple 1997). Developmentally appropriate practices are represented by the following teaching strategies:

- **Create an authentic/active environment:** Learning happens when the student is consciously engaged in meaningful activities that promote an active exploration of the environment. Students manipulate real objects and learn through hands-on, direct experiences. The curriculum provides opportunities for students to explore, reflect, interact, and communicate with other students and adults. Examples include: field trips, real-life experiences such as cooking, reenacting historical events, conducting scientific experiments, and participating in community service projects.

- **Encourage the use of varied instructional strategies:** The use of varied instructional strategies meets the learning needs of students. Such approaches may include process writing, peer coaching and tutoring, teacher-led instruction, thematic instruction, projects, problem-based learning, and literature-based instruction (Privett 1996; Stone 1995). By providing a wide variety of ways to learn, students with various learning styles are able to develop their capabilities. Teaching in this way also helps provide for multiple intelligences, and enables students to view learning in new ways.

- **Incorporate a balance between teacher-directed and student-directed activities:** Teacher-directed learning involves the teacher as facilitator who models learning strategies and gives guided instruction. Student-directed learning allows the student to assume some responsibility for learning goals.

- **Integrate curricula:** An integrated curriculum is one that connects diverse areas of study by cutting across subject matter lines and emphasizing unifying concepts. It combines many subject areas into a cohesive unit of study that is meaningful to students. An integrated curriculum often relates learning to real life. Whole language and writing across the curriculum are examples of integrated approaches.

- **Create learning centers:** Learning centers are independent stations set up throughout the classroom where students can go to actually engage in some learning activity. Students choose the center they will go to and decide on the amount of time to spend there. The learning center approach provides a time when students explore and practice skills to their own satisfaction. These centers provide students with opportunities for hands-on learning, cooperative learning, social interaction, real-life problem solving, autonomous learning, and open-ended activities. Learning centers should reflect the goal of active learning; they must not be workstations full of worksheets for students to complete. Learning centers offer an opportunity for students to be responsible for their own learning (Stone 1995; Sloane, 1998).

Learning becomes an interactive process. Teachers help students develop skills that can be applied in many different ways. Their goal is education for understanding (Gardner 1991), rather than acquisition of skills that can be used only in the narrow context in which they were learned. Learning is a search for meaning. Therefore, learning must start with the issues around which students are actively trying to construct meaning. Meaning requires understanding wholes as well as parts. And parts must be understood in the context of wholes. Therefore, the learning process focuses on primary concepts, not isolated facts. In order to teach well, teachers must understand the mental models that students use to perceive the world and the assumptions they make to support those models. The purpose of learning is for individuals to construct their own meaning, not just memorize the "right" answers and regurgitate someone else's meaning. Since education is inherently interdisciplinary, the only valuable way to measure learning is to make the assessment part of the learning process, ensuring it provides students with information on the quality of their learning. In short, many teachers are becoming facilitators of learning, rather than transmitters of facts and formulas.

Questions for Reflection

- How does constructivism differ from the traditional approaches of transmitting information to learners?

- What instructional strategies are commonly used in the constructivist classroom?

- How is authentic learning related to the constructivist principles?

Commentary on Standard #1

CLINT E. BRUESS, Ed.D. | CHES, Dean Emeritus and Professor, School of Education, Department of Human Studies, University of Alabama at Birmingham

There is no question that both subject matter and learning experiences are important when it comes to teaching. It is interesting, however, that many people seem to think that subject matter knowledge is all that is needed to be a good teacher. It is common to hear people suggest that a physicist would make a great science teacher, or that a retired accountant ought to be used to teach mathematics in schools. It would be interesting to see how some of these subject matter specialists do in real classrooms. Chances are they would not be very effective, and they might soon decide teaching is not for them.

Examples of programs designed to turn subject matter specialists into teachers have been common in recent years. Perhaps two of the better-known programs have been Teach for America and Troops to Teachers. In the first instance, liberal arts graduates are supposedly taught to teach in one summer and then given a teaching assignment. In the second instance, former military personnel are quickly turned into teachers. While it is certainly possible for subject matter specialists to learn to become good teachers, it is far less likely to happen in programs designed to do it in just a few weeks or months.

Another factor contributing to the underemphasis on teaching skills is the idea that anyone can teach. According to those who support this idea, courses about how to teach are a waste of time and subject matter specialists are supposed to simply fill students with knowledge. This has been called the "fallacy of the empty vessel"—meaning that students are like empty vessels and they can be filled with knowledge.

Fortunately, in recent years there has been excellent research that finally sheds some light on the relative importance of subject matter and learning experiences when it comes to teaching. Darling-Hammond[1] reported that diverse students and higher standards create greater demands on teachers. Her research indicated that teachers with more knowledge of teaching and learning were more effective. She concluded that knowledge of learning, curriculum, and methods are more important than subject matter.

None of this implies that subject matter knowledge is not important. However, those teachers who know how to create meaningful learning experiences for their students will be the most successful educators.

---

[1]Darling-Hammond, Linda. 2000. How teacher education matters. *Journal of Teacher Education* 51, 3 (May/June): 166–173.

Subject Matter Self-Assessment

The teacher understands the central concepts, tools of inquiry, and structure of the discipline and is able to create learning experiences that make these aspects of subject matter meaningful to students.

Knowledge/Performance Indicators	Yes*	Not Sure	No
1. I understand major concepts, assumptions, debates, processes of inquiry, and ways of knowing that are central to the discipline taught.	2	1	0
2. I understand how students' conceptual frameworks and misconceptions for an area of knowledge can influence the students' learning.	2	1	0
3. I can connect disciplinary knowledge to other subject areas and to everyday life.	2	1	0
4. I understand that subject matter knowledge is not a fixed body of facts but is complex and constantly developing.	2	1	0
5. I use multiple representations and explanations of subject matter concepts to capture key ideas and link them to students' prior understandings.	2	1	0
6. I use varied viewpoint, theories, ways of knowing, and methods of inquiry in teaching subject matter concepts.	2	1	0

7. I evaluate teaching resources and curriculum materials for comprehensiveness, accuracy, and usefulness for presenting particular ideas and concepts. 2   1   0

8. I engage students in generating knowledge and testing hypotheses according to the methods of inquiry and standards of evidence used in the discipline. 2   1   0

9. I develop and use curricula that encourage students to understand, analyze, interpret, and apply ideas from varied perspectives. 2   1   0

10. I design interdisciplinary learning experiences that allow students to integrate knowledge, skills, and methods of inquiry across several subject areas. 2   1   0

---

* A "Yes" response indicates that you can describe, document, and cite examples related to your student teaching assignment.

Self-Assessment Summary and Reflection

1. Which Knowledge/Performance Indicators can I currently describe, document, and cite examples?

   _____

   _____

2. Which Knowledge/Performance Indicators need some work or improvement?

   _____

   _____

3. What specific actions can I take to enrich my knowledge or skill in this area?

   _____

   _____

Activity 1.1   Scavenger Hunt

Context   Solid content knowledge provides the foundation for effective teaching. However, knowing and understanding the central concepts of the discipline is just the first step. Accomplished teachers recognize the power of connecting new knowledge and skills to existing ones and, thus, make connections within the discipline as well as to other disciplines and real life.

Purpose   This is an opportunity to analyze your lesson plans for examples of effective planning as supported by educational research.

Directions

- Select five lesson plans that you've written, and examine them to find evidence of best practice in planning, as listed in A, B, and C below.
- When you've found an appropriate example, write it in the space provided.
- For any of the following for which you cannot find an example, create a sample.

A.   Instructional Objectives: Find examples of . . .

1. A lesson objective that is clearly related to a unit/course goal.

   Objective: _____

   _____

   Course goal: _____

   _____

2. A lesson objective that can be met with more than one instructional task/activity.

   Objective: _____

   _____

   Explanation: _____

   _____

B.   Instructional Tasks and Activities: Find examples of . . .

3. Two activities/tasks/questions that prepared the students for the day's learning.

   Example a: _____

   _____

   Example b: _____

   _____

4. An instructional task/activity that required students to connect new information to their prior knowledge.

   Example: _____

   _____

5. An instructional task/activity that required students to reflect on new information or skills.

   Example: _____

   _____

6. An instructional task/activity that required a response from every student.

   Example: _____

   _____

7. An instructional task/activity (not quiz/test) that permitted a quick assessment of each student's understanding of information or performance of a skill.

   Example: _____

   _____

8. Two activities/tasks that provided rehearsal for students before they worked independently.

   Example a: _____

   _____

   Example b: _____

   _____

9. Two tasks/activities/questions that provided transitions for students while they moved from one task to the next.

   Example a: _____

   _____

   Example b: _____

   _____

10. Two questions that required students to use higher-order thinking skills.

    Example a: _____

    _____

    Example b: _____

    _____

11. Instructional task/activity that gave students the repetition necessary to learn new information/skills.

    Example: _____

    _____

12. Instructional tasks/activities that promoted high on-task student behavior.

    Example a: _____

    _____

Example b: _____

_____

13. Instructional tasks/activities that resulted in high student success.

   Example a: _____

   _____

   Example b: _____

   _____

14. An authentic instructional task/activity.

   Example: _____

   _____

15. An instructional task/activity that permitted differentiated instruction.

   Example: _____

   _____

C. Instructional Strategies: Find examples of . . .

16. Two instructional procedures that reflect the developmental needs of your students.

   Example a: _____

   _____

   Example b: _____

   _____

17. Two instructional strategies best suited for each learning modality.

   Visual Learners

   Example a: _____

   _____

   Example b: _____

   _____

   Auditory Learners

   Example a: _____

   _____

   Example b: _____

   _____

Tactile/Kinesthetic Learners

Example a: _____

_____

Example b: _____

_____

18. A modified assignment or test for students with special needs.

Example: _____

_____

19. Novelty/creativity that added interest and pizzazz to a lesson.

Example: _____

_____

20. Two predictable instructional procedures that fostered student independence and/or responsibility.

Example a: _____

_____

Example b: _____

_____

Activity 1.2   *Teaching: A Science or an Art?*

Context   Teachers who base learning tasks and activities on the five memory lanes will enable their students to remember more effectively and efficiently.

Purpose   Experiment with new ways to teach content information.

Directions

- Select some important information that you plan to teach your students. Because this information deals with words, students will be using semantic memory, the most fleeting memory. Write this information in the space provided below.
- Now create a mnemonic memory device (e.g., HOMES, Every Good Boy Does Fine, FACE) to help students remember this information better. Write it in the space provided below.
- Create either a graphic organizer (e.g., outline, webbing, flow chart, time line, graph, etc.) or song, rap, rhyme, rhythm, or physical movement to help your students remember this information better. Write it in the space provided below.

The important information your students need to remember:

_____

_____

_____

_____

_____

Your mnemonic device that will help them remember this information more easily:

_____

_____

_____

_____

_____

Your graphic organizer or musical/rhythmic activity that will help them remember this information more easily:

_____

_____

_____

_____

_____

Activity 1.3 Scope and Sequence

Context   What do students know about your subject matter at the beginning of the school year? Have they studied it before? What did students study last year to help them understand the concepts you'll be teaching? What will they need to know for future classes?

"No man is an island." To be effective, teachers must understand where the course they're teaching fits into the scope and sequence of district curriculum. For example, if the Biology 10 teachers know that students have studied the parts of the cell extensively in Life Science 7, they can build on this knowledge rather than reteaching the simpler concepts. When the English 9 teachers know that students study grammar as seventh and eighth graders, they can limit grammar study at ninth grade to a review unit.

In addition to the scope and sequence of district curriculum, teachers must also know state graduation standards for their content areas. Graduation standards were established to identify and describe what P–12 students need to know and be able to do in order to successfully live and work in today's society. Successful completion of these standards is required for graduation from public high schools. Often state graduation standards are embedded into high school courses as part of the curriculum.

Purpose   Through this activity, you will examine the placement of the course(s) you teach in district curriculum.

Directions   Choose one course that you're teaching and answer the following questions in the space provided. You will need to talk to other professionals to obtain the information. These may include your cooperating teacher, the department chair, the graduation standards technician, the principal, and counselor.

1. Is this a required course? If so, is it required at the local or state level? _____

2. Is this an elective course? If so, must students meet certain criteria for admittance? Please explain.

_____

_____

3. What content area courses do students study the year before and the year after the course you're teaching?

_____

_____

4. What state graduation standards are related to the course you're teaching?

_____

_____

5. Does the curriculum for this course include all or a part of a graduation standard? Please explain.

_____

_____

6. Are students promoted to the next grade based on their performance, attendance, effort? Please explain.

_____

_____

Case Study

Jenny was thrilled to be student teaching with Ms. Callahan, who had recently received national recognition from the National Council of Teachers of English for innovations in teaching. So, she was perplexed by the latest writing assignment that Ms. Callahan had given her ninth graders—a month-long project focused on self-discovery and reflection. Jenny was familiar with best practices in writing, having studied it in her university methods courses, so she realized that autobiographical writing was a time-honored topic. However, Jenny noticed that during this extensive project, the students did not share their writing with others, revise their own drafts, engage in peer editing and use other strategies identified as best practice. In fact, Ms. Callahan's approach seemed to contradict the research on practices that foster the development of confident, competent writers. When Jenny began to assume teaching responsibilities, the ninth graders had not completed this project and she was uncomfortable with using the same approach as Ms. Callahan. However, she felt obligated to learn from her seasoned cooperating teacher and was reluctant to introduce the best practices she had learned.

1. Is Jenny's concern valid? Please explain.
2. Jenny has met the other English teachers in the school. Should she visit with them? If so, how can she tap into their teaching practices without damaging Ms. Callahan's integrity?
3. What other options does Jenny have?
4. How might Jenny's situation be similar to student teachers in other subject areas?
5. How can Jenny best learn from her student teaching experience?

Student-to-Student Tips

✔ Get to know your cooperating teacher ahead of time if possible. Then you can focus on teaching right away. *Michelle, elementary student teacher*

✔ Get everything ready the night before. Have your clothes and lunch ready. Before I left school I had all the copying and materials ready and set up. You never know what might happen and you may not have the time in the morning. *Thaira, elementary student teacher*

✔ If you think you're a broke college student now, just wait until you are student teaching. *Emily, elementary student teacher*

✔ Eat healthy, exercise, take vitamin C—don't get sick. *Kim, elementary student teacher*

✔ You get as much out of student teaching as you put into it. If you want a good experience, you'll have to put in the time and effort. *Scott, elementary student teacher*

✔ Take notes while observing. Don't just sit and watch. *Lorraine, elementary student teacher*

✔ Stretch yourself. Get involved right away even if you are nervous. Don't sit back and wait. *Angie, elementary student teacher*

✔ Be prepared to get sick. I did. *Najma, elementary student teacher*

✔ Be ready to go through stages: excited to be there; tired and overwhelmed; "I want to get on with my life. This is going too slowly"; it's over already. *Tammy, secondary student teacher*

✔ Be ready with a lesson to teach the first day you are in the class. It can be a lesson that helps introduce yourself to the class. *Mohamed, secondary student teacher*

✔ Jump right in the first day. I was surprised when my cooperating teacher mentioned at the midterm how impressed she was by that. It's making a good first impression, I guess. *Ed, secondary student teacher*

✔ Student teaching takes a lot of energy—and time. Don't plan on doing anything else during your student teaching. You just don't realize how much time it takes to plan, prepare, and correct papers. And you still have the cooperating teacher helping you with many things. You don't have as many responsibilities as you will your first year of teaching. *Aish, secondary student teacher*

✔ Get involved right away. Sitting and observing for very long can be boring. Help the students and do things for the teacher (correct papers, hand out materials, etc.). *Carla, secondary student teacher*

✔ Don't worry too much; your supervisor is there to help you. *Andrea, elementary student teacher*

Bibliography

Anderson, C. W., and E. L. Smith. 1987. Teaching science. In *Educator's handbook: A research perspective*, ed. V. Koehler. New York: Longman.

Arends, R. I., N. E. Winitzky, and M. D. Tannenbaum. 2001. *Exploring teaching: An introduction to education.* 2nd ed. New York: McGraw Hill.

Bredekamp, S., and C. Copple. 1997. *Developmentally appropriate practice in early childhood programs.* Rev. ed. Washington, DC: National Association for the Education of Young Children.

Brooks, J. G., and M. G. Brooks. 1993. *In search of understanding: The case for constructivist classrooms.* Alexandria, VA: Association for the Supervision and Curriculum Development.

Danielson, C. 1996. *Enhancing professional practice: A framework for teaching.* Alexandria, VA: Association for Supervision and Curriculum Development.

Dewey, J. [1904] 1964. *John Dewey on education,* ed. R. Archambault. Chicago: University of Chicago Press.

———. 1938. *Experience and education.* New York: Macmillan.

Gardner, H. 1991. *The unschooled mind: How children think and how schools should teach.* New York: Basic Books.

Heuwinkel, M. 1996. New ways of learning and new ways of teaching. *Childhood Education* 73: 27–31.

Lowenberg, D. 2000. Bridging practices. *Journal of Teacher Education* 51, 3 (May): 241–252.

McNergney, R. F., and J. M. Herbert. 2001. *Foundations of education: The challenge of professional practice.* 3rd ed. Boston: Allyn and Bacon.

Papert, S. A., and I. Harel. 1991. *Constructionism.* Norwood, NJ: Ablex Publishers.

Piaget, J. 1948. *To understand is to invent.* New York: Viking.

Privett, N. B. 1996. Without fear of failure: The attributes of ungraded primary school. *School Administrator* 53, 1 (Jan.): 6–11.

Reynolds, A. 1992. What is competent beginning teaching? A review of the literature. *Review of Educational Research* 62, 1: 1–35.

Shulman, L. S. 1987. Knowledge and teaching: Foundations of the new reform. *Harvard Educational Review* 57, 1: 1–22.

Sloane, M. W. 1998. Engaging primary students. *Childhood Education* 75, 2 (Winter): 76–82.

Smith, L. R. 1985. A low-inference indicator of lesson organization. *Journal of Classroom Interaction* 21, 1: 25–30.

Stone, S. J. 1995. Teaching strategies: Empowering teachers, empowering students. *Childhood Education* 71, 3: 294–295.

Stykes, G., and T. Bird. 1992. Teacher education and the case idea. *Review of Research in Educational Research* 62, 1 (Aug.): 1–35.

Thompson, P., and A. Thompson. 1994. Talking about rates conceptually, Part I: A teacher's struggle. *Journal for Research in Mathematics Education* 25: 279–303.

Van Patton, J., C. Chao, and C. Reigeluth. 1986. A review of strategies for sequencing and synthesizing instruction. *Review of Educational Research* 56, 4: 437–471.

2
Student Learning

"A pupil needs a teacher who knows his work, who has the gift of teaching, who in patience and love will descend to the pupil's needs."
—*Andrew Murray*

Standard #2 The teacher understands how children learn and develop, and can provide learning opportunities that support their intellectual, social, and personal development.

Performance Indicators: *The teacher . . .*
- Draws upon well-established human development/learning theories and concepts and a variety of information about students to plan instructional activities.
- Consistently engages students in appropriate experiences that support their development as independent learners.

Vignette Antonio was assigned to student-teach in computer classes at the middle school. As the student teaching semester began, Antonio was excited about his classes. By the fourth week, he was aware that several of the students were not turning in their work. One of those students was Lety, a bright student and one never to cause a disturbance. Later in the week, Antonio notices Lety working on the keyboard but not doing the work she was suppose to. Antonio stopped the entire class from their work and said: "All right, now. I want to know why some of you are not working on your assignment." Lety replies: "I do not understand your directions on how to do the work" (Wentz 2001).

Fundamental Principles

People learn differently. Because we process information differently, some students will immediately understand the teacher's lesson, some will puzzle over it for a while and then "see the light," and some will not understand it and will become bored (Wentz 2001).

People often say that everyone can learn. And the reality is that everyone *does* learn. Every person is born with a brain that functions as an immensely powerful processor. As long as the brain is not prohibited from fulfilling its normal processes, learning will occur. Each brain is unique. Although we all have the same physiological systems, these systems of the human body are integrated differently in every brain (Kandel and Squire 2000). Moreover, because learning actually changes the structure of the brain, the more we learn, the more complex our brains become (Leamnson 2000).

During the past ten years, our understanding of the brain and how it works, as well as the kind of environment in which it works most effectively, has increased significantly. The following examples illustrate this explosion of information about how the human brain functions. Current brain research indicates that the brain undergoes physiological changes as a result of experience. Emotion influences learning. Intelligence is multiple. The learning environment can have serious impact on the learner, positively or negatively (Caulfield, Kidd, and Kocher 2000). A basic precept of brain-based research states that learning is best achieved when linked with the learner's previous knowledge of a given subject or concept (Perry 2000).

Recent studies of the brain and how it learns have given educators new insights about teaching and learning (Hardiman 2001). Caine and Caine (1990) stress the importance of educators developing an accurate model of how students learn by implementing twelve principles of brain-based learning into their curriculum:

- Every single brain is totally unique.

- Impact or threat or high stress can alter and impair learning.

- Emotions are critical to learning—they drive our attention, health, learning, meaning and memory.

- Information is stored and retrieved through multiple memory and neural pathways.

- All learning is mind-body—movement, foods, attentional cycles, drugs, and chemicals all have powerful modulating effects on learning.

- The brain is a complex and adaptive system—effective change involves the entire complex system.

- Patterns and programs drive our understanding—intelligence is the ability to elicit and to construct useful patterns.

- The brain is meaning-driven; meaning is more important to the brain than information.

- Learning is often rich and non-conscious; we process both parts and wholes simultaneously and are affected a great deal by peripheral influences.

- The brain develops better in concert with other brains; intelligence is valued in the context of the society in which we live.

- The brain develops with various stages of readiness.

- The brain can grow new connections at any age. Complex, challenging experiences with feedback are best. Cognitive skills develop better with music and motor skills.

Another general finding from brain research confirms what professionals have asserted in the past: The mind needs rich and stimulating experiences. Furthermore, emerging research from the neurosciences informs us that minds can do more at an earlier age than previously assumed (Puckett, Marshall, and Davis 1999). It is important then to recognize when a child is "ready to learn." McCart and Stief (1995) provide a definition of readiness that includes dimensions of child development associated with physical health and nutritional status, emotional well-being, social development, and language richness. The implications are that because it is impossible to isolate the cognitive from the affective domain, the emotional climate of the school and classroom must be monitored on a consistent basis, using effec-

tive communication strategies and allowing for student and teacher reflection (Sylvester 1994).

Research suggests that children must be mentally and physically active in the process of learning, that the brain best processes information when it is presented in integrated wholes, and that, while age-appropriate ranges exist, each child learns in his or her own particular way and time (Springer and Deutsch 1985; Bredekamp and Copple 1997). Good teaching necessarily builds understanding and skills over time because learning is cumulative and developmental. Therefore, presenting cognitive tasks that are inappropriate, meaningless, repetitive to the point of mental fatigue, or that present a perceived threat of failure, may affect the brain's ability to function at high levels or to engage in creative thought (Hart 1983; Lakoff 1987; Puckett, Marshall, Davis 1999). The brain learns best when confronted with a balance between stress and comfort: high challenge and low threat. The brain needs some challenge to activate emotions and learning (Caine and Caine 1995). Practically speaking, this means teachers should create places that are not only safe to learn (e.g., by caring deeply for each student, accepting and encouraging individuality, encouraging risk taking, and using unique student talents), but they should also spark some emotional interest (e.g., by displaying student work, varying instructional strategies, using multiage groups, and using community resources) (Green 1999).

How the brain works has a significant impact on what kinds of learning activities are most effective (Brandt, R. 1999). Teachers need to help students have appropriate experiences and capitalize on those experiences. Caine and Caine (1995) suggest three interactive elements essential to this process: (1) teachers must immerse learners in complex, interactive experiences that are both rich and real. Teachers must take advantage of the brain's ability to parallel process. (2) Students must have a personally meaningful challenge. Such challenges stimulate a student's mind to the desired state of alertness. (3) In order for a student to gain insight about a problem, there must be intensive analysis of the different ways to approach it, and about learning in general. This is what is known as the "active processing" of experience. Several additional tenets of brain-based learning include: (1) feedback from reality, rather than from an authority figure; (2) learning results when solving realistic problems; and (3) the big picture cannot be separated from the details. In this context, then, it is suggested that teachers design learning around student interests while structuring learning around real problems, encouraging students to also learn in settings outside the classroom and the school building.

Educators must be willing to develop individual learning profiles for each student and prepare for complex instruction. Complex instruction is multifaceted and involves providing a variety of instructional materials, resources, groupings, and assessment instruments. Moreover, structured classroom time devoted to social and emotional skill building, group problem solving, and team building strengthens academic learning. Brain and learning research indicates that the brain responds more to learning environments that are enriched and that involve as many of its processing centers as possible. Educators have to allow children to have rich experiences and then give them time and opportunities to make sense of their experiences by reflecting and finding connections in how things relate. Teachers need to use a great deal of real-life activity, including problem-solving techniques, journal writing, reading, stories, drama, and interaction of different subjects (Hinitz and Stomfay-Stitz 1999). Content needs to be relevant, integrating multiple aspects simultaneously.

Students should be given choices and encouraged to discuss their emotions and listen to others express *their* feelings. They should be challenged to ask their own questions and research plausible answers. When possible, activities should engage students' bodies and emphasize social interactions. Games, simulations, role-playing, field trips, dance, art, and music must be incorporated into the curriculum. Not all students need to be doing the same thing at the same time. Some group work is therefore appropriate. Students are not all at the same level of ability and they do not learn in the same way. It follows that different groups within the same class should be working at a variety of different levels of complexity and/ or difficulty simultaneously, but at different rates. Students need to be actively involved in making decisions and modifications to their learning efforts. They need appropriate challenges, a secure environment, and an opportunity to explore ideas and have fun learning.

Like cognitive development, social and emotional development are influenced by learning, maturation, and experience. Social development refers to the ways children learn to interact with others, whereas emotional or personal development refers to the ways they view themselves (Arends, Winitzky, and Tannenbaum 2001). Parents and educators alike want young people to succeed in their academic, personal, and social lives. They want children to have the motivation and ability to achieve; to establish positive re-

lationships with their peers and adults; to adapt to the complex demands of growth and development; to contribute to their peer group, family, school, and community; and to make responsible decisions that enhance their well-being. To help children accomplish these tasks, schools are increasingly challenged to offer more than basic instruction in the traditional academic areas.

Growing evidence suggests that social and emotional learning is critical to success in school and the workplace and to sustaining healthy relationships with family and friends. If children are not aware of their feelings, they will find it difficult to make reasoned decisions, control impulsive actions, or say what they really mean. A positive self-concept and the skills necessary for decision making, effective communication, and conflict resolution are central to a healthy social and emotional well-being. More definitively, personal development skills include self-discipline, impulse control, good judgment, integrity, courage, perseverance, and self-motivation. In addition, relationship skills include caring, kindness, courtesy, cooperativeness, helpfulness, honesty, respect, understanding, and tolerance (Kagan 2001). Gardner (1993) described these skills as necessary for social interaction and the understanding of one's own emotions and behaviors. These competencies enable individuals to identify their strengths and limitations and to develop positive feelings about themselves and others. Goleman (1995) emphasized that children can grow in cognitive skills when they develop socially and emotionally. When teachers use cooperative learning and other interactive teaching methods, they are supporting students' desire for close relationships with others and the need to feel competent (Arends, Winitzky, and Tannenbaum 2001).

Young people who lack social and emotional competence frequently cause discipline problems and are unsuccessful in learning. The lack of self-restraint and compassion for others may cause them to turn to violence or to withdraw from social interactions. Helping children develop socially and emotionally is as important as helping them progress academically. However, teachers hesitate to teach social and emotional skills systematically. Teachers may be concerned with time needed to teach affective instruction or with objections from parents. Media reporting of declining test scores has caused many schools to concentrate on teaching basic academic skills and to neglect the affective needs of students. In addition, many parents may view the teaching of social skills as "value education" and believe that such instruction belongs exclusively in the home (Richardson 2000).

Ryan and Bohlin (2001) have devised ideas to help make concepts of social and emotional development easy for teachers to integrate into their classrooms:

- Insist that quality matters. Homework should be handed in on time, neat and complete.
- Help students form friendships. When forming cooperative learning groups, keep in mind both the academic needs and emotional needs of students. These groups can represent an opportunity to group students who might not otherwise interact with one another.
- Do not underestimate the power of stories to build a child's character. Read aloud to students daily.
- Conduct literature discussions even in the youngest grades. Ask questions which encourage reflection.
- Build empathy in literature and social studies classes by teaching children to "put themselves in the shoes of" the people they are reading about and studying.
- Read and discuss biographies from all subject areas. Help students identify the person's core or defining characteristics.
- Assign homework that stimulates and challenges students. Engaging and demanding assignments will give rise to self-discipline and perseverance.
- Teach justice and compassion while helping the student separate the doer from the deed.
- Make classroom expectations clear and hold students accountable.
- Admit mistakes and seek to make amends. Expect and encourage students to do likewise.
- Lead by example. Pick up the piece of paper in the hall. Leave the classroom clean for the next teacher who will be using it.
- Employ the language of virtue in conversations with colleagues: responsibility, commitment, perseverance, and courage.

Several psychosocial and cognitive developmental characteristics of young adolescents suggest that the early adolescence developmental period is an optimal time to introduce multicultural education. In this period, their developmental growth focuses on forming cultural identities; establishing close friendships with, and positive opinions of, others; and developing a sense of justice and fairness. Middle school educators can promote harmony among young adolescents, and within the community, by providing multicultural ed-ucational experiences that address these three developmental characteristics (Manning 2000).

Opinions of one's self and one's culture play significant roles in academic achievement, social development, behavior, and one's overall outlook on life. In fact, the opinions of one's self and one's culture that are formed during early adolescence, whether positive or negative, may last a lifetime (Manning and Baruth 2000). Instructional materials should provide factual and objective information and perspectives; if sexism, racism, and ethnic, racial and gender stereotypes exist in texts and supplementary materials, teachers need to point them out to students. If the teacher does not challenge sexist or racist language, demeaning depictions of young adolescents' cultural groups or genders may affect their cultural identities, as well as their ability to live and work harmoniously with others in the classroom and in society (Manning 2000).

Educators know that young people place a high priority on forming friendships while in school. Research suggests that gender plays a role in the development of friendships; that is, both genders form like-gender friendships; and then later form cross-gender friendships (Crockett, Losoff, and Peterson 1984). Also, children's selection criteria usually include "like" characteristics and traits; that is, they tend to befriend those with similar characteristics and behavior patterns (DuBois and Hirsch 1990). Although teachers should refrain from trying to "make friends" on behalf of their students, they can arrange learning and social situations so that they have opportunities to learn and socialize with a variety of peers. Teachers can use cooperative learning to increase the likelihood of interethnic friendships, and to improve the attitudes and behaviors among students of different backgrounds (Manning and Lucking 1993).

School-age children are psychologically and cognitively capable of understanding injustices and unfair treatment. Most young people can detect ill treatment of others; some might actually engage in unfair behavior or fail to take a stand when others do. Regardless of their actions and stances toward others, their characteristics allow them to recognize the differences between how people treat one another and how they should be treated. Teachers can play vital roles in teaching the attitudes and ideals of a democratic society. Role-playing and case study investigations are but two means of teaching a sense of justice, a perception of fairness, and an overall sense of fair treatment (Manning 2000).

Students benefit when schools make clear the essential role of social and emotional skills in learning and life success. Elias, et al. (1997) believe that helping students develop and coordinate skills in emotion, cognition, and behavior is necessary in the classroom. Furthermore, they believe that competence in recognizing and managing feelings and social relationships is crucial for success in the home. An ongoing education to raise the social and emotional skills of children provides growth in their cognitive skills and behavior development. Social and emotional competencies can be taught and learned when schools integrate them into their academic environment.

Questions for Reflection

- What are the principles of brain-based learning?

- Is individual or group instruction best for learning? Why? Base your answer on current brain research.

- In what ways is constructivism similar to brain-based learning?

Commentary on Standard #2

CHARLOTTE DANIELSON | Lead Developer,
Educational Testing Service, Princeton, New Jersey

Every parent (indeed every aunt and uncle) knows that children of different ages are very different from one another. The activities that appeal to one age group are of little or no interest to those of another.

However, while parents all recognize the profound differences among children of different ages, the use they make of this information is very different from that of teachers. Parents' understanding of child and adolescent development is important to them as they plan birthday parties, and when they help their children through the rigors of growing up. It is essential for parents to be able to grant to their children in-

creasing amounts of responsibility, and to teach them important values of personal responsibility and strength in the face of peer pressure. Parents are, after all, their children's first teachers, and their influence is felt throughout a person's life.

Teachers, on the other hand, have a unique responsibility for the learning of young people; they have an obligation to design learning experiences for their students that are both engaging and productive, meaningful and rewarding, and in which students are both successful and challenged. This is not a simple matter, particularly since students in school, unlike children at home, are there in groups of 20 or 30 or more.

Children's thinking develops as they grow. Psychologists and educators have known this for many decades; it was documented with care and insight by Jean Piaget beginning in the 1920s. And while more recent work has served to refine our understanding of the process, the fundamental premise remains intact: young children understand their world in ways very different from that of adults. Adolescents see things differently than five-year-olds.

Teaching, then, involves not only understanding one's subject thoroughly. It includes that, and much more. It involves understanding one's students, their ways of knowing and understanding, and how to engage them in the content to be learned. In other words, not every great chemist is a great chemistry teacher. The skills are different.

This principle, then, embodies the heart of teaching. It requires exactly that aspect of the work that sets it apart from other work. It is in precisely understanding how our students think, in being able to enter their world, that gifted teachers work their magic. They are able to build the bridge between the inner world of the child (intellectually and socially) and the content to be learned. They engage students in important content, and through the methods they use, help student construct that understanding and make it their own.

Student Learning Self-Assessment

The teacher understands how children learn and develop, and can provide learning opportunities that support their intellectual, social, and personal development.

Knowledge/Performance Indicators	*Yes**	*Not Sure*	*No*
1. I understand how students internalize knowledge, acquire skills, and develop thinking behaviors.	2	1	0
2. I know how to use instructional strategies that promote student learning.	2	1	0

3. I understand that a student's physical, social, emotional, moral, and cognitive development influence learning.   2   1   0

4. I know how to address these factors when making instructional decisions.   2   1   0

5. I understand developmental progressions of learners.   2   1   0

6. I understand ranges of individual variation within the physical, social, emotional, moral, and cognitive domains.   2   1   0

7. I am able to identify levels of readiness in learning.   2   1   0

8. I understand how development in any one domain may affect performance in others.   2   1   0

9. I use a student's strengths as a basis for growth, and a student's errors as opportunities for learning.   2   1   0

10. I assess both individual and group performance and design developmentally appropriate instruction that meets the student's current needs in the cognitive, social, emotional, moral, and physical domains.   2   1   0

11. I link new ideas to familiar ideas.   2   1   0

12. I make connections to a student's experiences.   2   1   0

13. I provide opportunities for active engagement, manipulation, and testing of ideas and materials.   2   1   0

14. I encourage students to assume responsibility for shaping their learning tasks.   2   1   0

15. I use a student's thinking and experiences as a resource in planning instructional activities by encouraging discussion, listening, and responding to group interaction, and eliciting oral, written, and other samples of student thinking.   2   1   0

---

* A "Yes" response indicates that you can describe, document, and cite examples related to your student teaching assignment.

Self-Assessment Summary and Reflection

1. Which Knowledge/Performance Indicators can I currently describe, document, and cite examples?

    _____

    _____

2. Which Knowledge/Performance Indicators need some work or improvement?

    _____

    _____

3. What specific actions can I take to enrich my knowledge or skill in this area?

    _____

    _____

Activity 2.1   Student-Centered Classroom

Context   Teachers know that students need to be emotionally and cognitively involved in the learning process. They use a variety of strategies to connect with the varying needs, abilities, and experiences of their students. When planning your lessons, who is the focus, you or your students? Who does most of the work during the lesson? Is your classroom student-centered?

Purpose   This activity allows you to analyze strategies you are currently using and ones you plan to use in your lessons.

Directions   Rate yourself from 1 to 6 on the following indicators.

1 = I don't have a clue about this strategy.

2 = I know this is important, but I haven't tried it yet.

3 = I've tried this once or twice.

4 = I've tried this several times and was successful a few times.

5 = I've tried this a number of times and was mostly successful.

6 = I use this successfully and consistently.

_____ An important question before a teacher begins teaching is, "What do the students already know?" There are many ways to get this information, including KWL chart, web background information, warm-up activity eliciting/using prior knowledge, pretest, and skill survey.

_____ Catch the students' interest right from the beginning. Give the students reasons to want to learn. Pose a thought-provoking question, tie the new concept into the students' lives, begin the lesson with a surprise, set up the students the day before to make them want to come back to find out more, challenge the students, bring in an artifact or item related to the new lesson, or let the students have input on what they'll learn or do.

_____ Use meaningful examples that make use of the students' background knowledge. Use analogies that have meaning (H_2O is like a bicycle: for every oxygen molecule there are 2 hydrogen molecules, just like for every bike frame there are two wheels.). Define vocabulary words and give synonyms and examples that relate to the students' lives. Have students create their own examples to illustrate a concept.

_____ Use guided practice. Have students solve problems along with you; don't have just one person working (you or another student) while the others watch. Keep the students involved and on task throughout the lesson.

_____ Use every-student responses to gauge the learning of the students as you teach. This pairs nicely with guided practice. Students love to use individual chalkboards or white boards. Take advantage of that motivation to have them work individually on practice problems or record the efforts of their group. A quick flash of the boards allows you to check many students' answers at one time. Other every-student response techniques include the use of finger signals, yes/no cards, think pads, number cards, and partner discussions.

_____ Learning logs/journals. Students record such things as what they have learned, questions they have, opinions concerning activities, ideas to explore, and why learning this concept is important. It helps students to think about their thinking if their teacher models this metacognition process.

_____ Students have choices. They can help determine the direction for the class, offer suggestions and opinions, take responsibility for leading an activity, select an option from several that are offered, or create an activity.

Questions

1. Select an item that you rated a 1 or 2. Design two or more activities to help you implement this element into your teaching.

2. Select an item that you rated a 3 or 4. Analyze the differences between those activities that were successful and those that weren't. Use that information to restructure and improve an activity.

3. Select an item that you rated a 5 or 6. Analyze why those activities were successful. Reflect on the students' and your reactions.

Activity 2.2   What about Sherri?

Context   Each classroom has a wide variety of learners who come with various cognitive, social, emotional, and physical strengths and weaknesses. Teachers not only need to learn about each student, they plan instruction and decide on courses of action based on this knowledge. Are there students in your room who freeze up before a test or even before answering a question during a class discussion? Are there students who catch on to new skills very quickly? Is there anyone who amazes you with their answers because he/she always comes up with an idea different than anyone else's? Someone who really doesn't like the subject you teach and is only there because it's a required course? Someone who's sick a lot and misses class or seems very sleepy when in class? Someone who gets very upset when he/she makes a mistake and is unable to shrug it off?

Purpose   This activity will help you analyze your students' strengths and weaknesses and plan your lessons around that knowledge.

Directions

- Read the portrayal of Sherri and finish the analysis.

- Then analyze a student in your classroom. Don't select a student with extreme weaknesses or strengths, but choose someone with identifiable strengths and/or weaknesses. Pick a student who allows you to think about the cognitive, social, emotional, and physical development appropriate to your group of students.

- Determine what his/her strengths and weaknesses are, possible causes, and a course of action for you to take.

Example   Sherri works very hard and gets a lot of her homework done during class. Most of it is done correctly, but sometimes she seems to hurry and does not put in her best effort. Whatever work that she doesn't finish in class is very seldom finished as homework. If it is completed, it's poorly done.

1. What are Sherri's strengths?

- Works hard and completes work in class

- Generally does work correctly

- Seems to care about her work

- (How can you discover more of Sherri's strengths? For example, check Sherri's files—grades were quite good last year and there were few comments about incomplete homework.)

2. What are Sherri's weaknesses?

- Inconsistency in work standards

- Incomplete homework once or twice a week

3. What are some possible causes for these weaknesses?

- Disinterest in certain homework assignments

- Difficulty with certain concepts/skills

- Not enough sleep or ill

- Distractions during work time

4. How can you determine which of these are the cause(s), or if there is another cause?

- Talk with other teachers who work with Sherri

5. What are some steps you should take to help Sherri?

- Talk with cooperating teacher to learn more about Sherri

- Check Sherri's files

- Talk with Sherri's other teachers
- Talk with Sherri
- Talk with a school counselor/advisor
- Meet with Sherri's parents

Questions   Briefly describe one of your students and the situation.

_____

_____

_____

_____

1. What are the student's strengths?

_____

_____

_____

2. What are the student's weaknesses?

_____

_____

_____

3. What are some possible causes for these weaknesses?

_____

_____

_____

4. How can you determine what is the actual cause?

_____

_____

_____

5. What can you do to help the student?

_____

_____

_____

Activity 2.3   Active Participation

Context   Students learn when they interact with the concepts they are learning. They learn by experiencing and processing. Are your students actively involved in your lessons? Do you assume that they will pay attention and follow along, or do the words you use expect them to interact with the learning? As Harry Wong says, "The person who does the work is the *only* one who learns." Teachers strive to find as many ways as possible to get their students to be active learners.

Purpose   You will analyze your learning activities with an eye to how you can you involve your students more consistently and meaningfully.

Directions: Part 1   List at three concepts that you have taught the past week.

Example

1 linking verbs

2 vocabulary words

3 fractions

4 bicycle safety

1. _____

2. _____

3. _____

Directions: Part 2   Underline the active participation directions you used. If you had an example with no active participation, design directions for it. Describe the active participation you used in order to check what the students were learning. If there was no active participation, leave it blank.

Example

1. *linking verbs.* I had the students signal the number of the word that was the linking verb. (The{1} dog{2} is{3} frisky{4}.)

2. *vocabulary words.* The students showed an A, B, or C card to match with the vocabulary word that fit in the blank. (I really enjoyed the ___. A. delicious B. experience C. disappointment)

3. *fractions.* The students followed the directions on the overhead: Put the fractions in order from least to greatest. Show work. Raise your hand to have your work checked when you are finished.

4. *bicycle safety.* The students wrote or drew a picture of 2 things that are important for safe biking. They shared these with partners.

1. _____

2. _____

3. _____

Directions: Part 3   Select something that you will be teaching this/next week, and design an active participation technique that will require all the students to respond and allow you to check the students' understanding of the skill/concept while you are teaching it. (This is also called "guided practice.")

Active Participation   (Consistent involvement of the learner's mind with the learning)

Here are examples of directions to elicit *covert* (unobservable) behavior. Use them to get students to think and prepare answers and ideas.

think	fantasize	follow along
watch	smell	imagine
formulate	bring to mind	listen for
meditate	recall	say to yourself
envision	calculate	think back
figure out	mull over	remember
consider	be aware of	without pencil or paper
decide	expand your thoughts	pretend
put yourself in the story	pause for a moment to think	sense
suppose	reflect	make believe
in your head	visualize	
repeat	contemplate	

Here are examples of directions to elicit *overt* (observable) behavior. Use them to check students' answers and understanding of concepts.

match	sing	tell
read aloud	clap out	look up
show us	point to	dramatize
repeat	model	write
demonstrate	signal	hold cards up
tell me aloud together	thumbs up or thumbs down	ask the person next to you
describe to a neighbor	compare with a neighbor	share
say aloud	list	whisper to a neighbor
assist	jot down	
answer together	draw	

Concept: _____

Active Participation:　Description:

_____

_____

_____

_____

_____

_____

_____

_____

Case Study

Casey was observing her first-graders in their physical education class. The teacher, Mr. Caleb, was an excellent teacher. It was obvious that he had made his learning and behavior expectations clear to the students because his class ran so smoothly. The students loved going to phys ed and not just because they loved to burn off their energy. They really liked Mr. Caleb, and he kept everyone involved every moment of class. Everyone, that is, except Tabrisha. She hung out at the back of the gym and seemed to hide behind the other students. She really didn't participate much. Casey wasn't certain that Mr. Caleb noticed Tabrisha.

When her cooperating teacher came to walk the students back to their classroom, Casey walked next to Tabrisha and asked her if she had a good time in phys ed. Tabrisha just shrugged her shoulders and didn't say anything.

1. Should Casey continue her conversation with Tabrisha?

2. Is it proper for her to talk to her cooperating teacher about another teacher?

3. If Casey decides to talk to Mr. Caleb, what should she say?

4. Is Tabrisha just having a bad day, or is this something that Casey should pursue?

5. Should Casey have stepped in during the class and talked to Tabrisha then or helped her take part?

Student-to-Student Tips

✔ Be open to suggestions from anyone, even the students. Your main focus is for the students to learn, so be open to feedback. *Shafiei, elementary student teacher*

✔ Start right away working with individual students and with your classroom management. It helps you establish respect right away. *Stephanie, elementary student teacher*

✔ Be very caring and compassionate with students. Know when to be firm and when to be compassionate. *Theresa, elementary student teacher*

✔ Take notes those first days when you are observing, but also be part of the class. Help students. Get involved. It helps you develop a rapport with the students. *Julie, elementary student teacher*

✔ Have patience. Not every student will "get it" the first time. But don't be frustrated; it may work the next time around. *Nhu Thuy, secondary student teacher*

✔ Laugh with your students. Don't try to be so serious. *Jordan, secondary student teacher*

✔ Don't hold back. Get in there right away. Start learning about the individual students from the very beginning. *Ruth, secondary student teacher*

✔ Don't sit back. This is your time to show what you can do. Do your best. Do whatever you can to help the students. *Jill, secondary student teacher*

✔ Be professional with the students during the first week. Help them respect you as a teacher. *Mark, elementary student teacher*

✔ Think of the students first. Always worry about them before you worry about yourself. *José, elementary student teacher*

✔ Try to go to some of your students' outside activities and sports. They really notice that you are there and view it as something special. *Robert, elementary student teacher*

Bibliography

Arends, R. I., N. E. Winitzky, and M. D. Tannenbaum. 2001. *Exploring teaching: An introduction to education.* 2nd ed. New York: McGraw-Hill.

Brandt, R. 1999. Educators need to know about the human brain. *Phi Delta Kappan* 81: 235–238.

Bredekamp, S., and C. Copple. 1997. *Developmentally appropriate practice in early childhood education.* Rev. ed. Washington, DC: National Association for the Education of Young Children.

Caine, R., and G. Caine. 1990. Understanding a brain-based approach to learning and teaching. *Educational Leadership*, 47, 2 (Oct.): 66–70.

———. 1995. Reinventing schools through brain-based learning. *Educational Leadership* 52, 7 (April): 43–47.

Caulfield, J., S. Kidd, and T. Kocher. 2000. Brain-based instruction in action. *Educational Leadership* 58, 3 (Nov.): 62–65.

Crockett, L., M. Losoff, and A. Peterson. 1984. Perceptions of the peer group and friendship in early adolescence. *Journal of Early Adolescence* 4, 2: 155–181.

DuBois, D. L., and B. J. Hirsch. 1990. School and neighborhood friendship patterns of Blacks and

Whites in early adolescence. *Child Development* 61, 2: 524–536.

Elias, M., J. Zins, R. Weissberg, K. Frey, M. Greenberg, N. Haynes, R. Kessler, M. Schwab-Stone, and T. Shriver. 1997. *Promoting social and emotional learning: Guidelines for educators.* Alexandria, VA: Association for Supervision and Curriculum Development.

Gardner, H. 1993. *Multiple intelligence: The theory in practice.* New York: Basic Books.

Goleman, D. 1995. *Emotional intelligence: Why it can matter more than IQ.* New York: Bantam Books.

Green, F. E. 1999. Brain and learning research: Meeting the needs of diverse learner. *Education* 119, 4 (Summer): 682–691.

Hardiman, M. M. 2001. Connecting brain research with dimensions of learning. *Educational Leadership* 58, 3 (Nov.): 52–55.

Hart, L. A. 1983. Incredible brain: How does it solve problems? Is logic a natural process? *NASSP Bulletin* 67, 459 (Jan.): 36–41.

Hinitz, B. F., and A. M. Stomfay-Stitz. 1999. Peace education and conflict resolution through the expressive arts in early childhood and teacher education. Paper presented at the Annual Conference of the Eastern Educational Research Association. Hilton Head, SC.

Kagan, S. 2001. Teaching for character and community. *Educational Leadership* 57, 2 (Oct.): 50–53.

Kandel, E. R., and L. R. Squire. 2000. Neuroscience: Breaking down scientific barriers to the study of brain and mind. *Science* 290: 1113–1120.

Lakoff, G. 1987. *Linguistics as a cognitive science and its rule in an undergraduate curriculum.* Washington, DC: Linguistic Society of America.

Leamnson, R. 2000. Learning as biological brain change. *Change* 32, 6: 34–40.

Manning, M. L. 2000. Developmentally responsive multicultural education for young adolescents. *Childhood Education* 76, 2 (Winter): 82–87.

Manning, M. L., and L. Baruth. 2000. *Multicultural education of children and adolescents.* 3rd ed. Boston: Allyn and Bacon.

Manning, M. L., and R. Lucking. 1993. Cooperative learning and multicultural classrooms. *The Clearing House* 67, 1: 12–16.

McCart, L., and E. Stief. 1995. Governors' campaign for children: An action agenda for states. Washington, DC: National Governors' Association.

Perry, B. 2000. How the brain learns best. *Instructor* 11, 4: 34–35.

Puckett, M., C. S. Marshall, and R. Davis. 1999. Examining the emergence of brain development research. *Childhood Education* 76, 1 (Fall): 8–12.

Richardson, R. C. 2000. Teaching social and emotional competence. *Children and Schools* 22, 4 (Oct.): 246–251.

Ryan, K., and K. Bohlin. 2001 Now more than ever: Help kids build character. *Education Digest* (Nov.): 8–15.

Sylvester, R. 1994. How emotions affect learning. *Educational Leadership* 52, 2 (Oct.): 60–68.

Springer, S. P., and G. Deutsch. 1985. *Left brain, right brain.* New York: Freeman and Co., Pub.

Wentz, P. J. 2001. *The student teaching experience: Cases for the classroom.* Upper Saddle River, NJ: Merrill/Prentice Hall.

3

Diverse Learners

"The connectedness of things is what the educator contemplates to the limit of his capacity. No human capacity is great enough to permit a vision of the world as simple, but if the educator does not aim at the vision no one else will. And the consequences are dire when no one does."
—*Mark Van Doren*

Standard #3 The teacher understands how students differ in their approaches to learning and creates instructional opportunities that are adapted to diverse learners.

Performance Indicators: *The teacher . . .*

- Establishes a comfortable environment that accepts and fosters diversity. The teacher must demonstrate knowledge and awareness of varied cultures. The teacher creates a climate of openness, inquiry, and support by practicing strategies such as acceptance, tolerance, resolution, and mediation.
- Consistently provides opportunities that are inclusive and adapted to diverse learners.

Vignette Marta, a sixth grader, is often tardy and unprepared for class. She is tired, and frequently falls asleep after lunch. She is placed in a low-ability group for both reading and math. During whole class instruction, Marta's performance is generally below average. She presents no behavioral problems, preferring to withdraw from other students. Standardized tests show she is functioning below sixth-grade level. Stephanie, Marta's student teacher, observes that she reverses numerals when working mathematical problems. During reading Marta has difficulty sounding out new vocabulary words. Stephanie approaches her cooperating teacher with questions on how to create instructional opportunities for Marta that will not detract from learning for the other students in the class.

Fundamental Principles

Teaching to diversity allows all students to reach their potential regardless of their differences. Four major variables of diversity influence how teachers and students think and learn: race/ethnicity, gender, social class, and ability (Arends, Winitzky, and Tannenbaum 2001). Teaching for diversity creates an educational environment in which students from a variety of backgrounds and experience come together to experience educational equality (Banks 1994). Teaching to diversity assumes that children come from different backgrounds and helps them make sense of their everyday life. It focuses on how to learn rather than on what to learn.

Federal legislation and Supreme Court decisions require equal educational opportunities for all students regardless of gender, physical condition, socioeconomic level, racial or ethnic background, religion, or language. Children who were previously excluded from classes because of language, race, economics, and abilities are now learning together. Teaching now requires a pluralistic mindset and the ability to communicate across cultures. It means that teaching will capitalize on the strengths of student differences rather than on their weaknesses. It also means that teachers must learn to view cultural values from each group's perspective rather than from their own. This includes knowledge about racism, sexism, stereotypes, and prejudice. It also suggests that teachers understand the histories, characteristics, and intergroup differences among major racial and ethnic groups. It is, for example, nearly impossible for teachers to truly respect cultural differences among students and to communicate that respect to their students if they do not have accurate knowledge of those differences (McNergney and Herbert 2001).

If schools are to meet the challenge of educating increased numbers of children and youth with diverse needs, teachers must embrace instruction and curricula that engage and encourage all students (Ryan and Cooper 2000). Appendix E provides a list of educational resources for more specific information and services. How teachers perceive students strongly impacts their performance. Teachers who effectively teach for diversity hold high expectations for all students, particularly for ethnic minority children and youth. Research show that teachers tend to have lower expectations for ethnic minority youth (Vasquez 1988). These low expectations occur in interpersonal interactions and in how students are placed in opportunities for enrichment and personal growth. At-risk youth need a rich curriculum that allows no room for failure and provides the necessary support for success. To teach styles and strategies appropriate for only one group fails to meet the needs of all students from diverse backgrounds (Reiff 1997).

Current brain studies underscore the important role teachers play in facilitating a stimulating environment for students. The same research identifies educationally meaningful differences among individuals and equal opportunities for academic success. Each and every child has great capacity to learn when exposed to effective and relevant learning strategies (Green 1999). Many of these strategies exemplify standard practices of good teaching, and others are specific to working with students with diverse abilities (Burnette 1999).

The knowledge base regarding the use of classroom grouping includes findings from research on effective schools, effective teaching, student academic achievement, student perception of self and others, student motivation, student attitudes toward school, and student friendships and interactions in the classroom and school. A dominant theme in the research findings is that some types of instructional grouping contribute to more positive academic and affective outcomes for students. Other groups, particularly stable, long-term groups based on student ability, have a negative effect upon students (Sanchez, Li, and Nuttall 1995; Mueller and Fleming 2001). Common grouping types are: (a) learning cycle groups which consist of students with similar learning needs for the expressed purpose of mastering the content and skills

covered in a particular lesson or unit; (b) cooperative groups which require students with diverse ability and characteristics to work together and learn from one another to accomplish assigned learning goals or tasks; and (c) peer tutoring groups where students from a cross section of characteristics are formed to teach information and skills. Grouping is beneficial in assuring that all students learn. Research has found that both high- and low-ability students do better academically in classes where the total group includes students with a wide range of academic ability. Grouping also increases student engagement in learning. High levels of student on-task time occur in small groups. In particular, low-ability students spend much less time off task in cooperative small group situations than in total class instruction largely because they spend less time waiting for instructions and feedback. Grouping teaches students how to work with others. Students learn to cooperate with others when assigned group tasks that require each student to complete a task. Grouping facilitates social interaction among students. The more interdependent the group activities in which students engage, the more positive the prosocial outcomes are for the students. Grouping improves students' self-concepts and attitudes toward self and school. Grouping also teaches students how to learn in a variety of ways. Since most small-group activities do not involve direct instruction by the teacher, students are responsible for gathering information, coordinating work, helping one another, and solving problems. Students learn from one another. Particularly in groups, learning tasks expand beyond the listening, reading, and writing tasks that predominate in total class instruction.

It has sometimes been said that cooperative learning is only another teaching method in which students help one another learn the same thing, with capable students tutoring those less prepared. It is often characterized as an approach that encourages educators to teach to the middle, neglecting the academic needs of both particularly competent and struggling students. But when teachers implement cooperative learning thoughtfully and differentiate tasks within it, they can personalize student learning, help students collaborate while challenging each individual in the context of a group effort, and encourage students to appreciate their peers' diverse competencies and experiences (Schniedewind and Davidson 2000; Johnson and Johnson 2000; Siciliano 2001). The following principles illustrate how educators can differentiate learning within heterogeneous cooperative groups:

- Differentiate tasks by complexity and quantity. Students in a cooperative learning group can engage in tasks with different levels of complexity and learn different amounts of material.

- Use high-achieving students' work. Teachers can ask well-prepared students to integrate into the cooperative group task the advanced ideas they've worked on. The whole group benefits from ideas they otherwise would not have access to, and the advanced learner is appropriately challenged.

- Employ cooperative groups to enhance individualized work. Although students work on projects at their own levels, they check in with their group every few days to summarize what they have done and to get criterion-based feedback from cooperative group members.

- Add options for enrichment within cooperative learning. Such opportunities can challenge preconceived notions of student ability.

- Design cooperative activities for multiple intelligences. Students develop more sophisticated skills using intelligences in which they excel and build a broader range of skills by working in intelligences that are not as natural for them.

- Vary criteria for success. Within heterogeneous cooperative groups, students work on a common project but are assessed according to different criteria.

- Value cognitive, social, and emotional learning. Those who argue that "gifted students" are not challenged in cooperative groups typically define learning in academic terms only. Because many educators who use cooperative learning seek both cognitive and affective outcomes, differentiation can also focus on social and emotional competencies (Schniedewind and Davidson 2000).

Another teaching strategy of use in classrooms with students from diverse backgrounds is incorporating developmentally appropriate practice. Developmentally appropriate practice is "based on knowledge about how children develop and learn" (National Association for the Education of Young Children 1996). Instruction is based on: what is known about student development and learning; what is known about the strengths, interests, and needs of each individual child in the group; and knowledge of the social and cultural context in which students live. Developmentally appropriate practice is especially important in the diverse classroom because it encourages greater cultural sensitivity, recognizes a variety of cultural communication patterns, and allows for intervention in the natural course of teaching. Developmentally appropriate practices include the following teaching strategies: (a) providing active learning experiences; (b) incorporating a variety of instructional strategies; (c) providing a balance between teacher-directed and student-directed activities; (d) integrating/inclusive curriculum; and (e) using learning centers. These strategies emphasize the strengths but accommodate the needs of all students.

Another consideration for schools and teachers is to understand that students differ in the ways that they perceive and understand the world. Howard Gardner labels each of these ways a distinct "intelligence"—in other words, a set of skills allowing individuals to find and resolve genuine problems they face. Gardner's theory of multiple intelligences (1987, 1993) enables teachers to acknowledge positive strengths in all students and plan appropriate learning strategies for a more effective classroom environment.

Gardner's research led to the identification of eight intelligences.

- Linguistic learners have sensitivity to the meaning, sounds, and rhythms of words. Activities for linguistic learners could include reading/writing workshops, book sharing, dialogue writing, book-tape stories, word processing, and newspaper activities.

- Logical-mathematical learners enjoy number games, problem solving, pattern games, and experimenting. As teachers, challenge these students with problem-solving and patterning activities.

- Spatial learners respond to visual cues and are image-oriented. Maps, charts, diagrams, puzzles, and mazes are excellent resources. Provide manipulatives and use guided imagery and mind-mapping.

- Bodily kinesthetic learners enjoy creative dramatics, role-playing, dancing, and expressing themselves with movement and bodily action. These students derive much of what they learn through physical movement and from touching and feeling. They use movement, gesture, and physical expression to learn and solve problems. Provide physical exercises and hands-on activities.

- Musical learners thoroughly enjoy playing instruments and singing songs. Use a variety of music in the classroom as background and to teach skills.

- Interpersonal learners are very social and intuitive about other's feelings. They enjoy being part of a group and can help peers and work cooperatively with others. Students here would enjoy skits, plays, group work, discussions, debates, and cooperative learning.

- Intrapersonal learners like to work independently. They have the ability to understand their own feelings, motivations, and moods. Teachers should provide a quiet area for independent work, encourage writing in a personal journal, discuss thinking strategies, and suggest independent projects.

- The naturalist intelligence designates the ability to discriminate among living things, as well as a sensitivity to other features of the natural world (Checkley 1997; Reiff 1997; Adams 2000/2001). Students here would enjoy ecological field trips, outdoor work, specimen collection, charts, and video collection.

By applying multiple intelligences teachers can actively involve students in learning experiences, help develop particular intelligences that individual students may lack, and design approaches to reach students who have trouble learning. Gardner (1993) says that educators do not have to address all of the intelligences in everything they teach. Different projects can give students the option to explore a topic using their strongest intelligence. Students must learn about a topic in a manner that is appropriate for them. Traditional schooling heavily favors the verbal-linguistic and logical-mathematical intelligences. Gardner suggests a more balanced curriculum that incorporates the arts, self-awareness, communication, and physical education. Gardner also advocates instructional methods that appeal to all intelligences, including role-playing, musical performance, cooperative learning, reflection, visualization, and storytelling. This theory calls for assessment methods that take into account the diversity of intelligences, as well as self-assessment tools that help students understand their intelligences.

Each student processes and absorbs new information in a different way. The learning styles theory implies that how much individuals learn has more to do with whether the educational experience is geared toward their particular style of learning than whether

or not they are intelligent. The concept of learning styles is rooted in the classification of psychological types (Jung 1971). The learning styles theory is based on research demonstrating that, as the result of heredity, upbringing, and current environmental demands, different individuals have a tendency to perceive and to process information differently (Kolb 1984). The different ways of doing so are generally classified as concrete or abstract *perceivers*, and active or reflective *processors*. *Concrete perceivers* absorb information through direct experience, by doing, acting, sensing, and feeling. *Abstract perceivers*, however, take in information through analysis, observation, and thinking. *Active processors* make sense of an experience by immediately using the new information. Reflective processors make sense of an experience by reflecting on and thinking about it. A student may be a concrete perceiver and an active processor or a concrete percieiver and a reflective processor. Similarly, an abstract perceiver can be either an active or a reflective processor.

How does the learning style theory impact education? Teachers must emphasize intuition, feeling, sensing, and imagination, in addition to the traditional skills of analysis, reason, and sequential problem solving. Teachers should design their instruction methods to connect with all four learning styles, using various combinations of experience, reflection, conceptualization, and experimentation. Teachers can introduce a wide variety of experiential elements into the classroom, such as sound, music, visuals, movement, experience, and even talking. Teachers should employ a variety of assessment techniques, focusing on the development of "whole brain" capacity and each of the different learning styles.

Another learning style approach to teaching and learning is based on the idea that all students have strengths and abilities, but each student may have preferred ways of using these abilities (Dunn and Dunn 1995). Identifying learning styles and teaching to those learning styles can increase academic achievement and improve attitudes toward learning. They describe how children learn according to their visual, auditory, or kinesthetic learning style, which develops through interactions of biology and experience. Each child processes new information in ways that are related to environmental, emotional, sociological, physiological, and psychological elements. Dunn and Dunn (1995) also maintain that uniform teaching practices will invariably deny many students success in the classroom.

Analyses of the learning styles of underachieving students by Griggs and Dunn (1995) reveal that these students' learning styles (e.g., concrete) differ significantly from the learning styles of high achievers (e.g., abstract). Moreover, their research affirms that teaching and counseling these students congruently with their learning style preferences result in increased test scores and positive outlook on learning. However, Griggs and Dunn (1995) conclude from their studies on learning styles and cultures that there is great diversity within ethnic groups and fear that generalizations about a group of people often lead to incorrect inferences about individual members of that group. As a result, they recommend that teachers should concentrate not on cultural group characteristics but on learning style strengths of each individual student. Similarly, Guild (1994) maintains that although cultures have distinctive learning style patterns, one of the best ways to facilitate student diversity in group instruction is to vary the teaching methods. Combining instructional methods by explaining and then demonstrating gives students the opportunity to learn through different modes. Diversity can also be increased through discussion sessions. The greater the number of students participating, the better the chance for diverse and different points of view. When students are involved in discussions, they are usually attentive and participating in the learning process. Students are motivated by different approaches because they come from varied backgrounds. Getting to know students will increase the possibility of being able to effectively help them learn.

Success for the diverse populations that schools serve requires reexamination of beliefs about teaching, learning, the nature of human beings, and the kinds of environments that maximize growth for students and teachers alike. Teachers can meet diverse learning needs by intentionally applying multiple strategies and creating positive environments in which students can learn (Green 1999). Some teaching tips that can help increase instructional effectiveness in a diverse setting include (Lyter-Mickelberg and Connor-Kuntz 1995):

- At the start of the school year (and at regular intervals thereafter) speak about the importance of encouraging and respecting diversity.
- When doing group work, insist that groups be diverse with regard to race, gender, and nationality.
- Be understanding and respectful of different students groups. Refer to all students alike. Develop a consistent style for addressing all students regardless of their differences.
- Encourage all students to participate in discussions. Avoid allowing some students from certain groups to dominate interaction. Use a random method of picking students so all have an equal chance of contributing.
- Treat all students with respect and expect students to treat each other with dignity. Intervene if a student or group of students is dominating.
- When a difficult situation arises over a diversity issue, take a time-out and ask students to write down their thoughts and ideas. This allow all parties time to collect their thoughts and plan a response.
- Make sure evaluations and grades are written in gender-neutral or gender-inclusive terms.
- Encourage students to work with different partners every day. Do not allow students to have the same partner or group day after day. Students need to get to know other students in order to appreciate their differences.
- Invite guest speakers to the class who represent diversity in gender, race, and ethnicity even if they are not speaking about diversity issues.
- When students make comments that are sexist or racist, ask them to restate their ideas without offending others. Teach students that it is all right to express one's opinion but not in an inflammatory manner.
- Use rotating leaders when using groups. All students should have the opportunity to learn leadership skills.

Questions for Reflection

- When teaching students of varying abilities and diverse needs, what common grouping types are there?

- In what ways is grouping beneficial to student learning?

- How does Gardner's research on multiple intelligences meet the needs of diverse learners?

- Why is it important to select instructional methods that are congruent with student learning style preferences?

Commentary on Standard #3

GLEN OLSON | Principal of Ipalook Elementary
School in Barrow, Alaska

As a new teacher, you will find meeting the needs of
the diverse learners in your classroom to be a daunt-
ing task, requiring faith and humor along with a
dash of thoughtful practice, action, and reflection.
You will also be challenged to balance student needs
with the demands of the district's curriculum and
state-mandated assessments.

If you were to teach at Ipalook Elementary School
in Barrow, Alaska, you would contend with implementing a new reading curriculum, integrating state
and local standards into your teaching, and balancing
good learning with preparing students to succeed on
state-mandated tests. With twenty-one identified language groups, students with numerous difficulties,
and a dominant culture rich with subsistence activities focused on whaling, you would be expected to
adapt your attitudes and practices daily.

To effectively meet the needs of so many students
with differing and often conflicting needs, you must
thoughtfully plan activities that give each student
learning opportunities particular to their identified
needs and interests. You need to incorporate a cycle of
planning, action, and assessment into your routine
while paying attention to making the assigned work
relevant to the curriculum and meaningful to the lives
of your students. While a unit on harvest in some
parts of the United States may include the raising of
vegetables, harvest on the North Slope of Alaska entails berry picking, hunting of caribou, and whaling.
This makes the curriculum concept of harvest relevant to the local community, and gives students ways
to learn at their own rate and level of understanding.

Differentiating instruction or offering work relevant to the needs and interests of different students
is an excellent way to ensure the learning of all students. Cooperative learning, individualization, peer
tutoring, guest speakers, computer assisted instruction, project-based learning, activity centers, demonstrations, hands-on activities, and other educational
strategies are available to help you create constructive experiences supportive of the curriculum and
meaningful to the identified needs and interests of
each student.

You need to acknowledge and provide accommo-
dations for individual student differences whether
they are cultural, linguistic, or disability-related (social, emotional, or academic). Meeting individual
learning and assessment needs may be as simple as
allowing the student who struggles with handwrit-
ing to use a keyboard, to let the student who can't
read or write to demonstrate mastery verbally, to let
the builder build, the actor act, the writer write, the
artist create, and so forth.

You must understand the depth and scope of the
curriculum before you identify a student's needs and
interests and formulate a learning plan. A good
teacher determines each student's depth of subject
knowledge, level of skill development, and understanding of broader concepts. You will set class and
individual learning goals and plan learning experiences that engage all students in meaningful and relevant ways. Strong teachers work to ensure that
students treat each other with respect regardless of
individual differences.

Finally, as a new teacher, you must devote time
to reflect upon and adjust your practice to ensure
your students recognize and value the diversity of all
students.

Diverse Learners Self-Assessment

The teacher understands how students differ in their approaches to learning and creates instructional opportunities that are adapted to diverse learners.

Knowledge/Performance Indicators

	Yes*	Not Sure	No
1. I understand and identify differences in approaches to learning and performance, including varied learning styles and performance modes and multiple intelligences.	2	1	0
2. I know how to design instruction that uses a student's strengths as the basis for continued learning.	2	1	0

	2	1	0
3. I know about areas of exceptionality in learning, including learning disabilities, perceptual difficulties, and special physical or mental challenges, gifts, and talents.	2	1	0
4. I know about the process of second language acquisition and about strategies to support the learning of students whose first language is not English.	2	1	0
5. I understand how to recognize and deal with dehumanizing biases, discrimination, prejudices, and institutional and personal racism and sexism.	2	1	0
6. I understand how a student's learning is influenced by individual experiences, talents, and prior learning, as well as language, culture, family, and community values.	2	1	0
7. I understand the contributions and lifestyles of the various racial, cultural, and economic groups in our society.	2	1	0
8. I understand cultural and community diversity.	2	1	0
9. I know how to learn about and incorporate a student's experiences, cultures, and community resources into instruction.	2	1	0
10. I understand that all students can and should learn at the highest possible levels and that I must persist in helping all students achieve success.	2	1	0
11. I know about community and cultural norms.	2	1	0
12. I identify and design instruction appropriate to a student's stages of development, learning styles, strengths, and needs.	2	1	0
13. I use teaching approaches that are sensitive to the varied experiences of students and that address different learning and performance modes.	2	1	0
14. I accommodate a student's learning differences or needs regarding time and circumstances for work, tasks assigned, communication, and response modes.	2	1	0
15. I identify when and how to access appropriate services or resources to meet exceptional learning needs.	2	1	0
16. I use information about student's families, cultures, and communities as the basis for connecting instruction to students' experiences.	2	1	0
17. I bring multiple perspectives to the discussion of subject matter, including attention to a student's personal, family, and community experiences and cultural norms.	2	1	0
18. I develop a learning community in which individual differences are respected.	2	1	0

* A "Yes" response indicates that you can describe, document, and cite examples related to your student teaching assignment.

Self-Assessment Summary and Reflection

1. Which Knowledge/Performance Indicators can I currently describe, document, and cite examples?

_____

_____

2. Which Knowledge/Performance Indicators need some work or improvement?

_____

_____

3. What specific actions can I take to enrich my knowledge or skill in this area?

_____

_____

Activity 3.1   Do I Have to Write This Down?

Context   Remember writing book reports? For some of us, reading the book was okay, maybe even fun, but writing the book report was torture. But were you ever lucky enough to have an English teacher who gave you choices? If so, perhaps, you first were given a choice of what book to read, perhaps from a list of suggested titles or from ones that the teacher had given book talks on. Then you were given a choice on the way you wanted to share the book after you'd finished reading it. You could discuss the book with a parent, share with others in a book discussion, videotape a book talk, draw a poster or make a mobile, read an excerpt of the book to the class, or write a book review. No matter how you chose to report on the book, the teacher would evaluate you according to the same criteria: an understanding of the book, making connections to real life, knowledge of the characters, an opinion of the book supported by details, and the preparation put forth to share the book. Now this teacher may or may not have had intimate knowledge of Gardner's eight intelligences, but her book report options were based on a similar premise, that students do not learn the same thing in the same way at the same time. By providing choices where possible, she built on the strengths of individual students.

Purpose   Through this activity you will generate a list of instructional strategies that would be appropriate for different types of learners.

Directions   This activity is based on Howard Gardner's theory of multiple intelligences. (You may want to review the "Fundamental Principles" section of this chapter.)

Activity 1   Categorize each instructional activity/task under the type of learner it is best suited for. Some activities/tasks may be written in more than one category. A few have been done to get you started.

Instructional Activities/Tasks

demonstrate the word "slouch"

read from a textbook

present data in a graph

write a poem

dissect a frog

analyze ancient drawings

create and bury artifacts

classify objects on a table

learn the steps to a line dance

write a short story

create a human sculpture

create a song with hand movements

respond to a journal prompt

use manipulatives to solve problem

solve a murder mystery

determine the rate of population growth

Type of Learner

Linguistic	Tactile/Kinesthetic	Logical/Mathematical
write a poem	*dissect a frog*	*solve a murder mystery*
_____	_____	_____
_____	_____	_____
_____	_____	_____
_____	_____	_____
_____	_____	_____
_____	_____	_____

Activity 2   Suppose your students were working in groups of three to classify the shoes worn by all their classmates that day and then present their findings. List five ways students might classify the shoes. List different means through which students might present or illustrate their findings.

Possible Shoe Categories

1. _____

2. _____

3. _____

4. _____

5. _____

Possible Ways to Present or Illustrate

_____

_____

_____

_____

_____

_____

_____

_____

_____

Activity 3.2   I Don't Get It

Context   No matter what the content area, all teachers are faced with (1) teaching vocabulary, (2) connecting concepts to real life, (3) showing the relationship between ideas, and (4) teaching the steps in a process or procedure. For vocabulary, teachers might use textbook activities supplemented by a daily review. To connect a concept to real life, they might draw from an article in a recent newspaper. To demonstrate the relationship between two ideas, a Venn diagram could serve the purpose. Finally, to teach the steps of a process, a poster might be helpful. Imagine the frustration when, despite the teacher's good efforts, some students don't "get it." Simply repeating the information in the same way will not help these students. True, to learn the information, students must have it repeated, but it must be repeated in a variety of ways.

Keep in mind Gardner's multiple intelligences: linguistic, logical/mathematical, bodily kinesthetic, spatial, musical, interpersonal, intrapersonal, and naturalistic. For example, a linguistic learner might learn vocabulary by reading and studying words in a textbook. However, a tactile/kinesthetic learner would be more successful by "showing" the meaning of a word with facial expressions or body language.

Purpose   This activity will require that you "think outside the box" to create a variety of activities/tasks that would help all learners meet the same lesson objective.

Directions   With each of the four general learning objectives listed below, jot down a list of possible instructional activities for each objective. Each list should include activities that would be appropriate for a minimum of two different types of intelligences. Examples have been provided to get you started. (Hint: Look back at Activity 3.1 to get a few ideas.)

Learning objective 1   Learn five new vocabulary words specific to content area.

Instructional ActivityType(s) of Intelligence

Use flash cards with words & graphics to teach vocab.   *spatial, linguistic*

_____   _____

_____   _____

_____   _____

_____   _____

_____   _____

Learning objective 2   Connect a concept to real life.

Instructional ActivityType(s) of Intelligence

Bring in guest speaker on WWII.   *interpersonal, linguistic*

_____   _____

_____   _____

_____   _____

_____   _____

_____   _____

Learning objective 3   Show the relationship between two ideas.

Instructional Activity Type(s) of Intelligence

Use analogy to explain similarity of speech to composition.   *logical, linguistic*

_____   _____

_____   _____

_____   _____

_____   _____

Learning objective 4   Know and use the steps of a process.

Instructional Activity Type(s) of Intelligence

Make up song to teach the steps to the scientific method.   *musical, kinesthetic*

_____   _____

_____   _____

_____   _____

_____   _____

List four new ideas that you learned from this activity that you could use in your teaching to accommodate different types of learners.

New Ideas for Activities   Type(s) of Intelligence

_____   _____

_____   _____

_____   _____

_____   _____

_____   _____

Activity 3.3 Actions + Words = Successful Communication

Context   We've all heard the adage "Actions speak louder than words," and we realize the truth in this saying. In teaching, it's important that our actions and words match, that we are not sending mixed messages. The manner in which you treat students and allow them to treat one another sends a very loud message. As teachers, we must be models of what we expect because our students learn by example, example, example.

Purpose   To examine how you demonstrate respect for all students, their diverse backgrounds, experiences, and needs.

Directions   Indicate the extent to which you demonstrate the following behaviors.

	Frequently	Sometimes	Rarely
1. I show enthusiasm for all students when I work with them.	3	2	1
2. I show empathy when a student is struggling.	3	2	1
3. I show respect for every student regardless of race, gender, ability, or social status.	3	2	1
4. I exhibit an open-minded attitude toward differences in student beliefs and values.	3	2	1
5. I encourage students to give their own opinions.	3	2	1
6. I treat all students fairly.	3	2	1
7. I avoid favoritism.	3	2	1
8. I pay attention to everyone.	3	2	1
9. I am careful not to embarrass students when praising or correcting them.	3	2	1
10. I prevent students from treating each other rudely or insensitively.	3	2	1
11. I avoid using sarcasm to discipline students.	3	2	1
12. I know all of my students' names and call them by their first names.	3	2	1
13. I give students more than one chance to earn back my trust and support.	3	2	1
14. I avoid acting like a "buddy" or friend.	3	2	1
15. I am considerate of students' feelings even when they seem immature.	3	2	1
16. I know some positive, unique quality about every student.	3	2	1
17. I acknowledge to my students that not everyone learns the same thing in the same way at the same time.	3	2	1
18. I provide my students with choice of instructional tasks or activities.	3	2	1
19. I modify assignments for students who are struggling.	3	2	1

Total score = _____. The higher the score (maximum 57), the more you exhibit positive actions and words.

Name two areas that represent your strongest attributes.

1. _____

2. _____

Name two area that you believe need some work.

1. _____

2. _____

Set two goals designed to improve your "actions and words" behavior.

1. _____

2. _____

Activity 3.4   No Place for the Meek

Context   Teaching has been referred to as a "stream of decisions" and Charlotte Danielson has been quoted as saying that teachers make 3000 non-trivial decisions a day! No wonder teachers are exhausted by the day's end! Many of the decisions made by teachers are responses to their students' words and actions. Effective teachers listen and watch their students for clues about their learning; they monitor and adjust according to the feedback students give. Even when students give extremely subtle hints about how they learn, savvy teachers discern the subtleties and make on-the-spot changes to foster better learning.

Purpose   Through this activity, you will identify instructional activities suitable for a student's preferred learning style.

Directions

- Read Case Study A and Case Study B.

- Answer the questions at the end.

Case Study A   Take the case of Josh, a likable winsome student who has a passion for sports, dogs, and bass guitar. He's often the last one to sit down in his desk at the beginning of the class period, taps and bites on his pencil during seatwork, often volunteers to pick up assignments, chooses math projects that involve building, and is most on-task during activities using manipulatives. From a close observation of his behaviors, Josh's teacher, Ms. Gillispie, suspects that his preferred learning style is tactile/kinesthetic, and she tries to find approaches to build on Josh's need to "learn through doing."

Case Study B   Angie is another student in Ms. Gillispie's class who usually comes into classroom just as the bell rings (after finishing a conversation with two or three friends). She's involved in Student Council, sports, band, choir, and theater and seems happiest when she's in a group of people. Angie often talks to nearby students about the assignment during quiet seatwork, always chooses partner-work when given a choice, sometimes complains about not being paired with her friends, has good success on group projects, and volunteers to read to first graders. Ms. Gillispie suspects that Angie's preferred learning style is through personal interactions with others, and she tries to find strategies that will give Angie legitimate opportunities to learn through group and paired activities.

Often students who learn through movement or social interactions with others can be viewed as discipline problems. If instead we view their behaviors as *clues to their learning styles*, we will be more able to accommodate them and foster an appreciation for diversity.

1. How do Josh's behaviors suggest that he is a tactile/kinesthetic learner?

   _____

   _____

2. What kinds of tasks and activities can Ms. Gillispie incorporate into her math class that would accommodate his preferred way of learning?

   a. _____

   b. _____

   c. _____

3. How do Angie's behaviors suggests that she learns through personal interactions?

   _____

   _____

4. What kinds of tasks and activities can Ms. Gillispie incorporate into her math class that would accommodate Angie's preferred way of learning?

   a. _____

   b. _____

   c. _____

5. List your students who seem to prefer to learn like Josh. List your students who learn like Angie.

   Like Josh: _____

   _____

   Like Angie: _____

   _____

6. Think of instructional strategies that you could use in your class with students who prefer to learn like Josh and Angie and list them below.

   Josh: _____

   Angie: _____

7. What have you learned from this activity that will help you as a teacher?

   _____

   _____

   _____

   _____

Activity 3.5   Lingo Diverse

Context   Today, at most any public school in the United States, there may be students who are not proficient in English. Schools throughout the United States are becoming more ethnically and linguistically diverse. Most of the United State's immigrants come from non-English-speaking countries. In response to this trend, schools continue to develop specialized programs designed to ensure appropriate achievement of students with limited English proficiency. Many of these programs also include extensive teacher training.   School programs that focus on the needs of students who have limited English proficiency have many diverse names, including acronyms. Some of the program acronyms and names include:

ESL	English as a Second-Language	NES	Non-English Speaking
ELL	English Language Learner	SI	Sheltered Instruction
LEP	Limited English Proficient	ESOL	English Speakers of Other Languages

To better assist and prepare new teachers in the instruction of limited English proficient students, more and more colleges and universities are now including pedagogical training in their teacher preparation programs. Unfortunately, one common mistake made by many new teachers is to equate limited English proficiency with special education or low ability.

Limited English proficiency (LEP) students arrive at U.S. schools with a wide range of academic backgrounds and abilities. Some LEP students will enter the school, possibly your classroom, with substantial knowledge and skills. In their native language, they are literate. They may be well above grade level in several core subjects. On the other hand, some LEP students who enter our classrooms are not literate, even in their native language. For an immense number of possible reasons, they have not attained the knowledge and skill necessary for academic competence.

As you can see, the academic range of LEP students is representative of *all* students. And, as with all students, varying instructional approaches are necessary to ensure academic success.

Purpose   Through this activity, you will analyze your lessons in regard to best ELL teaching and learning practices.

Directions   Review your last five lessons. Considering these five lessons as a composite, rate yourself on the frequency of each strategy according to the following scale (not every lesson can or will contain all strategies):

3   = Frequent use of this strategy
2   = Occasional use of this strategy
1   = Limited use of this strategy
0   = No use of this strategy
NA = Not Applicable

1. _____ I used a high level (over 80% of class time) of student engagement—active learning.

2. _____ I used a variety of room and seating arrangements.

3. _____ I was clear on the students' learning expectations, objectives, and goals.

4. _____ I created classroom predictability—routines and procedures.

5. _____ I used a variety of student groupings—individuals, pairs, small groups.

6. _____ I used a variety of student mixing—LEP and non-LEP students; at times, I allowed students to be in groups according to their dominant language.

7. _____ I integrated language, culture, out-of-school experiences, and community issues in my lessons.

8. _____ I used modeling and demonstrations.

9. _____ I connected past learning with new learning.

10. _____ I used drama, hands-on, and role-play.

11. _____ I created frequent opportunities for student/teacher and student/student interaction.

12. _____ I used lower-level (or modified) texts and native language materials when available.

13. _____ I used cooperative learning.

14. _____ I taught vocabulary in authentic, meaningful ways—I didn't just give the students a word list and a dictionary.

15. _____ I taught study skills—e.g., note taking, outlining, planning, homework, organization, time management, prioritizing, footnotes, and documentation.

16. _____ I used a variety of visual aids—maps, photographs, posters, transparencies, videos, cassettes, graphs, charts, and newspapers.

17. _____ I used electronic/computer resources.

18. _____ When possible, at times, I used the native language of the LEP student(s).

19. _____ I established a peer tutoring experience for LEP students.

20. _____ I was enthusiastic; I enjoyed teaching these lessons.

Total score = _____. The higher the score(maximum 60), the more frequently you used beneficial LEP teaching and learning strategies.

1. What were your most frequently used strategies?

_____

_____

2. What strategies where not used?

_____

_____

3. What two strategies can you improve?

_____

_____

Conclusion   As you can see, many of the strategies suggested for LEP students are good teaching and learning strategies for all students. Many schools have staff and/or resources to assist teachers with LEP students. Take advantage of these resources. Your cooperating teacher or building administrator should be able to direct you to these resources. Your university supervisor and other university staff may also be a valuable resource for assistance in LEP instruction.

Case Study

Tonya was enjoying her student teaching at Kennedy. She appreciated the cultural diversity of her students. In fact, the ELL teacher had just finished a project supported by the school and the PTO. Hanging in the cafeteria was a flag from every country represented by the students at Kennedy; over forty in all.

As an African American, Tonya had looked forward to an inner-city teaching experience, and felt that this was a great school to be in. The teachers were concerned about each and every student and went out of their way to help everyone fit in and be successful. That's why it was a surprise to Tonya that her cooperating teacher, and the school for that matter, didn't have anything special planned for Black History Month. In fact, she was a bit put out that there didn't seem to be any recognition by the staff and felt that she should do something about it.

1. Is Tonya right to expect the school to recognize Black History Month?

2. Should she talk to her cooperating teacher or university supervisor about her concern?

3. What are some things that Tonya might suggest that the school do?

4. What are some things that she could do herself in her own classroom or for the school?

5. Why do you suppose that the school had not done anything to recognize Black History Month?

Student-to-Student Tips

✔ Make sure that over the course of a week you have activities for auditory, kinesthetic, and visual learners. You don't need each in every lesson, but you should have a variety of task each day. *Beverly, elementary student teacher*

✔ Find out about your students' interests and use that when planning examples and stories. *Starr, secondary student teacher*

✔ Don't forget to talk to students about respecting one another, especially when doing group work. *Dreena, secondary student teacher*

✔ Make sure you assess students by their ability. Not everyone can accomplish the same things. *Tasha, secondary student teacher*

✔ Turn negatives into positives. Let the bossy kid be a group leader and the talker be the reporter. *Seth, secondary student teacher*

✔ Remember that you are an example for your students. Treat all of them with respect. They're watching and listening to you. *Soren, elementary student teacher*

✔ Don't be so concerned about teaching lessons. Focus on the students to make sure that they are learning the concepts. *Yohan, secondary student teacher*

✔ Be sure to read your students' IEPs so you know how to work with each of them. *Breck, elementary student teacher*

✔ Build relationships with the students by observing them and learning about them. Focus on them rather than yourself. *Rosha, elementary student teacher*

✔ Make notes about your students' interests, abilities, and strengths. Remember to review those notes when planning your lessons. *Marcus, secondary student teacher*

✔ Volunteer to chaperone dances, supervise sports, go on field trips so that you get to know your students better and they get to know you. *Carrie, secondary student teacher*

Bibliography

Adams, T. L. 2000/2001. Helping children learn mathematics through multiple intelligences and standards for school mathematics. *Childhood Education* (Winter): 86–92.

Arends, R. I., N. E. Winitzky, and M. D. Tannenbaum. 2001. *Exploring teaching: An introduction to education.* 2nd ed. New York: McGraw-Hill.

Banks, J. A. 1994. *Multiethnic education: Theory and practice.* Boston: Allyn and Bacon.

Burnette, J. 1999. Critical behaviors and strategies for teaching culturally diverse students. *Eric Digest E584.* Reston, VA: ERIC Clearinghouse on Disabilities and Gifted Education.

Checkley, K. 1997. The first seven . . . and the eight. A conversation with Howard Gardner. *Educational Leadership* 55, 1: 1–8.

Dunn, R., and K. Dunn. 1995. *Teaching students through their individual learning styles.* Reston, VA: Reston, Publishing.

Gardner, H. 1987. *Frames of mind: The theory of multiple intelligences.* New York: Basic Books.

———. 1993. *Multiple intelligence: The theory in practice.* New York: Basic Books.

Green, F. E. 1999. Brain and learning research: Implications for meeting the needs of diverse learners. *Education* 119, 4 (Summer): 682–691.

Griggs, S., and R. Dunn. 1995. Hispanic-American students and learning style. *Emergency Librarian* 23, 2 (Nov.–Dec.): 11–14.

Guild, P. 1994. The culture/learning style connection. *Educational Leadership* 51, 8 (May): 16–21.

Jung, C. 1971. *Psychological types.* Princeton, NJ: Princeton University Press.

Johnson, R. T., and D. W. Johnson. 2000. How can we put cooperative learning into practice? *Science Teacher* 8, 6 (Jan.): 39.

Kolb, D. 1984. *Experiential learning: Experience as the source of learning and development.* Englewood Cliffs, NJ: Prentice Hall.

Lyter-Mickelberg, P., and F. Connor-Kuntz. 1995. Stop stereotyping students. *Strategies* 8, 6: 16–21.

McNergney, R. F. and J. M. Herbert. 2001. *Foundations of education: The challenge of professional practice.* Boston: Allyn and Bacon.

Mueller, A. and T. Fleming. 2001. Cooperative learning: Listening to how children work at school.

Journal of Educational Research 94, 5 (May–June): 259–265.

National Association for the Education of Young Children. 1996. Developmentally appropriate practice in early childhood programs. [Online]. Available: http://www.naeyc.org/resources/positionstatements/deptoc.html

Reiff, J. C. 1997. Multiple intelligences, culture and equitable learning. *Childhood Education* 73, 5 (Summer): 302–304.

Ryan, K., and J. Cooper. 2000. *Those who can teach.* Boston: Houghton Mifflin.

Sanchez, W., C. Li, and E. V. Nuttall. 1995. Working with diverse learners and school staff in a multicultural society. *ERIC Digest* [Online]. Available: http://www.edgove/databases/ERICDigests/ed390018.html

Schniedewind, N. and E. Davidson. 2000. Differentiating cooperative learning. *Educational Leadership* 58, 1 (Sept.): 24–27.

Siciliano, J. I. 2001. How to incorporate cooperative learning principles in the classroom: It's more than just putting students in teams. *Journal of Management Education* 25, 1 (Feb.): 8–20.

Vasquez, J. 1988. Contests of learning for minority children. *Educational Forum* 52, 3: 243–253.

4
Instructional Strategies

"The thirst to think is the desire that is never fulfilled."
—*Thomas Edison*

Standard #4   The teacher understands and uses a variety of instructional strategies to encourage students' development of critical thinking, problem solving, and performance skills.

Performance Indicators: *The teacher . . .*

- Uses performance assessment techniques and strategies that measure higher-order thinking skills in students and continues to build a repertoire of realistic projects and problem-solving activities designed to assist all students in demonstrating their ability to think creatively.

- Consistently uses a variety of active learning strategies to develop students' thinking, problem-solving, and learning skills.

Vignette   Choa's cooperating teacher informed her that she would be teaching a unit on suicide. One of her greatest fears had been met, that of teaching a sensitive issue. Choa was concerned not only with student questions, administrative apprehension, and general community controversy; but also how was she going to teach this unit to her students without indirectly suggesting ideas on how to carry out a suicide? Choa had remembered reading a study that was published some time back indicating that media attention to suicide causes copycat suicides. If she were to broach the subject, would she be placing her students at a greater risk? What strategies would be important in making a distinction between the topic of suicide and the highly emotional reactions that sometimes follow suicide?

Fundamental Principles

To help learners improve how they think, "teaching has changed from covering the content to ensuring that students understand and know what they have learned. The switch has been to a less-is-more philosophy" (Halpern and Nummedal 1995, 82–83). If the education reform efforts of the 1990s are to be remembered for anything, it will be the emphasis upon building the capacity of all children and youth to engage in higher-order thinking. This capacity enables a learner not merely to remember facts, but also to develop the curiosity and mental discipline necessary to pursue answers to questions about the world. Although numerous frameworks and labels have been applied to describe critical thinking, the "basic process is knowledge through inquiry" (Young 1992, 48). Two thousand years ago, Socrates observed that wisdom begins in wonder. Asking why, why not, who says, and what would happen if, and letting each answer lead to further questions, are all part of this active wondering.

Many educators have long advocated the teaching of critical thinking skills such as reasoning and problem solving (Fernandez-Balboa 1993). From an examination of the vast literature on critical thinking, various definitions of critical thinking emerge. Here are some samples:

- "Critical thinking is the intellectually disciplined process of actively and skillfully conceptualizing, applying, analyzing, synthesizing, and/or evaluating information gathered from, or generated by, observation, experience, reflection, reasoning, or communication, as a guide to belief and action" (Scriven and Paul 1996).

- "Critical thinking is the intentional application of rational, higher order thinking skills, such as analysis, synthesis, problem recognition and problem solving, inference, and evaluation" (Angelo 1995, 6).
- "Critical thinking is the ability to reach sound conclusions based on observation and information" (Paul 1988).
- According to Norris (1985) critical thinking helps students to apply everything they already know and feel, to evaluate their own thinking, and especially to change their behavior.
- Ennis (1987) suggests that critical thinking refers to a purposeful means of reasoning.

Perhaps the simplest definition is offered by Beyer (1995, 8): "Critical thinking means making reasoned judgments." Basically, Beyer sees critical thinking as using criteria to judge the quality of something, from cooking to a conclusion of a research paper. Based on these definitions, then, critical thinking is intended to help students evaluate the worth of ideas, opinions, or evidence before making a decision or judgment.

What are the characteristics of critical thinking? In his book, *Critical Thinking,* Beyer (1995) elaborately explains what he sees as essential aspects of critical thinking. These are:

- **Dispositions:** Critical thinkers are skeptical and open-minded. They respect evidence and reasoning, look at different points of view, and will change positions when reason leads them to do so.
- **Criteria:** To think critically, one must apply criteria. Conditions must be met for something to be judged as believable.
- **Argument:** Critical thinking involves identifying, evaluating, and constructing arguments with supporting evidence.
- **Reasoning:** Critical thinkers have the ability to infer a conclusion after examining logical relationships among statements and data.
- **Point of view:** In a search for understanding, critical thinkers view phenomena from many different points of view.
- **Procedures for applying criteria:** Critical thinking makes use of many procedures including asking questions, making judgments, and identifying assumptions.

Constructivist theory suggests that learners construct and reconstruct information to learn (Brooks and Brooks 1993). These constructions (and understandings) evolve when learners actively gather, generate, process, and personalize information rather than passively receive knowledge from teachers and other resources. Learning, therefore, is simply the process of adjusting one's mental models to accommodate new experiences. We can explicitly teach learners to organize existent and new information by using concept organizers (Bellanca 1992; Carter and Solmon 1994; Maylath 1989; Wooley 1995). Wurman (1989) claims that "knowing how things are organized is the key to understanding them" (8). He offers these guiding questions for consideration: "How can I look at this information? How would reorganizing the information change its meaning? How can I arrange the information to shed new light on the problem? How can I put the information in a different context?" When existing information is reorganized and connected in different ways, new patterns can lead to new meanings and interpretations. Consequently, a higher level of knowing results; this is called understanding. Constructivism calls for the elimination of a standardized curriculum. Instead, it promotes using curricula customized to the student's prior knowledge. Also, it emphasizes hands-on problem solving. Under the theory of constructivism, teachers focus on making connections between facts and fostering new understanding in students. Teachers tailor their instructional strategies to student responses and encourage students to analyze, interpret, and predict information. Teachers also rely heavily on open-ended questions and promote extensive dialogue among students. Assessment becomes part of the learning process rather then the use of grades and standardized testing.

King (1995) suggests that learners can exhibit "the habit of inquiry by learning to ask thoughtful questions of themselves and of each other, about the material they read, hear in lectures, and encounter during class discussions." She states: "Good thinkers are always asking 'What does this mean? What is the nature of this? Is there another way to look at it? Why is this happening? What is the evidence for this? And, how can I be sure?' Asking questions such as these and using them to understand the world around is what characterizes critical thinking" (13).

In the classroom where students are engaged in critical and creative thinking, learners can be encouraged to be inquisitive and learn to generate questions about themselves and their world. In teaching for understanding, it is suggested to focus on the developmental needs, interests, and backgrounds of the learners (Wilen 1987). A developmental perspective focuses continually on how students learn, rather than focusing more typically on the content of the lesson, and/or the methodology for delivering the content. Grundy and Henry (1995) remind us "to think of classroom interactions in terms of learning experiences rather than teaching strategies." Experiences to develop critical thinking in the classroom might include:

- **CATS (Classroom Assessment Techniques):** Angelo (1995) stresses the use of ongoing classroom assessment as a way to monitor and facilitate students' critical thinking. An example of a CAT is to ask students to write a "Minute Paper" responding to questions such as "What was the most important thing you learned in today's class? What question related to this session remains uppermost in your mind?" The teacher selects some of the papers and prepares responses for the next class meeting.

- **Cooperative learning strategies:** Cooperative learning consists of instructional techniques that require positive interdependence between learners in order for learning to occur. Cooper (1995) argues that putting students into group learning situations is the best way to foster critical thinking. "In properly structured cooperative learning environments, students perform more of the active, critical thinking with continuous support and feedback from other students and the teacher" (8). Methods for implementing cooperative learning have been articulated by Siciliano (2001), Slavin (1995), Johnson and Johnson (1999), and Quin, Johnson, and Johnson (1995). Depending on the strategy selected, teachers can impart factual material, basic skills, conceptual understanding, or problem solving. All cooperative learning strategies develop communication and group interaction skills. One of the first decisions teachers must make in implementing cooperative learning is how to group students. Cooperative learning necessitates purposeful grouping, in which teachers match a grouping pattern to their instructional purpose. If the goal is to maximize test scores, students are mixed by their ability levels. When teachers place high, middle, and low achievers in cooperative learning teams, academic achievement is increased. Other goals, such as developing social skills, broadening student

friendships, and promoting cross-racial understanding, can be maximized by different grouping patterns. Structures to ensure individual accountability can be critical to the success of cooperative learning. Individual accountability means that each student is held responsible for personally learning the material. Students may help each other in the learning process, but in the final analysis, each student must demonstrate that he or she can reason, understand, remember, analyze, solve, and evaluate.

- **Case study/discussion method:** McDade (1995) describes this method as the teacher presenting a case (or story) to the class without a conclusion. Using prepared questions, the teacher then leads students through a discussion, allowing students to construct a conclusion for the case.

- **Using questions:** King (1995) identifies ways of using questions in the classroom: (a) *Reciprocal peer questioning:* Following a lecture, the teacher displays a list of question stems (such as, "What are the strengths and weaknesses of . . ."). Students must write questions about the lecture material. In small groups, the students ask each other the questions. Then, the whole class discusses some of the questions from each small group. (b) *Reader's questions:* Require students to write questions from an assigned reading and turn them in at the beginning of class. Teachers then select a few of the questions as the impetus for class discussion.

- **Use writing assignments:** Wade (1995) sees the use of writing as fundamental to developing critical thinking skills. "With written assignments, a teacher can encourage the development of dialectic reasoning by requiring students to argue both (or more) sides of an issue" (24).

- **Dialogues:** Robertson and Rane-Szostak (1996) identify two methods of stimulating useful discussions in the classroom: (a) *Written dialogues:* Give students written dialogues to analyze. In small groups, students must identify the different viewpoints of each participant in the dialogue. They must look for biases, presence or exclusion of important evidence, alternative interpretations, misstatement of facts, and errors in reasoning. Each group must decide which view is the most reasonable. After coming to a conclusion, each group acts out their dialogue and explains their analysis of it. (b) *Spontaneous group dialogue:* One group of students is assigned roles to play in a discussion (such as leader, information giver, opinion seeker, and disagreer). Four observer groups are formed with the functions of determining what roles are being played by whom, identifying biases and errors in thinking, evaluating reasoning skills, and examining ethical implications of the content.

Students who are critical thinkers do not merely follow steps out of a workbook, but have developed a sense of wonder, questioning, and skepticism. For them, if we have been successful, curiosity and inquiry become a vibrant part of who they are and who they will become.

Questions for Reflection

- How is critical thinking significant to learning?

- Define critical thinking.

- What are the characteristics of critical thinking?

- List several classroom strategies that help students develop critical thinking.

Commentary on Standard #4

ANN C. SLATER, ED.D., CHES | Lead
Teacher/Strategies for Success
White Knoll High School, Lexington School District
One, Lexington, South Carolina

"It's going to be a long quarter," I said to myself as I observed my new class of 30 sixth-grade students. I had been assigned a section of a middle school study-skills course. It was my task to teach this intellectually, culturally, and economically diverse group how to write research papers. I also had many "behavioral" problems because these kids would not stay seated! I would get one seated and two would pop up. I would get those two seated and three different ones would pop up! However, when I assessed their learning styles, I discovered that these students were more similar than different. Every one of them was a tactile-kinesthetic learner. Most were also interpersonal learners.

In addition to revising my instructional methods to include more strategies to accommodate their

learning styles, I also found it necessary to revise my classroom management strategies. If I had tried to enforce my "stay in your seat" rule, we would have ended up with a lose-lose situation. So students were permitted to stand up and move around as long as their movement was related to the task at hand. Teaching these students became a wonderful adventure. One student wrote a paper about tornadoes. I watched him twirl around clockwise and then counterclockwise. Then he wrote a paragraph about the movement of a tornado. This strategy exemplified the typical technique used by many of the students. They would physically go through the motions and then write something into their papers. Hardly anyone sat at a desk. They would stand and bend over to write while their bottoms swayed to imaginary music. After writing their first drafts, they traded papers and discussed ways their partners could improve spelling, grammar, and other linguistic elements of their papers.

Many wrote papers about their beloved animals. When the day came to present their research papers to their classmates, I permitted them to bring their pets to class. One very shy boy confidently stood in front of the class with his cockatiel on his shoulder during his presentation. He made many new friends that day as fellow students later gathered around him to ask questions about the bird. Other students wore animal costumes or brought their dog, cat, or iguana to school for the presentations. Those who wrote papers on foreign countries treated us to foods from those countries. All students in this class produced excellent research papers.

I am now teaching high school freshmen a required course called Strategies for Success, which combines comprehensive health education and career development. While the purpose of the course is to teach the students strategies to be successful, I understand that I too must use a variety of instructional strategies to be a successful teacher. It is impossible for educators to encourage students' development of critical thinking, problem-solving, and performance skills unless they utilize a variety of instructional strategies. Teachers must also match strategies to students' specific needs. Learning styles, socioeconomic status, family characteristics, health status, gender, ethnicity, age, and other variables should be considered when selecting strategies for instruction *and* for assessment and evaluation. Frequently a teacher will successfully use a variety of strategies to help the students learn the concepts. However, when the teacher evaluates whether these concepts have been learned s/he resorts to traditional paper and pencil tests. Alternative assessment strategies, including but not limited to portfolios, should be adopted to fairly evaluate students' performance.

Every successful teacher I know has a collection of *at least 50* different instructional strategies. Most have many more. They also possess the ability to appropriately and enthusiastically implement them.

Instructional Strategies Self-Assessment

The teacher understands and uses a variety of instructional strategies to encourage students' development of critical thinking, problem-solving, and performance skills.

Knowledge/Performance Indicators	Yes*	Not Sure	No
1. I understand our state's graduation standards and how to implement them.	2	1	0
2. I understand the cognitive processes associated with various kinds or learning and how these processes can be stimulated.	2	1	0
3. I understand principles and techniques, along with advantages and limitations, associated with various instructional strategies.	2	1	0
4. I enhance learning through the use of a wide variety of materials and human and technological resources.	2	1	0
5. I nurture the development of student critical thinking, independent problem solving, and performance capabilities.	2	1	0
6. I demonstrate flexibility and reciprocity in the teaching process as a necessary for adapting instruction to student responses, ideas, and needs.	2	1	0
7. I design teaching strategies and materials to achieve different instructional purposes and to meet student needs including developmental stages, prior knowledge, learning styles, and interests.	2	1	0
8. I use multiple teaching and learning strategies to engage students in active learning opportunities that promote the development of critical thinking, problem solving, and performance capabilities and that help students assume responsibility for identifying and using learning resources.	2	1	0
9. I monitor and adjust strategies in response to learner feedback.	2	1	0
10. I vary the instructional process to address the content and purposes of instruction and the needs of students.	2	1	0
11. I develop a variety of clear, accurate presentations and representations of concepts, using alternative explanations to assist students' understanding.	2	1	0
12. I present varied perspectives to encourage critical thinking.	2	1	0
13. I use educational technology to broaden students knowledge about technology, to deliver instruction to students at different levels and paces, and to stimulate advanced levels of learning.	2	1	0

* A "Yes" response indicates that you can describe, document, and cite examples related to your student teaching assignment.

Self-Assessment Summary and Reflection

1. Which Knowledge / Performance Indicators can I currently describe, document, and cite examples?

   _____

   _____

2. Which Knowledge / Performance Indicators need some work or improvement?

   _____

   _____

3. What specific actions can I take to enrich my knowledge or skill in this area?

   _____

   _____

Activity 4.1   Me, My Students, and Bloom

Context   Students need to demonstrate their competency at several different cognitive levels. Teachers need to provide a variety of questions and activities to guide the students' development of thinking and performance skills.

Purpose   This activity will help you analyze your objectives and the questions you ask to ensure that you are having students demonstrate their abilities at a variety of cognitive levels.

Directions

Videotape and/or audiotape segments from three different lessons. For each lesson, list your objectives and identify the level of cognition you are asking your students to demonstrate. Under each objective, list the questions you asked and directions you gave for activities. (Refer to *Bloom's Taxonomy Prompts* listed at the end of this activity.)

Lesson #1

Objective(s): _____

_____

Cognition Level: _____

Questions you asked: _____

_____

Directions you gave: _____

_____

Lesson #2

Objective(s): _____

_____

Cognition Level: _____

Questions you asked: _____

_____

Directions you gave: _____

_____

Lesson #3

Objective(s): _____

_____

Cognition Level: _____

Questions you asked: _____

_____

Directions you gave: _____

_____

Based on these three lessons, answer the following reflection questions.

1. Did you have a variety of cognitive levels in your objectives? _____

2. Did your students have the prior knowledge necessary for them to successfully meet your objectives? How do you know? _____

   _____

   _____

3. Highlight the questions and directions that match the cognitive level of your objective. _____

   _____

   _____

4. Did your questions and activities allow the students the opportunity to move to higher cognitive levels?

   _____

5. Give an example of a question where the students' answers showed that they were thinking at different cognitive levels. _____

   _____

   _____

6. How can you extend the learning in these lessons or connect them to future lessons?

   _____

   _____

Bloom's Taxonomy Prompts

Level 1: Knowledge • *Students remember and recall information.*

Define. . . .	Locate. . . .
How did . . . happen . . . ?	What is . . . ?
How is . . . ?	When did . . . happen . . . ?
Label. . . .	Where is . . . ?
List. . . .	Who . . . ?

Level 2: Comprehension • *Students explain, understand, and translate information into terms that are meaningful to them.*

Describe. . . .	Discuss. . . .
What is the main idea of . . . ?	Clarify. . . .
Interpret or put in your own words. . . .	What can you say about . . . ?
Compare. . . .	Which is the best answer . . . ?
How are . . . alike/different . . . ?	Which comes first, . . . or . . . ?

Arrange the . . . in order.

Why did . . . ?

Give reasons for. . . .

Explain. . . .

What if . . . ?

Level 3: Application • *Students solve problems or use acquired skills and knowledge in new situations.*

Find an example of . . . ?

Graph. . . .

How can we solve . . . ?

How can you use . . . ?

Organize . . . to show. . . .

Show your understanding of . . . by. . . .

Solve . . . using what you have learned.

Level 4: Analysis • *Students take apart information and identify key ideas and their connections.*

Classify/categorize. . . .

How is . . . related to . . . ?

Identify. . . .

Infer. . . .

Outline or diagram. . . .

Simplify . . . to its basic components.

What are the parts or features of . . . ?

What evidence can you find to . . . ?

What does . . . tell us about . . . ?

What do you think . . . ?

Level 5: Synthesis • *Students combine key ideas and concepts in unique and original ways.*

Adapt or modify. . . .

Combine. . . .

Create or invent. . . .

Delete . . . from. . . .

Design a new. . . .

Design a new use for. . . .

Develop. . . .

Elaborate. . . .

How can we improve . . . ?

If you had . . . how would you . . . ?

Minimize or maximize. . . .

Reorganize. . . .

Suppose you could . . . ?

What is another way . . . ?

What will happen if . . . ?

Level 6: Evaluation • *Students judge the value of material based on previously established criteria or criteria they have determined.*

Assess the value or importance of. . . .

Prioritize. . . .

Prove/disprove that . . . is better than. . . .

What is your opinion of . . . ?

Why do you think or agree . . . ?

Would it be better if . . . ?

Activity 4.2   Extend Thinking

Context   Students often look to teachers for the right answer. Teachers can be the source of all information or they can encourage students to search for an answer and thus develop creative and critical-thinking abilities.

Purpose   This activity will help you recognize opportunities for extending students' thinking and devise ways to use those opportunities appropriately.

Directions: Part 1   Observe your cooperating teacher on three different days. Check (✔) each time you observe the strategy.

Day 1	Day 2	Day 3	*Strategies to Extend Thinking*
_____	_____	_____	*Alert students to expectations:* Teacher lets the students know that there isn't one right answer to the question and demonstrates this by calling on a number of students to share answers. e.g., "There are many possible solutions to this problem. Let's see how many we can come up with."
_____	_____	_____	*Answer a question with another question:* Teacher extends the students' thinking by responding to an answer with: "Why? How do you know? Do you agree? Will you give an example? Can you tell me more?"
_____	_____	_____	*Create a question:* Teacher provides opportunities for students to generate their own questions. These questions can then be asked of the class, used to discuss or review with a partner, or used as the basis for a quiz at the end of class or a review at the beginning of the next lesson.
_____	_____	_____	*Devil's advocate:* Teacher asks students to support their answer by bringing up a different point of view or asks, "But what if . . . ?"
_____	_____	_____	*Metacognition:* Teacher asks student to think about thinking. "Describe how you arrived at your answer. What steps led you to that conclusion? Tell us about your thought process. How did you get that answer?" Teacher models this by describing his/her own thinking process.
_____	_____	_____	*Poll the class:* Teacher polls the students by asking questions like, "Signal if you agree with the author's point of view. Raise your hand if you solved the problem in a different way."
_____	_____	_____	*Random selection:* Teacher uses a random way of calling on students such as using sticks with students' names on them drawn from a cup or drawing a number that corresponds with the students' roll call number. Students get in the habit about thinking and preparing an answer for every question since they don't know when they will be called on.
_____	_____	_____	*Student calls on student:* Teacher asks a student to call on another student to give an answer or opinion or to help first student come up with an answer.
_____	_____	_____	*Summarize/process:* Teacher breaks lessons into manageable learning chunks and gives students time to process what they've learned. "Summarize our discussion thus far. Record in your journal two key points. Show your partner the strategy you used to solve the problem."
_____	_____	_____	*Think—pair—share:* Teacher asks a question and allows individual thinking time. Then the students discuss their answers with a partner. After a couple of minutes, the teacher opens up the question for class discussion.

_____   _____   _____   *Wait time:*   Teacher pauses to allow at least five seconds of think time after a question. Teacher pauses to allow at least five seconds of think time after a student's response.

Directions: Part 2   Look at your weekly lesson plan outline. Find situations where you will have a class discussion, be questioning students, review previous lessons, provide time for students to process a concept, etc. Include in your lesson plan at least one of the strategies to extend the students' thinking. After the lesson, reflect on the effectiveness of the strategy.

1. Were your directions clear? _____

2. Did students do what you asked? Explain.

   _____

   _____

3. How successful was the strategy? Explain. _____

   _____

   _____

4. If the strategy was unsuccessful, how will you modify it? _____

   _____

   _____

5. What was the students' reaction? _____

   _____

   _____

6. What feedback did your cooperating teacher give you? _____

   _____

   _____

Activity 4.3   Class Discussion

Context   Teachers help students process and make meaning out of what they are learning through class discussion. To make the most productive use of class discussion time, teachers should prepare themselves and the students for the discussion and direct it through effective questioning techniques.

Purpose   By watching a videotape of a class discussion, you will be able to identify strategies that you use effectively and those which you need to improve.

Directions   Videotape a class. Watch the videotape once, then watch it again and rate yourself on the following items. Use "+" to indicate strong evidence; "0" to indicate satisfactory evidence; "–" to indicate weak or no evidence.

_____ I am familiar and comfortable with subject under discussion.

_____ Students have background knowledge about subject under discussion.

_____ Materials, displays, and examples are provided to aid understanding.

_____ Questions are directed to all students.

_____ All students have opportunity to contribute to discussion.

_____ I ask a variety of questions, low and high cognitive levels.

_____ I respond to students by validating their answers and encourage them to expand upon them.

_____ I provide wait time that allows students to formulate quality answers and responses.

_____ I correct errors in a manner that does not embarrass or belittle the students.

_____ I guide students to complete answers or to correct answers through prompts and leading questions.

_____ I model good listening skills and expect students to do the same.

_____ I facilitate discussion and students are able to question and respond to each other.

_____ I move discussion back to the topic when necessary.

_____ I provide students with opportunities to summarize what is being discussed.

_____ Students demonstrate that they have met lesson objective(s).

Activity 4.4   Terms and Products

Context   New teachers often have a difficult time aligning the words of a student assignment to the expected learning or product. For example, a teacher should not ask student to merely "list" the organs of the digestive system if the learning expectation is to "describe" the sequence and function of the digestive system.

Purpose   To provide and generate examples of terms and products for student assignments (tasks). The final product of this activity will serve as a model or guide as you develop and create learning tasks for your students.

Directions: Part 1   Match the six levels of Bloom's Taxonomy (classification) to the proper definition/explanation.

Level

_____ Knowledge

_____ Comprehension

_____ Application

_____ Analysis

_____ Synthesis

_____ Evaluation

Definition/Explanation

A. The ability to break down information (e.g., facts, concepts) and determine its relation/organization to associated parts and to the whole.

B. The ability to recall information (e.g., facts, content, principles, rules, steps).

C. The ability to make judgments and/or choices and support/defend the decision.

D. The ability to create a new product (e.g., hypothesis, result, solving a problem) by combining, integrating, organizing, or transferring prior knowledge.

E. The ability to apply knowledge and understanding to a new situation (e.g., solving a problem).

F. The ability to explain, interpret, paraphrase or recount something in one's own words.

Directions: Part 2   Listed below, in Group 1, are possible student assignment terms—terms used to help define the task. In Group 2 are possible student products—the end result of the task. For each of the six taxonomic categories, find ten "terms" and ten "products" that support the essence of that category. Write them in the table at the end of this activity. You will end up with a total 60 terms and 60 products (try not to repeat a term or product).

Group 1: Assignment Terms

acquire	analyze	apply	appraise
argue	arrange	assemble	assess
calculate	categorize	change	choose
classify	communicate	compare	compose
conduct	consider	construct	contract
create	criticize	critique	debate
decide	deduce	describe	design
detect	develop	diagram	differentiate
discriminate	discuss	dissect	distinguish
dramatize	draw	employ	evaluate
examine	experiment	explain	express
estimate	formulate	generalize	identify

illustrate	imagine	improve	infer
inspect	interpret	invent	inventory
investigate	judge	justify	know
label	list	locate	manage
manipulate	match	measure	memorize
modify	name	observe	operate
organize	paraphrase	plan	practice
predict	prepare	produce	propose
question	rate	recall	recognize
recommend	record	relate	remember
repeat	report	restate	restructure
revise	role-play	schedule	score
select	separate	sequence	set up
show	sketch	solve	speculate
state	summarize	suppose	survey
teach	tell	transfer	transform
translate	underline	use	validate
verify	write		

Group 2: Assignment Products

advertisements	analogies	book reviews	bumper stickers
cartoons	chart	collages	comic strips
commercials	confessions	construction	conclusions
critiques	dances	debates	design plans
diagrams	diaries	dictionaries	dioramas
displays	essays	forecasts	games
ghost stories	graphs	how-to guides	illustrations
interviews	inventions	jokes	laws
lessons (student taught)	letters	machines	maps
metaphors	mobiles	models	movie reviews
murals	myths	news article (student written)	pantomimes
petitions	photographs	pictures	poems
protest letters	puppet shows	questionnaires	radio shows
recipes	recommendations	recordings	report
research	résumés	scrapbooks	sculptures
self-evaluation	set of rules	sketches	songs
speculations	speeches	stitchery	
stories	surveys	tests	
time lines	valuing	worksheets	

Level	Possible Terms	Possible Products
Knowledge		
Comprehension		
Application		
Analysis		
Synthesis		
Evaluation		

Case Study

Joleen was looking forward to the next student teaching seminar and sharing time. She wanted to talk about her science lesson that had gone beautifully. The first graders really were into the brick making and seemed to understand the connection between the clay and the bricks.

She had been well organized for the cooperative learning groups by having all the materials out, directions written on the board, and the job cards ready. Each student enjoyed having a different job to do in the group and, for once, they didn't seem to fight about who was to do what. They even did a good job of taking turns. The lesson lent itself to a variety of higher-order thinking questions. Joleen was pleased with all the different answers and hypotheses the students came up with as they worked.

The highlight of the whole lesson was a comment from Brandon. He often refused to cooperate, but really was on target during this lesson. When Joleen asked the students to compare the brick to the beads they had made, Brandon said, "I know why we're making the bricks today. We have a vacation and there will be more time for them to dry." What a surprise! And he was right!

- What were some reasons that Joleen's lesson had gone so well?
- Why do you suppose the students did better than usual in the groups?
- Compare Joleen's cooperative group lesson with a time that you used learning groups.
- Building on the success of this lesson, what are some ways that Joleen can help students be effective group members?
- What are the advantages and disadvantages of cooperative groups?

Student-to-Student Tips

✔ This is a good time to try things that you are curious about to see how they'll work in the classroom. *Crista, elementary student teacher*

✔ Subscribe to a teacher idea magazine such as "Mailbox." *Yean, elementary student teacher*

✔ Have lots of resources. Don't be afraid to take ideas from other teachers. *Dan, secondary student teacher*

✔ Be organized. Have your ideas and samples from methods classes organized so that you can pull them easily. They'll be a start, but you'll have to find more resources. *Carlos, elementary student teacher*

✔ Observe specialists and as many classroom teachers as you can. You can get so many ideas and techniques for working with the students. *Sarah, elementary student teacher*

✔ I bought two books from Barnes and Noble about teaching activities. The store has a great selection of "teacher books." I realize it gets expensive to buy these books, but there is nothing wrong with bringing a pencil and notebook to Barnes and Noble and taking notes. *Meg, secondary student teacher*

Bibliography

Angelo, T. A. 1995. Beginning the dialogue: Thoughts on promoting critical thinking: Classroom assessment for critical thinking. *Teaching of Psychology* 22, 1: 6–7.

Bellanca, J. 1992. *The cooperative think tank II: Graphic organizers to teaching thinking in the cooperative classroom.* Palatine, IL.: IRI Skylight Training and Publishing, Inc.

Beyer, B. K. 1995. *Critical thinking.* Bloomington, IN: Phi Delta Kappa Educational Foundation.

Brooks, J. G., and M. G. Brooks. 1993. *In search of understanding: The case for constructivist classrooms.* Alexandria, VA: Association for Supervision and Curriculum Development.

Carter, J. A., and M. A. Solmon. 1994. Cognitive mapping: An activity for health education. *Journal of Health Education* 25, 2: 108–109.

Cooper, J. L. 1995. Cooperative learning and critical thinking. *Teaching of Psychology* 22, 1: 7–8.

Ennis, R. 1987. A taxonomy of critical thinking dispositions and abilities. In *Teaching Thinking Skills: Theory and Practice*, ed. Joan Baron and Robert Sternberg. New York: W. H. Freeman.

Fernandez-Balboa, J. M. 1993. Critical pedagogy: Making critical thinking really critical. *Analytic Teaching* 13, 2: 61–72.

Grundy, S., and M. Henry. 1995. Which way home economics? An examination of the conceptual orientation of home economics curricula. *Journal of Curriculum Studies* 27, 3: 281–297.

Halpern, D. F., and S. G. Nummedal. 1995. Closing

thoughts about helping students improve how they think. *Teaching of Psychology* 22, 1: 82–83.

Johnson, R. T., and D. W. Johnson. 1999. *Learning together and alone: Cooperative, competitive, and individualistic learning*. Boston: Allyn and Bacon.

King, A. 1995. Designing the instructional process to enhance critical thinking across the curriculum: Inquiring minds really do want to know: Using questioning to teach critical thinking. *Teaching of Psychology* 22, 1: 13–17.

Maylath, N. S. 1989. Constructing concept maps for health instruction. *Journal of School Health* 59, 6: 269–270.

McDade, S. A. 1995. Case study pedagogy to advance critical thinking. *Teaching of Psychology* 22, 1: 9–10.

Norris, S. P. 1985. Synthesis of research on critical thinking. *Educational Leadership* 42 (May): 40–45.

Paul, R. 1988. Critical thinking in the classroom. *Teaching K–8* 18 (April): 49–51.

Quin, Z., D. W. Johnson, and R. T. Johnson. 1995. Cooperative versus competitive efforts and problem solving. *Review of Educational Research* 65, 2: 129–144.

Robertson, J. F., and D. Rane-Szostak. 1996. Using dialogues to develop critical thinking skills. A practical approach. *Journal of Adolescent and Adult Literacy* 39, 7: 552–556.

Scriven, M., and R. Paul. 1996. Defining critical thinking: A draft statement for the National Council for Excellence in Critical Thinking. [On-Line] Available: http://www.criticalthinking.org/University/univlibrary/library.nclk

Siciliano, J. I. 2001. How to incorporate cooperative learning principles in the classroom: It's more than just putting students in teams. *Journal of Management Education* 25, 1 (Feb.): 8–20.

Slavin, R. E. 1995. *Cooperative learning*. 2nd ed. Boston: Allyn and Bacon.

Wade, C. 1995. Using writing to develop and assess critical thinking. *Teaching of Psychology* 22, 1: 24–28.

Wilen, W. 1987. *Questions, questioning techniques, and effective teaching*. Washington, DC: National Education Association.

Wooley, S. F. 1995. Behavior mapping: A tool for identifying priorities for health education curricula and instruction. *Journal of Health Education* 26, 4: 200–206

Wurman, R. S. 1989. *Information anxiety*. New York: Doubleday.

Young, L. E. 1992. Critical thinking skills: Definitions, implications for implementation. *NASSP Bulletin* 76, 548: 47–54.

5
Learning Environment

"The most important method of education has always consisted of that
in which the students are urged to actual performance."
—*Thomas Edison*

"Tell me, and I'll listen. Show me, and I'll understand. Involve me, and I'll learn."
—*Teton Lakota Indian*

Standard #5 The teacher uses an understanding of individual and group motivation and behavior to create a learning environment that encourages positive social interaction, active engagement in learning, and self-motivation.

Performance Indicators: *The teacher . . .*

- Understands the importance of setting up effective learning environments and has techniques and strategies to use to do so, including some that provide opportunities for student input into the processes. The teacher understands the need for a variety of techniques and is working to increase his or her knowledge and skills.

- Consistently creates a safe and positive learning environment that encourages social interaction, civic responsibility, active engagement in learning, and self-motivation.

Vignette Scott was very excited about finally getting to teach. He began the first two weeks by observing his cooperating teacher and learning student names. In addition, he assisted in handing out and collecting assignments as well as working with individual students during class time. During this observation period, Scott noticed the numerous visuals on display in the classroom. One entire wall was a window that faced an outside courtyard where often times other classes convened. While the blackboard was filled with the daily and weekly agendas along with due dates for as-

signments, the remaining two walls were covered with bulletin boards, calendars and pictures. Scott felt this classroom was much too busy for some of the students to learn efficiently; that it might be too distracting for students.

Fundamental Principles

Effective teachers work in many ways to build positive classroom interactions. These teachers recognize that involving students in this endeavor not only promotes growth in personal and social responsibility but also enhances the development of democratic and social values. Group rapport is enhanced as students and teachers work cooperatively to establish classroom norms and rules. Teaching and modeling effective problem-solving techniques such as conflict resolution provide motivation for learning, positive social interaction among children, and positive self-esteem for all. Thus, the effective teacher strives to create a learning community that fosters group decision making, collaboration, individual responsibility, and self-directed learning (Campbell, et al. 1995, 23).

What are the elements that make up school climate? What does a school with a positive climate look like, and how does it operate? Teachers at all levels have made efforts to motivate students and to enhance their learning by fostering self-concepts and by establishing positive classroom environments. Purkey and Novak (1996) present a framework for looking at how schools become "invitational" by focusing on five elements: physical environment, policies, programs, processes, and people. In the same regard, Danielson (1996) suggests that the prerequisites to good instruction are the physical environment, attention to routines and procedures, and the establishment of norms and expectations for student behavior. Research by Wang, Haertel, and Walberg (1993) suggests that classroom instruction and management and the immediate environment of the student influence academic performance as well as good student–teacher interaction. Organization and policies of the school and nature of the community, however, did not appear to affect students' learning.

Every child deserves a school that is inviting, academically challenging, and safe. The ambiance of a school has a significant, if unconscious, effect on students' learning. The significance of the learning should not be underestimated. A school building that was designed with the students' needs in mind fulfills its objective of providing the students with a feeling of belonging (Hebert 1998). A school's inviting exterior and cheerful, warm interior set the tone of an environment in which both parents and students feel welcomed and wanted. An overall climate in which all feel comfortable leads to a productive learning environment that has a positive impact on the achievement of the students. The brain learns faster in challenging, creative, accommodating, and healthy environments.

Research (Hebert 1998) has also shown that classroom designs affect students' attitudes and behavior. Children unconsciously display courteous attitudes in environments that are physically adjusted to their needs. The organization of space has a profound effect on learning (Arends, Winitzky, and Tannenbaum 2001). As examples: lower than usual classroom ceilings create an intimate space suitable for small children; windowed walls in classrooms invite the outdoors inside; wide hallways give students personal space to move about the building throughout the day; teachers' desks are not alienated from the rest of the class but near students to increase the security of belonging; students' accomplishments decorate the walls, heightening the students' sense of achievement; and public areas are designed to foster a sense of community, cooperation, and comfort throughout the building. Research suggests that color and lighting may influence learning. Birren (1977) reported that warm colors and brilliant lighting increased mus-

cular tension, respiration rate, pulse, blood pressure, and brain activity. Insufficient lighting causes visual fatigue. Distracting color combinations can lead to task confusion and slow reaction. Quality lighting and appropriate colors improve visual processing and reduce stress (Birren 1972).

Classroom climate refers to the socio-psychological dimensions of classroom life, including cooperation among teachers and students, common interests and values, the pursuit of common goals, a clear academic focus, well-organized and well-planned lessons, explicit learning objectives, an appropriate level of task difficulty for students, and an appropriate instructional pace (Haertel, Walberg, and Haertel 1981). Teachers have to ensure that the classroom environment adopts a positive social climate (Shapiro 1993). Direct influences include the amount of time a teacher spends on a topic and the quality of the social interactions teachers have with their students. Classroom instructional variables such as enthusiasm, clarity, feedback, and correctives are also key elements. The teacher's expertise and experience are not sufficient to achieve the goal of a positive social climate. Constructive student and teacher social interactions have a documented effect on school learning. The frequency and quality of these interactions contribute to students' sense of self-esteem and foster a sense of membership in the class and school (Wang, Haertel, and Walberg 1993). The teacher who can help students develop positive self-concepts has a better chance of increasing academic achievement and motivation. Positive teacher practices produce improvement in student performance, including attentiveness, achievement, and discipline, regardless of task level or student ability (Vacha 1977).

The reason some students feel disconnected in school is because they were consistently overlooked. No one encouraged them to participate in activities, and they seldom related to faculty and staff. Teachers returned papers with no more than a letter grade and did not seem to notice students' absences. "These students suffered from a 'caring disability'; not enough educators cared to invite them to participate in school life" (Purkey and Novak 1996, 14). The difference between classrooms in which students are achieving and those in which they are not is due to the amount of negative or positive interaction (1) between the individual students, (2) among the class as a whole, and (3) between the class and the teacher. If the climate is supportive and positive, the students succeed. When this form of cooperative learning is successful in the classroom, teachers report better student participation, increased learning, enhanced student self-esteem, and a more positive classroom environment (Klemp, Hon, and Shorr 1993). Such a setting has been defined by Schmuck and Schmuck (1975) as one in which the students expect one another to do their intellectual best and to support one another. Educators need to examine why children fail and provide schools in which children can succeed. Youth who feel the concern and acceptance of a teacher can gain self-confidence, which in turn enhances self-motivation. These factors constitute the foundation for success. A student experiencing success is much more likely to anticipate each learning activity and participate in an orderly way than a student who is not experiencing success. Once the cycle of success within each student is in operation, class control is more effective. The learning climate is a result of the effects of the teacher's attitudes and behavior on students' feelings and thoughts about their personal safety and self-esteem (Faust 1980). The personality, self-confidence, and attitudes of the teacher communicate to the students that the teacher cares about them and about the subject that is being taught. Effective instruction communicates to students that they are capable, important, and self-sufficient. Stressing a positive self-concept and offering experiences to promote success are invaluable aids to learning.

Research also claims that attention to class routines and procedures is important to creating a positive learning environment. Danielson (1996) states that "teaching requires good management before good instruction is possible. Teachers must develop procedures for the smooth operation of the classroom and the efficient use of time before they can address instructional techniques" (83). In fact, she mentions, the opposite is also true; when students are engaged deeply in the content, classroom management is not an issue. Doyle (1986) says the difference is that the rules and procedures in effective learning environments are explicit, concrete, and functional. Brophy (1987) mentions not only the need for establishing clear routines as a means to stemming undesirable student behavior but also its impact on increasing the time available for student learning to occur. Effective classroom management increases student engagement, decreases disruptive behaviors, and makes good use of instructional time. Kounin (1977) identified several principles of effective management that correlated significantly with high task involvement and low deviancy of students. These were (1) with-it-ness and overlapping, (2) smoothness and momentum, (3) group alerting and accountability, and (4) chal-

lenge and variety. With-it-ness was defined as teachers' communicating to students by their actions that they know what is going on in the classroom. Overlapping refers to the ability of a teacher to attend to two activities simultaneously without neglecting one or the other. Smoothness and momentum involve the ability to move students quickly and smoothly from one activity to another at a good pace, without losing the focus on learning. Group alertness is created by using techniques that keep students actively participating in the content of the lesson. Accountability is created when students feel that they are held accountable for their time in class.

The key to effective classroom management is to minimize off-task and deviant behaviors by (1) establishing and practicing class routines; (2) providing developmentally appropriate, challenging activities for each student; (3) holding students accountable for learning; (4) ensuring sufficient opportunities to practice so success is possible; (5) moving at a rapid pace as dictated by student progress; and (6) ensuring that each student experiences success regularly. Good teachers understand students' backgrounds, abilities, interests, and attention spans and plan class activities to meet the needs of each student. Teachers who operate a structured teaching-learning environment appear to be more effective.

Successful teachers effectively manage student behavior. Management skills may vary among teachers in emphasis and focus, but collectively they characterize quality teaching. Effective teachers make three assumptions: teaching is a profession, students are in school to learn, and the teacher's challenge is to promote learning. Effective management means maintaining an environment in which all children have the opportunity to learn. It is the responsibility of the teacher to fashion a learning environment in which all children can learn and feel comfortable.

Many class management and discipline problems can be prevented through anticipation and planning (Arends, Winitzky, and Tannenbaum 2001). It is important to anticipate the types of problems that might occur and to have a plan for dealing with them when they do. The following are some suggestions for preventing behavior problems:

- Anticipate and explain the rules rather than waiting for them to be broken.
- Talk with students' parents and ask for suggestions for dealing with misbehavior.
- Avoid placing students in situations that give rise to misbehavior; be aware of individual students'

tolerance for failure; some students are never willing to fail in front of peers.

- Call attention regularly to desirable behavior.
- Talk with students and try to better understand their feelings. For example, the student may feel that the teacher does not like him or her.
- If feasible, give problem students added responsibility they are capable of handling. For example, make them student helpers or teacher's assistants.
- As a teacher, model the behaviors expected of students. For example, ask students to do things politely, and discuss problems in a caring manner.

Additional research has demonstrated the relationship between effective instructional practices of teachers and appropriate on-task classroom behavior of students (Christenson and Ysseldyke 1989; Gettinger 1988; McKee and Witt 1990; Wehby, et al. 1998). These investigations found that teachers can prevent problem behaviors from occurring by teaching in ways that promote high levels of academic engagement. In other words, when teachers implement specific instructional practices effectively and match their tasks to each student's individual needs, students are more likely to remain engaged with the process of learning, to complete academic tasks, and are less likely to engage in off-task and problem behaviors (Martens and Kelly 1993). In contrast, when teachers implement less effective instructional practices and assign tasks that are mismatched to the student's individual needs, students are more likely to fail and then engage in off-task and problem behavior (Pacchiano 2000). Children who frequently engage in disruptive behaviors, such as talking out of turn or hitting other children, often perform poorly in school, while children who engage in constructive behaviors are more likely to perform well (Wang, Haertel, and Walberg 1993).

Danielson (1996) suggests that approaches to managing student behavior in well-run classrooms share certain characteristics: (a) expectations are clear to everyone; (b) standards of behavior are appropriate to the developmental levels of the students; (c) expectations are consistently applied; (d) teachers are aware of what is going on in the classroom at all times; (e) teachers refrain from losing their tempers; (f) any chastisement of conduct focuses on a student's behavior, not on the student; and (g) teachers encourage students to monitor their own behavior. The formulation of classroom rules has been found to be an important component of effective classroom discipline as well (McGinnis, Frederick, and Edwards 1995; McKee and Witt 1990; Ringer et al. 1993). Almeida (1995) suggests that rules include: (a) clarity, (b) providing consequences for unacceptable behavior, (c) consistency in bestowing rewards and punishments, (d) caring about the students and understanding, and (e) change which may be necessary to create an effective learning environment. Nevertheless, rules alone will not stop misbehavior unless they are integrated with a positive and warm classroom atmosphere. Teachers who care and respect their students create an environment that maximizes learning (Geiger 2000). The proper balance between warmth and discipline is often hard to find, especially for novice teachers (Johnson 1994).

If we believe that most students want to learn and to feel competent, then we must accept that when the instructional conditions in a classroom do not meet the student's needs, teaching and learning can become unpleasant experiences for the student (Pacchiano 2000). Effective teachers perform multiple activities simultaneously that facilitate student learning and prevent problems from occurring (Kounin 1970). The activity that most distinguishes effective teachers from less effective teachers, however, is the ability to implement effective instructional practices that keep students engaged and motivated to learn (McKee and Witt 1990). The role of the teacher is to increase student motivation and develop the skills or strategies that make a student more competent and to structure the learning environment so that students are able to take ownership of their own learning. Fortunately, many of the strategies that "empower" and "engage" students also lead to increased motivation. Motivation and achievement have long been recognized to have a close cause-effect relationship, as of course have ability and achievement.

Research has identified general strategies of teaching that enhance student motivation and learning. Establishing specific class routines and procedures can minimize class disruptions (Maehr and Midgley 1996; Raffini 1993). These strategies are:

- Capitalize on students' existing needs and strengths. Students learn best when incentives for learning in a classroom satisfy their own motives for being in the class. Building on strengths first gives students an opportunity to use their talents to achieve success. Success is motivating when students understand why they are succeeding and are able to develop their confidence and competence.

- Make students active participants in learning. It is good to involve students in activities, group problem-solving exercises, or working with each other in some way. Give them opportunities and strategies to develop their creativity. Students perform with higher motivation when their creativity is engaged. Challenge students to construct original and creative products to support their written reports.

- Challenge students. This gives students an opportunity to discover the relationship between effort and success and between success and motivation, and to develop higher self-concept. Hold high but realistic expectations for students. If the teacher expects students to be motivated, hardworking, and interested in class, they are more likely to be so.

- Help students set achievable goals for themselves. Teach them how to make their tasks more manageable. Narrowing or broadening the topic to a challenging but manageable size is very important for developing motivation. Failure to attain unrealistic goals can disappoint and frustrate students. Help students evaluate their progress by encouraging them to critique their own work, analyze their strengths, and work on their weaknesses.

- Tell students what they need to do to succeed in the class. Do not let students struggle to figure out what is expected of them. Students need to understand the relevance of all their school activities. Clearly establish the expected goal and required method. Let the students know the benefits that will be realized.

- Strengthen students' self-motivation. Avoid messages that reinforce the power of the teacher or that emphasize rewards. Help students develop an internal locus of control. Students who feel they have the power to control some events in their lives are more likely to become self-motivated than students who see themselves as powerless.

- Help students feel connected. Approaches such as cooperative learning, peer mentoring, peer counseling, and community service are essential for promoting students' academic and social development. It is through their collaboration with peers that students learn the importance of attending to others, supporting each other, and negotiating differences.

- Be enthusiastic about the subject. A teacher's enthusiasm is a crucial factor in the student's motivation to learn.

- Teach students to evaluate themselves. Self-evaluation needs to address the questions: "What was done well?" and "How can it be improved?" The ability to realistically evaluate one's own performance improves with practice and is both empowering and highly motivating. These motivational strategies need to be applied individually and changed frequently so that they do not become ineffective through overuse.

As Campbell, et al. (1995) have remarked: "Teachers interested in building and sustaining a positive learning climate are aware of the range of behavioral phenomena confronting them and use this knowledge along with their classroom experiences to construct an ever-evolving student motivation and management philosophy. This philosophy is specific enough to guide classroom actions yet flexible enough to accommodate the individual needs of students" (39).

Questions for Reflection

- In what ways might the school foster a positive learning environment?

- How does classroom design affect student attitudes and behavior? Base your answer on research findings.

- What is meant by "classroom climate"?

- What impact do instructional practices have on classroom management? Base your answer on research findings.

- How can teachers help all students develop enthusiasm for and a deep knowledge of the subject matter?

Commentary on Standard #5

CAROL CUMMINGS | Ph.D., Educational Consultant, Author and Researcher, Seattle Pacific University, Seattle, Washington

Imagine going to the gym for a workout. Chances are you'll use a variety of machines, getting a full-body workout. Purposefully you avoid overuse of any one muscle group—to avoid both boredom and fatigue. Now, apply this same concept to the classroom. Novelty will prevent both boredom and mental fatigue. Too much of the same, whether it be teacher talk or working alone, forces learners to seek their own novelty. More often than not, this results in off-task behavior. Veteran teachers know that it's more difficult to get students to stop doing something than to prevent them from doing it in the first place. How do we prevent off-task behavior while at the same time promote active engagement? Develop a lesson plan that uses all four sociological learning styles: teacher talk (direct instruction), small group work (cooperative learning), independent learning, and whole group interaction (i.e., discussion). Then, apply the concept of multiple intelligences across the four styles. For example, teacher talk might include lecture (verbal-linguistic), showing graphic organizers (spatial), bodily-kinesthetic (interactive slide lecture), intrapersonal (connecting the lesson to personal problems), using numbers, graphs, and logic (logical-mathematical), playing music to illustrate a point (musical), provide examples of social issues relevant to the lesson (interpersonal), and include environmental, ecological problems (naturalist). You could find examples of the eight intelligences to fit small group, independent work, as well as whole group interaction. The guiding principle, however, is: "Don't force a fit!" That is, only include those intelligences that align with the lesson objective; it's unlikely you'll use all of them.

Planning for the use of multiple intelligences and sociological learning styles is not enough, however, to sustain focus. Limit the time spent in any given activity. Eight to ten minutes of teacher lecturette, filled with graphics and intrapersonal examples, might be followed by a ten-minute small group activity where students are emotionally involved in debating the idea presented in the lecturette. A lively whole group debate follows with students lined up on one side of the room or the other to signify their side of the issue. The remaining 10–12 minutes of class find students working independently, writing about their own position on the topic.

The science of teaching tells us about the importance of the active involvement of the learner's brain in the lesson. It is the art of teaching, the teacher designing and implementing the lesson, that makes it happen.

Learning Environment Self-Assessment

The teacher uses an understanding of individual and group motivation and behavior to create a learning environment that encourages positive social interaction, active engagement in learning, and self-motivation.

Knowledge/Performance Indicators	Yes*	Not Sure	No
1. I understand human motivation and behavior and draw from the foundational sciences of psychology, anthropology, and sociology to develop strategies for organizing and supporting individual and group work.	2	1	0
2. I understand how social groups function and influence people, and how people influence groups.	2	1	0
3. I know how to create learning environments that contribute to the self-esteem of all persons and to positive interpersonal relations.	2	1	0
4. I know how to help people work productively and cooperatively with each other in complex social settings.	2	1	0
5. I understand the principles of effective classroom management and use a range of strategies to promote positive relationships, cooperation, and purposeful learning in the classroom.	2	1	0
6. I know factors and situations that are likely to promote or diminish intrinsic motivation and how to help students become self-motivated.	2	1	0

	2	1	0
7. I understand how participation supports commitment.	2	1	0
8. I establish a positive climate in the classroom and participate in maintaining a positive climate in the school as a whole.	2	1	0
9. I establish peer relationships to promote learning.	2	1	0
10. I recognize the relationship of intrinsic motivation to student lifelong growth and learning.	2	1	0
11. I use different motivational strategies that are likely to encourage continuous development of individual learner abilities.	2	1	0
12. I design and manage learning communities in which students assume responsibility for themselves and one another.	2	1	0
13. I participate in decision making, work both collaboratively and independently, and engage in purposeful learning activities.	2	1	0
14. I engage students in individual and group learning activities that help them develop the motivation to achieve, by relating lessons to students' personal interests, allowing students to have choices in their learning, and leading students to ask questions and pursue problems that are meaningful to them and the learning.	2	1	0
15. I organize, allocate, and manage the resources of time, space, activities, and attention to provide active engagement of all students in productive tasks.	2	1	0
16. I maximize the amount of class time spent in learning by creating expectations and processes for communication and behavior along with a physical setting conducive to classroom goals.	2	1	0
17. I develop expectations for student interactions, academic discussions, and individual and group responsibility that create a positive classroom climate of openness, mutual respect, support, inquiry, and learning.	2	1	0
18. I analyze the classroom environment and make decisions and adjustments to enhance social relationships, student motivation and engagement, and productive work.	2	1	0
19. I organize, prepare students for, and monitor independent and group work that allows for full, varied, and effective participation of all individuals.	2	1	0

* A "Yes" response indicates that you can describe, document, and cite examples related to your student teaching assignment.

Self-Assessment Summary and Reflection

1. Which Knowledge/Performance Indicators can I currently describe, document, and cite examples?

_____

_____

_____

2. Which Knowledge/Performance Indicators need some work or improvement?

_____

_____

3. What specific actions can I take to enrich my knowledge or skill in this area?

_____

_____

Activity 5.1   Enhancing the Learning Environment

Context   When teachers provide a warm, inviting learning environment, they do so intentionally using a myriad of strategies that range from subtle and unusual to conspicuous and expected.

Purpose   To recognize teacher behaviors that enhance the learning environment.

Directions   Look at the following teacher behaviors and categorize each by using the following letters. There will be more than one correct answer for some of these.

C = provides a positive *climate* in which to learn
E = establishes a high *expectation* for learning and student behavior
P = provides a safe, accessible, inviting *physical environment*

1. _____ Calls students by their first names.

2. _____ Uses words of respect such as "please," "thank you," "It would be helpful if . . ."

3. _____ Gives specific, positive feedback: "Good answer. I can tell you did your homework."

4. _____ Greets students at the door or as they enter.

5. _____ Has classroom expectations posted: "Work, Respect, Belong."

6. _____ Smiles at and laughs with students.

7. _____ Reacts to mistakes that s/he has made as a fact of life, no big deal.

8. _____ Has a daily agenda and/or weekly agenda.

9. _____ Posts homework assignments in the same place.

10. _____ Begins the class with an interesting quote of the day.

11. _____ Plans transitions between tasks so there's little empty time.

12. _____ Has trash can, pencil sharpener, reference materials in an area that has easy access.

13. _____ Has student work displayed.

14. _____ Has pictures of students working on a big project.

15. _____ Has a bulletin board with newspaper articles/pictures featuring school events.

16. _____ Has arranged room in a modified "U" shape so that s/he can be in close proximity to all students.

17. _____ Has posters, bean bag chairs, flowers, reading nook.

18. _____ Has student folders for in-class assignments and make-up work.

19. _____ Has students help determine the classroom rules and regulations.

20. _____ Attends extracurricular events.

21. _____ Has established standards for neatness and accuracy of assignments.

22. _____ Has students attend study sessions and retake quizzes/tests on core knowledge if they score below a C.

Activity 5.2 Proactive Classroom Management

Context To be proactive is the opposite of being reactive. Rather than wait for something to happen and then move into action, the proactive teacher looks at a situation and structures the environment to reduce the potential for disruptions and the amount of time spent on transitions.

Purpose This exercise asks you to look at common classroom occurrences and analyze them for ways to reduce the time spent on non-instructional activities (e.g., taking attendance) and the potential for disruptions.

Directions Read the 26 situations below. Following the list, select five situations and describe how each might create classroom management problems. Finally, plan a proactive strategy for each to avoid potential problems.

1. The teacher plunges into the work before having the attention of all the students.

2. Too much thought is given to the teaching and too little to the students' learning.

3. The teacher fails to make clear the lesson's purposes (what is to be learned and why).

4. The teacher fails to motivate students (create within the students the desire to learn).

5. The teacher does not know the names of his/her students.

6. Lessons aren't prepared and teaching materials aren't organized until the last minute.

7. The teacher talks too rapidly or too slowly.

8. The teacher sits at the desk all of the time.

9. The teacher does all the explaining and answering of questions.

10. The teacher speaks in a low, monotonous tone.

11. The teacher allows him/herself to be sidetracked by irrelevant questions or comments.

12. The teacher is tied to the textbook or to a written lesson plan.

13. The teacher repeats each student's answer.

14. The teacher expresses ideas using vocabulary unfamiliar to the students.

15. The teacher leaves a concept before the students understand it fully.

16. The teacher interrupts the students' work to add or change the directions.

17. The teacher has little idiosyncrasies and mannerisms, either physical or vocal.

18. In assigning work the teacher says, "I want you to do _____ for me tomorrow."

19. The students' responses are greeted with a monotonous "all right" or "OK."

20. The teacher calls the name of a particular student before stating a question.

21. The teacher has not developed a sense of "with-it-ness" (eyes in the back of the head).

22. During class discussion the teacher frequently fails to notice indifferent or off-task students.

23. Directions are given in the form of a question. ("Will you open your books?")

24. The teacher works with individual students but does not monitor the entire class.

25. A teacher overemphasizes interpersonal relationships in an attempt to get the students to like him/her.

26. The students who misbehave get the most attention, while the teacher ignores the students who are following directions correctly.

*Situation #*_____

Potential Problem: _____

Proactive Approach: _____

*Situation #*_____

Potential Problem: _____

Proactive Approach: _____

*Situation #*_____

Potential Problem: _____

Proactive Approach: _____

*Situation #*_____

Potential Problem: _____

Proactive Approach: _____

*Situation #*_____

Potential Problem: _____

Proactive Approach: _____

Activity 5.3   Classroom Procedures and Routines

Context   Teachers know that time is a precious commodity in the classroom. By teaching procedures and routines to their students, they are able to spend less time on transitions and procedural behavior and more time on learning. A procedure is the method used to perform a task that is required on a regular basis. A procedure becomes routine when the students do it *automatically* or with only a brief reminder. Teachers also know that the expectations they have help the students assume responsibility and develop a sense of belonging.

Purpose   This exercise helps you focus your observations of your cooperating teacher. Your students don't come into your classroom knowing how you want them to hand in their papers or deal with pencil sharpening. They've been in a variety of classrooms and performed those tasks in a variety of ways. You have to decide how you want them to perform the students in your classroom and then teach that procedure.

Directions   Describe what the teacher and students are doing at these times.

1. Class/Day begins (right after bell rings or students come into the room)

   Teacher: _____

   _____

   Students: _____

   _____

2. Students are absent or tardy

   Teacher: _____

   _____

   Students: _____

   _____

3. Students are dismissed

   Teacher: _____

   _____

   Students: _____

   _____

4. Assignments and tests are corrected, collected, graded, and returned

   Teacher: _____

   _____

   Students: _____

   _____

5. Materials and equipment are needed (books, reference material, lab equipment, classroom library)

   Teacher: _____

   _____

   Students: _____

   _____

6. Students are expected to go to their seats

   Teacher: _____

   _____

   Students: _____

   _____

7. Students have make-up assignments

   Teacher: _____

   _____

   Students: _____

   _____

8. Student leave the room (for lavatory, office, locker)

   Teacher: _____

   _____

   Students: _____

   _____

9. Students answer questions or give ideas during class discussions

   Teacher: _____

   _____

   Students: _____

   _____

10. Students finish an assignment/test early

    Teacher: _____

    _____

    Students: _____

    _____

11. Students are given a homework assignment

   Teacher: _____

   _____

   Students: _____

   _____

12. Classroom jobs are assigned and carried out ("line leader," running errands, taking care of the class pets and plants, handing out papers/materials)

   Teacher: _____

   _____

   Students: _____

   _____

13. There are expectations for class discussion, seatwork, group work

   Teacher: _____

   _____

   Students: _____

   _____

14. There is an agenda for the day

   Teacher: _____

   _____

   Students: _____

   _____

Activity 5.4   Classroom Rules

Context   Teachers need to establish a safe and positive learning environment to maximize student achievement. This can be accomplished in a variety of ways. The teacher can involve the students in setting rules and expectations, can inform the students what the rules are, or can let the students determine all the rules, and many things in between. The degree of collaboration conveys roles and responsibilities to the students.

Purpose   This activity will help you think through your philosophy on classroom rules *before* you start working with your students.

Directions   Answer the questions below.

1. What rules do you think are important in your classroom?

2. Who should determine the rules—you, your students? Mark the continuum to indicate your answer.

Teacher   Both   Student

  1   2   3   4   5   6   7   8   9   10

3. How will you and/or your students determine the rules?

4. How do you make the students aware of the rules—tell them, show them, post them?

5. Who is responsible for enforcing the rules? Mark the continuum to indicate your answer.

Teacher   Both   Student

  1   2   3   4   5   6   7   8   9   10

6. Who determines the consequences when a rule is broken? Mark the continuum to indicate your answer.

Teacher   Both   Student

  1   2   3   4   5   6   7   8   9   10

7. What are the consequences when a rule is broken?

8. Who determines the reward when students follow the rules? Mark the continuum to indicate your answer.

Teacher   Both   Student

1   2   3   4   5   6   7   8   9   10

9. What are the rewards when students follow the rules?

_____

_____

10. How do you add rules or change rules, if necessary?

_____

_____

Activity 5.5   Following Through on Classroom Rules

Context   Teachers establish classroom rules to facilitate a smooth-running classroom, maximize learning time, and help students develop responsibility. The rules are designed to serve most students in most situations. They are not set up to address every single situation or every student. This could result in a "laundry list" of don'ts that becomes unmanageable. Teachers know they will have to enforce the rules and are prepared to do so.

Purpose   This activity will help you plan ahead and think about how you will react when a student breaks one of the rules.

Directions   Read through these scenarios. Pick three that you have experienced. Use the checklist to help analyze how you responded. Put a "+" if you met the criteria, a "–" if you did not meet the criteria, or a "✔" if the criteria is not applicable to that scenario.

Scenarios:

A. One student is constantly blurting out during class discussions.

B. Several students are exhibiting off-task behavior after they have completed the learning activity.

C. One student hasn't completed any assignments missed during an absence.

D. Two students are visiting with each other while the teacher is giving directions.

E. During small group work half the students are chatting and not on task.

F. Three or four students are tardy to class almost every day.

Write the letter of the Scenarios you chose.

____	____	____	Acted in a manner that respected the students' dignity
____	____	____	Expressed disapproval but not anger
____	____	____	Talked with the student privately or at a later time
____	____	____	Made certain student knew what behavior was inappropriate
____	____	____	Gave the student a chance to respond/explain
____	____	____	Listened to the student
____	____	____	Maintained a professional demeanor and relationship
____	____	____	Tied disapproval with students' behavior not with students' personality
____	____	____	Followed established consequence
____	____	____	Held student to same standards as other students
____	____	____	Made certain student understood what behavior was expected
____	____	____	Provided choices/alternatives for student
____	____	____	Evaluated own behavior to make changes to lessen the likelihood the student will repeat the behavior

Activity 5.6 Intervention vs. Prevention

Context   Teachers establish classroom rules to facilitate a smooth-running classroom, maximize learning time, and help students develop responsibility. They also realize that there are things that they can do in their teaching and in structuring the classroom that will reduce the likelihood that students will disregard the rules. But teachers are also realistic and expect that they will have to enforce the rules at some point in time and are prepared to do so.

Purpose   This activity will help you plan ahead to lessen the chance that students will violate a rule and to think about how you will react when a student does break a rule.

Directions

Read through these scenarios. Pick two that you have experienced or are likely to experience. Describe strategies that you can use to avoid the situation (prevention) and strategies that you can use to respond to the situation (intervention).

Scenarios:

A. One student is constantly blurting out during class discussions.

B. Several students are exhibiting off-task behavior after they have completed the learning activity.

C. One student hasn't completed any assignments missed during an absence.

D. Two students are visiting with each other while the teacher is giving directions.

E. During small group work half the students are chatting and not on task.

F. Three or four students are tardy to class almost every day.

Scenario Letter _____

Prevention Strategies: _____

_____

_____

Intervention Strategies: _____

_____

_____

Scenario Letter _____

Prevention Strategies: _____

_____

_____

Intervention Strategies: _____

_____

_____

Activity 5.7 An Ounce of Prevention

Context Effective teachers design lessons that keep students actively engaged, anticipate potential problems and develop prevention strategies to avoid them, and use intervention strategies when behavior problems arise.

Purpose Use these techniques to increase your ability to manage a class effectively.

Directions Label each classroom management technique by using *L* for *lesson design*, *P* for *presentation strategy*, and *I* for *intervention strategy*.

Teacher's action:

1. _____ Posts class guidelines and expectations

2. _____ Communicates lesson outcomes to students

3. _____ Welcomes students as they enter the classroom

4. _____ Provides a variety of instructional tasks during a single class period

5. _____ Praises student privately but acknowledges student publicly

6. _____ Looks in the direction of a disturbance made by student in the back of the class

7. _____ Calls on a student whose attention appears to be wandering

8. _____ Uses a sign-out procedure for lavatory use

9. _____ Writes the day's agenda on the board and begins class by reviewing it

10. _____ Provides opportunity for student choice for partner activity

11. _____ Modifies the tasks for those who are not learning

12. _____ Uses "I" statements rather than "you" statements

13. _____ Describes the behavior she wants of students during group activity

14. _____ Gets closer to a student when giving him/her a directive

15. _____ Makes a request with a statement, rather than a question

16. _____ Says, "maybe so, let's talk about it later, I understand what you're saying" to a student who is argumentative

17. _____ Uses words of respect: "please, " "thank you, " "it would be helpful"

18. _____ Provides students an opportunity to practice with feedback before assigning independent work

19. _____ Pauses to wait for talkative students to stop talking

Activity 5.8   Steps to Successful Discipline

Context   Even the most skilled teachers experience behavior problems in their classrooms. However, they realize that dealing with student behavior and misbehavior is part of the job. Over time and with training they accrue a huge "bag of tricks" to draw from when deciding (often in a split second) how to best react to student misbehavior and extinguish it while maintaining the dignity of the student. Some of the interventions that teachers use are subtle and permit classroom instruction to continue. Other discipline strategies may interrupt instruction, but the matter is handled in the classroom. More serious discipline situations may be resolved outside of the classroom and involve school administration. The most serious discipline problems may involve authorities outside of the school.

Purpose   This activity will help you analyze appropriate responses (interventions) to student misbehavior.

Directions

- Read through the following teacher interventions, and indicate the level of discipline for each:

  1 = Level 1: The flow of instruction is maintained.

  2 = Level 2: The flow of instruction is disrupted, but matter is handled in the classroom.

- Put a ✔ by the interventions you have used. Be ready to explain their effectiveness. Be ready to share other interventions not listed.

	Level	Teacher interventions
1.	_____	Teacher pauses
2.	_____	Teacher writes student's name on board
3.	_____	Teacher stares at student who's out of line
4.	_____	Teacher moves in the direction of the disturbance
5.	_____	Teacher moves student to another desk
6.	_____	Teacher writes a warning note and puts it on a student's desk
7.	_____	Teacher calls on the student who's distracted
8.	_____	Teacher touches the shoulder or desk of a student who's off-task
9.	_____	Teacher isolates student within classroom
10.	_____	Teacher stops and gives student a verbal reprimand
11.	_____	Teacher requests a change in behavior ("I" message)
12.	_____	Teacher catches student's eye, walks over and points to posted guideline that's not being followed
13.	_____	Teacher gives the class an assignment and then takes a disruptive student into the hallway for quiet discussion
14.	_____	Teachers gives misbehaving student a choice of consequences

Activity 5.9 Prevention Strategies

Context "An ounce of prevention . . ." Classroom management is the way you do all those things teachers do in the classroom. One of the many classroom management topics is disruptive behavior. Suggestions from experts in the field on ways to deal with disruptive behavior in the classroom often begin with guidelines focusing on the "prevention" of disruptive behavior. Several prevention strategies are listed below to help you develop and maintain a well-managed classroom.

Directions Listed below are several suggested intervention strategies. Using the words listed under each section, fill in the statement blanks.

Provide effective instruction

1. _____ class guidelines and expectations

2. _____ lesson outcomes/objectives to students

3. _____ engage students in learning

4. _____ which produce many correct answers

5. _____ informal feedback to students during the instruction

    a. Post   b. Ask questions   c. Communicate   d. Actively   e. Provide

Help students experience more success than failure

1. _____ a positive, cooperative learning environment: high five, handshake, smile, smile, smile

2. _____ students as they enter

3. _____ of respect: "Please," "Thank you," "It would be helpful"

4. _____ space and materials thoughtfully

5. _____ learning tasks to students' level: students need to be successful 80% of the time to achieve

6. _____ instructional tasks (3 or 4 per class period)

7. _____ opportunity for student choice

8. _____ practice and feedback before independent work

9. _____ an "mistakes are part of learning" atmosphere

10. _____ tasks for those who are not succeeding

11. _____ that "students do things that have worked for them in the past."

12. _____ student work

    a. Use words   b. Modify   c. Variety   d. Display   e. Establish   f. Create

    g. Encourage   h. Provide   i. Welcome   j. Realize   k. Adjust   l. Arrange

Recognize positive behavior

1. _____ at student

2. _____ student privately

3. _____ student publicly

4. _____ motivation: raise students' level of concern, provide a pleasant learning environment, plan for student success, pique student interest, provide students with results/feedback, remember intrinsic and extrinsic motivation

5. _____ attribution theory to help students understand what they did that attributed to their success

    a. Praise   b. Acknowledge   c. Smile   d. Increase   e. Apply

Respect your students and show it

1. _____ "I" statements rather than "you" statements

2. _____ and don't assume you already know the answer

3. _____

4. _____ feelings

    a. Listen   b. Acknowledge   c. Use   d. Ask

Summary   Review the entire list of "prevention" suggestions and circle the ones you do regularly.

List three of these "prevention" suggestions that you plan to use more frequently.

1. _____

   _____

2. _____

   _____

3. _____

   _____

Activity 5.10   *Intervention Strategies*

Context   Classroom management is often the most frequently mentioned concern of new teachers. Shocking stories, whether true or not, about classroom behavior can cause a great deal of distress and even fear for the new teacher. Although there is not just one way to handle classroom management, there exist some common suggestions. Also remember that the classroom management style that works well for one teacher may not work for another teacher. Observing the classroom management style of several teachers will help you develop a style that works well for you. And finally, remember, no matter how hard you try, sometime a student's behavior will be disruptive.

Directions   Listed below are several suggested intervention strategies. Using the words listed under each section, fill in the statement blanks.

Give early attention to potentially disruptive behavior

1. Make _____, smile, ask for student attention.

2. Walk _____ student and chat privately, touch shoulder, put hand on student desk.

3. Provide _____ to student privately.

4. Move, move, move _____ the students while teaching.

    a. feedback   b. scan   c. toward   d. eye contact

Use redirection strategies

1. _____ minor negative behaviors and recognize positive ones.

2. _____ student behavior nonverbally: gesture, point to work that needs to be completed.

3. Ask for status or rule: _____ and quietly, "What are you supposed to be doing?" "What is the expectation for taking a test?"

4. Request a change of _____ : quietly and while making eye contact, state what behavior you want. Acknowledge the student when behavior changes.

5. _____ student within the room to complete a task.

6. Give _____.

    a. redirect   b. isolate   c. privately   d. ignore   e. choice   f. behavior

Teach responsibility

1. Assign a _____: "Homework is due at the beginning of class."

2. When _____ arises: "You don't have your homework?"

3. Lead with _____: "How upsetting."

4. Use _____: "What happens when it's not turned in?"

5. _____ the responsibility: "Homework is due at the beginning of class."

    a. logical consequences   b. responsibility   c. empathy   d. reassign   e. problem

Hold problem-solving session

1. _____ "Tough problem, huh."

2. _____ Question: "What do you plan to do about this?"

3. _____ to Share: "Would you like to know what others have tried?"

4. _____ Consequences: "How do you think these might work for you?"

5. _____ to Solve or Not: "Good luck! Let me know how it works out."

6. Or . . . Take _____: "We can go with my ideas." "Feel free to . . ."

   a. permission   b. empathy   c. allow   d. sincere   e. possible   f. ownership

Conduct a conference on misbehavior

1. _____ "What were you doing?" "How did it help you?" "What were you supposed to be doing?" "What are you going to do about it?" "What should happen if you do it again?"

2. _____ have student write the answers and sign.

   a. ask student   b. conduct in private

Summary   Review this list of intervention strategies and circle the ones that you have used effectively.

List three of these intervention strategies that you plan to use more frequently.

1. _____

_____

2. _____

_____

3. _____

_____

Case Study

Terry taught an elective English course. Most of the students in the class were highly motivated to be there and worked hard to do their best. When the discussion at seminar centered around classroom management, Terry felt that this was one area that he didn't need to worry about. The kids in his class were easy to teach and didn't cause any discipline problems.

After the first day of his three-day cooperative group activity, however, he began to think that he should have paid more attention in seminar. It wasn't that the students were disruptive or off-task, it was more the fact that so much time was spent getting into groups and handing out materials that they did not have time to complete all their tasks. Also, the students were so involved in the work it was hard to get their attention to give more directions. At times, the noise level got to the point where Terry had to close the door because they were disturbing the class across the hall. But the students were involved and working hard on their projects.

- Did Terry confuse the concepts of classroom management and discipline?

- What could he do to reduce the time it takes the groups to get started?

- Should Terry's cooperating teacher have given him some management tips, or was it good for him to learn from his experiences?

- What does classroom management look like at the senior high level compared to the primary grades?

- How important is classroom management to being a good teacher?

Student-to-Student Tips

✔ Try not to be "Mr. Nice Guy." Follow through on your discipline. *Bunthoeun, elementary student teacher*

✔ Be firm from the beginning. Stand your ground. Make your expectations clear and then follow through on them. *Tim, elementary student teacher*

✔ Look for books with "filler" activities like puzzles, crosswords, etc. *Nicole, secondary student teacher*

✔ Organize, organize, organize. The more you have prepared, the easier it is to handle a situation or have a different approach when needed. *Katie, secondary student teacher*

✔ Stick to what you say when disciplining the students. Don't be afraid to follow through, especially the first time that you need to. *Jen, elementary student teacher*

✔ Set down ground rules for discipline and respect right away, even if the students aren't acting up. *Maria, secondary student teacher*

Bibliography

Almeida, D. A. 1995. Behavior management and the 5 Cs. *Teaching pre K–8* 26, 1: 88–89.

Arends, R. I., N. E. Winitzky, and M. D. Tannenbaum. 2001. *Exploring teaching: An introduction to education.* 2nd ed. New York: McGraw-Hill.

Birren, F. 1972. The significance of light. *The AIA Journal* (Aug.): 27–30.

———. 1977. Color it color. *Progressive Architecture* (Sept.): 129–133.

Brophy, J. E. 1987. Educating teachers about managing classrooms and students. *Occasional Paper No. 115.* East Lansing, MI: Institute for Research on Teaching, Michigan State University.

Campbell, D. M., P. B. Cignetti, B. J. Melenyzer, D. H. Nettles, and R. M. Wyman. 1995. *How to Develop a Professional Portfolio.* Boston: Allyn and Bacon.

Christenson, S. L., and J. E. Ysseldyke. 1989. Assessing student performance: An important change is needed. *Journal of School Psychology* 27: 409–425.

Danielson, C. 1996. *Enhancing professional practice: A framework for teaching.* Alexandria, VA: Association for Supervision—Curriculum Development.

Doyle, W. 1986. Classroom organization and management. In *Handbook of Research on Teaching* (p. 410), ed. M. C. Wittrock. 3rd ed. New York: Macmillan.

Faust, V. 1980. *Self-esteem in the classroom.* San Diego: Thomas Paine.

Geiger, B. 2000. Discipline in K–8 grade classrooms. *Education* 121, 2 (Winter): 383.

Gettinger, M. (1988). Issues and trends in academic engaged time of students. *Special Services in the Schools* 2: 1–17.

Haertel, G. D., J. H. Walberg, and E. H. Haertel. 1981. Social-psychological environments and learning: A quantitative synthesis. *British Educational Research Journal* 7: 27–36.

Hebert, E. A. 1998. Design matters: How school environment affects children. *Educational Leadership* 56, 1 (Sept.): 69–74.

Johnson, V. 1994. Student teachers' conceptions of classroom control. *Journal of Educational Research* 88, 2: 109–117.

Klemp, R. J., J. Hon, and A. Shorr. 1993. Cooperative literacy in the middle school: An example of a learning strategy based approach. *Middle School Journal* 24: 19–27.

Kounin, J. S. 1970. *Discipline and group management in the classroom.* New York: Holt, Rhinehart, and Winston.

———. 1977. *Discipline and group management in the classroom.* Huntington, NY: Krieger.

Maehr, M. L., and C. Midgley. 1996. Enhancing student motivation: A schoolwide approach. *Educational Psychology* 26, 3/4: 399–427.

Martens, B. K., and S. Kelly. 1993. A behavioral analysis of effective teaching. *School Psychology Quarterly* 8, 1: 10–26.

McGinnis, J. C., B. P. Frederick, and R. Edwards. 1995. Enhancing classroom management through proactive rules and procedures. *Psychology in the Schools* 32: 220–224.

McKee, W. J., and J. C. Witt. 1990. Effective teaching: A review of instructional and environmental variables. In *Handbook of social psychology* (pp. 821–846). New York: Wiley.

Pacchiano, D. M. 2000. A review of instructional variables related to student problem behavior. *Preventing School Failure* 44, 4 (Summer): 174.

Purkey, W. W., and J. M. Novak. 1996. *Inviting school success.* Belmont, CA: Wadsworth.

Raffini, J. 1993. *Winners without losers: Structures and strategies for increasing student motivation to learn.* Boston: Allyn and Bacon.

Ringer, M. M., P. F. Doerr, J. H. Hollenshead, and G. D. Witt. 1993. Behavior problems in the classroom: A national survey of interventions used by classroom teachers. *Psychology in the Schools* 30: 168–175.

Schmuck, R. A., and P. A. Schmuck. 1975. Helping teachers improve classroom group process. *The Journal of Applied Behavioral Science* 4, 4.

Shapiro, S. 1993. Strategies that create a positive classroom climate. *The Clearing House* 67, 2 (Nov.–Dec.): 91–98.

Vacha, E. 1977. *Improving the classroom and social climate.* Orcutt, CA: Holt, Rinehart and Winston.

Wang, M. C., G. D. Haertal, and J. H. Walberg. 1993. What helps students learn? *Educational Leadership* 51, 4 (Dec.–Jan.): 74–86.

Wehby, J. H., F. J. Symons, J. A. Cancle, and F. J. Go. 1998. Teaching practices in classrooms for students with emotional and behavioral disorders: Discrepancies between recommendations and observations. *Behavioral Disorders* 24, 1: 51–56.

6
Communication

"Do not train youths to learning by force and harshness, but direct them to it
by what amuses their minds so that you may be better able to discover
with accuracy the peculiar bent of the genius of each."
—*Plato*

"Nothing new that is really interesting comes without collaboration."
—*James Watson, winner of the Nobel prize for codiscovering the double helix*

Standard #6   The teacher uses knowledge of effective verbal, nonverbal, and media communication techniques to foster active inquiry, collaboration, and supportive interaction in the classroom.

Performance Indicators: *The teacher . . .*

- Recognizes the need for effective communication in the classroom and constantly acquires new techniques to be used in the classroom.
- Consistently enriches communication in the learning environment.

Vignette   Within several days of her student teaching experience, Karen notices that Brielle, a third grader, is very shy. She sits quietly in her seat after completing her assignments, putting her head down on the table. While her written academic work is at grade level, she rarely contributes to class discussions. At recess she stays by herself, rejecting classmates' requests to play with her. Brielle is a frail child, but always clean and neatly dressed. Karen wants to be accurate and sensitive in describing her students without labeling them in ways that may be both inaccurate and potentially damaging. She ponders her concerns and at the same time wonders how she can encourage Brielle to interact with other students her age and participate in classroom activities.

Fundamental Principles

Communication refers to the transfer of information from one person to another. It includes the ways that people send and receive information: conversations, written messages, media sources, public speeches, body language, signs and other symbols. Communication can be verbal or nonverbal: e.g., reading, writing, speaking, and listening. Through this process, we understand others, and in turn try to be understood by them. Good teachers are good communicators. They communicate clearly both verbally and nonverbally. These communication skills may be applied to transmit information about subject matter. Such skills may also be used to communicate with parents, administrators, and other teachers. But they can just as well be used to communicate expectations for student performance, empathy, and feedback (McNergney and Herbert 2001).

Clear communication between teacher and student is important to the teaching/learning process (Guskey 1996; McNergney and Herbert 2001; Tjeerdsma 1997). "For students to become engaged in learning, they must be exposed to clear directions and explanations. In addition, a teacher's use of vivid and expressive language can enhance a learning experience. Clear and accurate communication has two elements. The first element is clarity of directions and procedures.

The second element is the quality of oral and written communication" (Danielson 1996, 90).

Clarity refers to how clear and interpretable the information is. For example, are the points presented understandable at the student's developmental level? Is the teacher able to explain concepts clearly? Is the teacher's oral delivery audible? Clarity is related to the teacher's organization of the content, familiarity with the lesson, and delivery strategies. Clear messages are specific so that students perceive their intent. As an example, when giving directions for an assignment, the teacher should communicate what should be done, how, and when it should be completed.

In a related way, research also indicates that variability or flexibility in the type of feedback given to students enhances student achievement. Feedback is information teachers provide to students about their progress in learning (Danielson 1996). It lets students know what is correct and how to judge response quality, and it can contribute to students' motivation (Arends, Winitzky, and Tannenbaum 2001). According to Danielson, to provide feedback, teachers must carefully watch and listen to students, who reveal their level of understanding through the questions they ask, their approaches to projects and assignments, and the work they produce. In other words, feedback should be provided on all significant work such as papers, tests, and classroom work, thereby helping students judge their own progress. She also emphasizes that to be effective, feedback should be accurate, constructive, substantive, specific, and timely; and that in most cases, student use of feedback requires planning by the teacher, and time must be made available for it.

Hoy (1987) argues that feedback improves the communication process by reducing the chances of major disparities between the information or ideas received and the one intended (in other words, clarifying the message). Steps to ensure adequate feedback are essential to maintaining effective communication. This requires careful preparation and planning.

When feedback is provided for student written work, the teacher should clearly explain to the students that the purpose of writing assignments is to help the teacher understand the students' views. First, the teacher must decide on the criteria such as: What does good performance on this task for this age group look like? Or how do I decide if a student is giving a high or low effort? What behaviors do I believe show high effort? Merely deciding on criteria is not enough; teachers must communicate clearly what is expected of the students and how their learning

will be evaluated. Both corrective and positive feedback should be stated in specific and congruent terms.

Perhaps one of the most popular and effective ways of providing feedback during instruction is to ask questions. All teachers ask questions. Asking questions can accomplish a wide variety of goals: reinforcing the content, developing critical thinking, and enhancing communication skills. The effective teacher needs to know something about the art of asking questions and must have the ability to discriminate among different types of question formats. Questioning plays a critical role in the teaching and learning process. When teachers use skilled questioning, they engage their students in an exploration of content. Carefully framed questions enable students to reflect on their understanding and consider new possibilities (Danielson 1996). Teachers must design and ask questions which will help students to meet the stated performance objectives or a given learning experience. Questions are also essential elements to stimulate students' thinking. Orlich, et al. (2001) notes that questions may be used to (1) diagnose student progress, (2) determine entry-level competence, (3) prescribe additional study, and (4) enrich an area of study. Although questions serve a variety of purposes, teachers often ask low-level knowledge questions which focus on the memorization of information. In order for students to develop critical thinking skills, it is essential that teachers ask more questions which are thought provoking, encourage higher-order thinking skills, and actively involve students in the learning process (Arends, Winitzky, and Tannenbaum 2001; Cinelli, et al. 1995).

Questioning strategies are divided into four categories: (1) convergent, (2) divergent, (3) evaluative, and (4) reflective (Orlich, et al. 2001). The convergent questioning pattern is narrow in focus. These questions require students to respond or focus on a central theme. These types of questions typically elicit a short response from the student. Also, these questions focus on the lower levels of the cognitive taxonomy, namely the knowledge and comprehension levels.

Divergent questioning strategies are broad and evoke student responses which vary greatly. These questions also elicit longer and more developed student responses. Divergent questions often have few "right" or "wrong" answers. A frequent type of divergent questioning encourages students to employ a critical thinking process and elicit a variety of possible responses to a given situation.

Evaluative questioning is based on the divergent strategy. The basic difference is that evaluative questions have a built-in set of evaluation criteria. For example, an evaluative question might ask why something is good or bad, why something is important, or why one theory explains the facts better than another. A major component of the teacher's role in the evaluative strategy is to help students develop a logical basis for establishing evaluative criteria.

Reflective questioning strategies are based on the classical Socratic method of questioning (Elder and Richard, 1998). While this approach stimulates a wide range of student responses (as do divergent questions), it also has an evaluative element. The goal of using the reflective strategy is to require students to develop a higher-order thinking. Rather than asking a student a "why" or "what," the student is encouraged to ponder, to think of implications, and to search for unintended consequences.

Discussion is probably the most familiar and commonly used procedure of oral instruction. Discussions generally begin with a lecture by the teacher, students, or a resource person. Discussion generally permits students to ask questions, make recitations, perform surveys, and participate in numerous other ways in the learning process (Danielson 1996). They provide opportunities for the exchange of information between students and teachers. The goal of discussion is to arrive at a decision by identifying relevant information, detecting bias, determining logical fallacies, and evaluating the strength of an argument or claim (Garmston and Wellman 1998). Group discussion is especially valuable because it is conducive to helping students gain understanding and respect for each other's feelings and viewpoints. To achieve this, the teacher must foster an open and trusting classroom environment where students feel comfortable in expressing their own thoughts and feelings.

Skilled discussions are organized, collective efforts in critical thinking. Skilled discussions:

1. Encourage and stimulate student questions, because they provide information about needs, interests, and concerns.

2. Try to involve all students in the class to participate or be involved.

3. Do not hurry or rush the discussion, but do not let it drag.

4. Listen carefully to all contributions and relate them to the topic. Compliment and encourage students who make remarks. It may be necessary to have students elaborate their statements.

5. When students are reluctant to engage in discussions, mention of a personal experience or anecdote or asking a pertinent question may help increase participation (Garmston and Wellman 1998).

Feedback is also considered an important method of improving communications. Researchers contend that a good teacher is always interested in the reaction from students. The student who falls asleep in class provides as much feedback to the teacher as the student who responds to questions. Feedback must not be viewed as criticism since it is not evaluative, but rather, descriptive (Simiyu 1990). It is important for the teacher to be aware of communication barriers. No matter how clearly a person thinks he/she communicates, the actual message received can be affected by many factors. The communication barriers are a type of interference that can ultimately confuse the meaning of the message. Poor communication often results when people have different perspectives of the same events. If they try to communicate with one another based on different perspectives, misunderstandings can occur, resulting in student frustration, decreased learning, and inappropriate student behavior (Tjeerdsma 1997). When communication fails, the teacher must recognize the cause and find a solution to minimize or prevent miscommunication in the future. Most communication barriers can be overcome by paying special attention to clarity and accuracy.

It is not only what teachers say in the classroom that is important, but it's how they say it that can make the difference to students. Nonverbal messages are an essential component of communication in the teaching process. Nonverbal communication, e.g., using symbols, signs, or body language to convey a message, can sometimes tell others more than words that accompany it. Nonverbal cues provide additional information that can help clarify the verbal message. Teachers should be aware of nonverbal behavior in the classroom for three major reasons. (1) An awareness of nonverbal behavior will allow teachers to become better receivers of students' messages. (2) Teachers will become better senders of signals that reinforce learning. (3) This mode of communication increases the degree of the perceived psychological closeness between teacher and student.

Eye contact is an important channel of interpersonal communication. Teachers who make eye contact with students convey interest, concern, warmth, and credibility. Smiling, another area of nonverbal behavior, is a powerful cue that transmits happiness, friendliness, warmth, and approachability. Smiling is often contagious, and students will react favorably and learn more. Teachers who fail to gesture while speaking may be perceived as boring, stiff, and unanimated. A lively and animated teaching style captures students' attention, makes the material more interesting, and facilitates learning. Teachers also communicate numerous messages by their body language. The way teachers walk, talk, stand, and sit; their facial expressions; and their body movements are all clues to their thoughts and feelings. Standing erect, but not rigid, and leaning slightly forward communicates to students that the teacher is approachable, receptive, and friendly. Furthermore, interpersonal closeness results when the teacher and the students face each other. Speaking with one's back turned or looking at the floor or ceiling should be avoided; it communicates disinterest. Cultural norms dictate a comfortable distance, or proximity, for interaction with students. Teachers may raise their eyebrows, shrug their shoulders, cross their arms, or use hand or facial gestures while sending a message or in response to something they have heard. Teachers should look for signals of discomfort caused by invading students' space such as rocking, leg swinging, tapping, and/or gaze aversion.

Another facet of nonverbal communication includes vocal elements or paralinguistics. For example, one of the major criticisms registered by students is teachers who speak in a monotone. Listeners perceive these teachers as boring and dull. For maximum teaching effectiveness, teachers should learn to vary the elements of voice such as tone, pitch, rhythm, loudness, and inflection. Students report that they learn less and lose interest more quickly when listening to teachers who have not learned to modulate their voices. Humor is often overlooked as a teaching tool. Laughter releases stress and tension for both teacher and student. Teachers should develop the ability to laugh at themselves and encourage students to do the same. It fosters a friendly classroom environment that facilitates learning.

Obviously, adequate knowledge of the subject matter is crucial to teacher success; however, it is not the only crucial element. Creating a climate that facilitates learning and retention demands good nonverbal and verbal skills. It is difficult to give a verbal message without accompanying body language. As a result, it is important to become aware of nonverbal messages and be sure that these messages do not contradict the verbal message.

Schools also recognize the importance and the need for effective communication between parents and teachers (Ysseldyke, Algozzine, and Thurlow 1992). Three reasons help to explain why: First, students with special needs are receiving more of their instruction in regular classrooms. Second, parents raising their families under challenging social and economic conditions need teachers to assist them with their educational responsibilities at home. Three, student success in school also depends on the support they receive at home (Sicley 1993).

The methods of communication considered most effective, according to surveys conducted with parents, are (1) the direct approach by phone or in person and (2) parent/teacher conferences (Cattermole and Robinson 1985). These researchers concluded that parents prefer interactions with the school that are direct and personal. In the same study, parents also expressed a desire to be kept informed of school-related matters. Turnbull and Turnbull (1990) stressed the importance of using methods of communication that provide opportunities for parents and teachers to exchange information, allowing parents to actively participate in their child's education.

Communication—the ability to clearly express one's thoughts, feelings, beliefs, opinions, reactions, values, and hopes—is a skill that must be learned. A teacher's ability to communicate effectively to his/her students can have a direct effect on the quality of the relationship as well as student learning. Poor communication can cause misunderstanding, which can lead to feelings of frustration and mistrust in relationships between teachers and students.

Questions for Reflection

- What are the two prerequisites to clear and accurate communication?

- How does feedback improve communication?

- How does asking questions serve to develop critical thinking skills?

- What types of questioning strategies are commonly used during instruction?

Commentary on Standard #6

CHET BRADLEY | Director, Region II: College of Education, Cardinal Stritch University, Madison, Wisconsin

The teacher uses knowledge of effective verbal, non-verbal and media communication techniques to foster active inquiry, collaboration, and supportive interaction in the classroom.

After thirty-eight years as a professional educator, I am convinced that success in education is all about building relationships. I believe teachers are and must be in the business of building positive relationships with their students and their colleagues every time they come into contact with them. I also believe that the key to these relationships is effective two-way communication. While knowledge of effective verbal, nonverbal, and media communication techniques is an important base for teachers to have, practicing and living these communication skills on a daily basis is critical to effective teaching and student learning.

As a teacher, when you walk into a classroom of students for the first time you only have one opportunity to make a good first impression. This first impression will be largely determined by your facial expressions, the way you speak, the tone of your voice, the way you move throughout the room, the eye contacts you make, and how you welcome students to your classroom. All of these little communication elements tell a very first story about who you are. Obviously, the more time you spend with students and your colleagues, the more the real you is revealed and the more long-lasting meaningful friendships and positive student/teacher relationships will grow and develop.

If classrooms are to be alive, interactive, and supportive in nature, teachers must create a learning environment that promotes open dialogue, nurtures a cooperative approach to problem solving, and pro-vides opportunities for exploring collaborative projects among students. The daily demonstration by the teacher of effective communication skills sends a clear message to students that these skills are basic to positive personal and professional relationships for the rest of their lives.

In closing, words from an anonymous old poem which I used to share with teachers when I did staff development workshops during my years as a Department of Public Instruction Health Education Consultant come to mind when I think about effective communication skills and building positive relationships.

The poem reads as follows:

> I'd rather see a sermon, than hear one any day, and
> I'd rather one would walk with me, than merely show the way.
> The eye is a better pupil and more trusting than the ear,
> fine counsel can be confusing but example is always clear.
> I soon can learn to do it, if you let me see it done,
> I can see your hands in action but your tongue too fast may run.
> And the lectures you deliver may be very fine and true,
> But I'd rather learn my lesson by observing what you do.
> For I may misunderstand you and the high advice you give,
> But there is no misunderstanding of how you act and how you live.

Communication Self-Assessment

The teacher uses knowledge of effective verbal, nonverbal, and media communication techniques to foster active inquiry, collaboration, and supportive interaction in the classroom.

Knowledge/Performance Indicators	Yes*	Not Sure	No
1. I understand communication theory, language development, and the role of language in learning.	2	1	0
2. I understand how cultural and gender differences can affect communication in the classroom.	2	1	0
3. I understand the importance of nonverbal as well as verbal communication.	2	1	0

4. I know effective verbal, nonverbal, and media communication techniques.	2	1	0
5. I understand the power of language for fostering self-expression, identity development, and learning.	2	1	0
6. I use effective listening techniques.	2	1	0
7. I foster sensitive communication by and among all students in the class.	2	1	0
8. I use effective communication strategies in conveying ideas and information and in asking questions.	2	1	0
9. I support and expand learner expression in speaking, writing, and other media.	2	1	0
10. I know how to ask questions and stimulate discussion in different ways for particular purposes, including probing for learner understanding, helping students articulate their ideas and thinking processes, promoting productive risk taking and problem solving, facilitating factual recall, encouraging convergent and divergent thinking, stimulating curiosity, and helping students to question.	2	1	0
11. I use a variety of media communication tools, including audiovisual aids and computers and other educational technology, to enrich learning opportunities.	2	1	0

* A "Yes" response indicates that you can describe, document, and cite examples related to your student teaching assignment.

Self-Assessment Summary and Reflection

1. Which Knowledge / Performance Indicators can I currently describe, document, and cite examples?

   _____

   _____

2. Which Knowledge / Performance Indicators need some work or improvement?

   _____

   _____

3. What specific actions can I take to enrich my knowledge or skill in this area?

   _____

   _____

Activity 6.1 "But You Didn't Tell Us to Do That!"

Context   Giving clear directions is an important teaching skill, and is as much a science as it is an art. Teachers know that students receive and process information using three modalities: visual, auditory, and tactile/kinesthetic. Effective teachers use this information when they give directions for an assignment by telling students, showing them, and providing them practice.

How do you know if your directions are clear? It's a numbers game. If, after you've given the instructions, many students ask questions about how to proceed, or engage in off-task behavior, then your instructions were not clear enough or you did not provide enough guidance. If, however, only a few students ask questions about how to complete the assignment, then your directions were clear enough and these students simply need reassurance.

Purpose   Through this activity, you will identify your strengths in giving directions and set goals to improve areas of weakness.

Directions

- Read this list of strategies before writing directions to an upcoming assignment.
- Select some of these strategies to incorporate when you write directions for the assignment.
- Show your cooperating teacher this checklist and then arrange to have your teacher in class when you'll be giving the directions to the assignment.
- Ask your cooperating teacher to listen to your directions and mark the checklist using this legend:

  E = effective

  S = pretty good

  N = needs some work

- Have your cooperating teacher share this information as feedback.

1. _____ Had all students looking at me when giving directions.

2. _____ Spoke loudly, clearly, and slowly enough for all students to hear and understand.

3. _____ Made sure students knew what they were supposed to learn from the activity.

4. _____ Gave concise directions in sequential order.

5. _____ Used both verbal and visual directions.

6. _____ Modeled how to complete the assignment.

7. _____ Made sure the students understood the directions by having them paraphrase.

8. _____ Placed directions where they could be seen (and checked) by students (e.g., as a handout, on a transparency, on the whiteboard).

9. _____ Had students complete practice "problems" before starting the assignment while I walked around and checked their understanding.

10. _____ Clarified the directions based on any confusion I noticed when students were completing the "practice" items.

11. _____ Described (or showed) the quality of a successfully completed assignment.

12. _____ Provided time and opportunity so that students could ask questions.

13. _____ Had students write tips or special instructions before starting the assignment.

14. _____ Showed that the assignment had been carefully thought out.

15. _____ Explained how students could get assistance.

16. _____ Explained what students should do with completed assignment.

17. _____ Prepared an instructional task or activity to follow the completion of this assignment.

18. What are your strengths in giving clear directions?

_____

_____

19. What weaknesses did you exhibit in giving directions?

_____

_____

20. Set a goal for each weakness. Select two goals and include them in your lesson plans for next week.

_____

_____

21. Of what value was this activity to your development as a teacher?

_____

_____

Activity 6.2   Nobody's Perfect

Context   Have you ever watched a videotape of yourself teaching a lesson, presenting some information or accepting an honor? What were the first things you noticed? Your appearance? Your mannerisms? The sound of your voice? Some linguists contend that the words we speak express only about 35 percent of our messages and that the rest is conveyed nonverbally by our facial expressions, our body language, the tone, volume, and rate of our voice—even by the clothes we wear! Are you aware of how you communicate with your students, peers, and colleagues? How is it possible to self-assess and evaluate this indispensable teaching skill?

Purpose   Through this activity you will identify the barriers to effective communication.

Directions

- Read through this list of communication distracters.

- Videotape yourself teaching a twenty- to thirty-minute segment.

- Now watch the videotape and mark (✔) any of the distracters that you demonstrated during the videotaped lesson. Provide specific examples.

- Remember, nobody's perfect!

1. _____ My voice is sometimes too loud, too soft, or too muffled for the situation.

    I did this when _____

2. _____ I overuse a certain expression such as "like" or "okay."

    I frequently used the expression _____. I said it _____ times!

3. _____ I need to avoid slang expressions such as "listen up" or "you guys."

    I used these slang expressions: _____

4. _____ I need to use standard English rather than words such as "gonna" or "had went."

    The words I need to work on are _____

5. _____ I have a physical mannerism that may be annoying because I use it too often.

    I kept doing this: _____

6. _____ I need to say "please" "thank you" and/or "excuse me" more often.

    I omitted this when _____

7. _____ I need to use students' first names more often.

    I did not call students by their first names _____ times.

8. _____ I need to get students' attention without shouting at them.

    I could do this by _____

9. _____ I need to use facial expressions to show that I am actively listening.

    I could have _____

10. _____ I need to smile more to show students that I enjoy teaching them and am confident.

    I smiled only in these situations: _____

11. _____ I need to move around the classroom more.

My usual movement pattern was _____

12. _____ I need to develop a "teacher voice" that differs from my more casual conversational style.

I could have used a "teacher voice" in this situation: _____

13. _____ I dress more casually than the teachers in this building.

I may have given the impression that _____

14. _____ I need to address students on both sides of the room as well as in the front and back of the room.

I directed most of my teaching to _____

15. _____ I need to change the pace and inflection of my voice.

I need to do this especially when _____

Activity 6.3 "Life Is Like a Box of Chocolates"

Context   In the film *Forrest Gump*, when the main character says, "Life is like a box of chocolates," he is using the comparison to explain life's little surprises. Perhaps when you were in preschool or kindergarten, your teacher gave "object lessons" in which she held up a familiar object to help explain a more complex idea. Thus, diversity could be explained by showing a box of crayons; reliability could be illustrated by using a clock; the magic of multiplication could be introduced with a slight-of-hand magic trick. Good teachers use comparisons to teach because it's a proven teaching strategy, and recent brain research provides the rationale. Simply put, we learn more quickly when we connect new information or skills to something we already know or can do, as the following examples illustrate.

Adult beginners can understand e-mail, for example, when it is compared to the postal mail system. Slices of pizza have helped students understand fractions; a balance scale can demonstrate equations; a sandwich can illustrate the parts of an essay; video clips can show point of view. Using comparison is a very powerful way to teach new complex information.

Purpose   This activity will help you create comparisons that you can use to connect new information to your students' interests and background.

Directions

- Make a list of ten items that you know are of interest to your students or relate to their age and background.

- For each item, think of a comparison or analogy that would connect with a fact, concept, or skill that you are (or will be) teaching. The first one has been done for you.

	Student Interests and Background	*Comparison or Analogy*
1.	*Example:* My students wear t-shirts that reveal their participation in sports.	*Example:* I could use a team t-shirt to introduce the concept of goal setting.
2.		
3.		
4.		
5.		
6.		

7.		
8.		
9.		
10.		

Case Study

Pete Schmidt was an enthusiastic student teacher who devoted considerable time, thought, and energy in his planning and preparation. His cooperating teacher, Mr. Kvebak, was impressed with Pete's depth of knowledge about social studies, his easy rapport with his eighth graders, and his commitment to thorough planning and preparation. However, Mr. Kvebak was concerned about Pete's frequent incorrect use of grammar, spelling, and usage. He sometimes misspelled words as he wrote them on a transparency or on the white board, and whenever he said "had went" or "I seen it," Mr. Kvebak cringed. Strong communication skills are indispensable for teachers and making blatant errors can undermine the credibility and effectiveness of a beginning teacher. To complicate the situation, Pete came from an area of the state known for its vernacular and idioms and grew up hearing and using incorrect grammar. Although Mr. Kvebak accepted as his responsibility the task of providing Pete with feedback about his communication skills, he wanted to accomplish this in a professional and non-judgmental manner.

- Is Mr. Kvebak's concern about Pete's misuse of language a valid one? Please explain.

- What ways might Pete discover his use of incorrect grammar and misspellings without Mr. Kvebak's involvement?

- If you were Pete, how would you like this situation to be handled?

- How can Pete learn to use correct grammar, usage, and spelling?

Student-to-Student Tips

✔ Use "The Teacher Look" or a poignant pause. You don't always have to say something to get students' attention. *Allysa, secondary student teacher*

✔ Have lots of resources. Don't be afraid to take ideas from other teachers. *Soumen, secondary student teacher*

✔ Write important information and directions on the overhead or board. Keep it covered until you're ready for it. *Sonny, elementary student teacher*

✔ Be sensitive to the needs of the students and co-operating teacher. Appear eager, but don't step on toes. *Gideon, secondary student teacher*

✔ Don't be afraid to admit you made a mistake. If a lot of kids do something wrong, it might be because of your directions. *Latonya, secondary student teacher*

✔ Get to know your cooperating teacher ahead of time if possible. Then you can focus on teaching right away. *Michelle, elementary student teacher*

✔ Let the students help you out. Have the computer whiz set up the computers for you or have a student run the VCR. That way you can monitor the rest of the class. *Rosie, elementary student teacher*

✔ This is a good time to try things that you are curious about to see how they'll work in the classroom. *Guillan, elementary student teacher*

✔ Make sure the students understand what you're saying. Don't use vocabulary that's too hard or too easy for them. *Jasmine, secondary student teacher*

✔ Establish a good working rapport with other staff members. They can help you out, support you, and are fun to be with. *Zachary, secondary student teacher*

✔ Practice writing on the chalkboard. *Ginny, elementary student teacher*

✔ Don't send home any written communication without proofreading it. Have your cooperating teacher proof it also. Take it from me, mistakes are embarrassing. *Madonna, elementary student teacher*

✔ Don't be afraid to try new ideas. Ask your cooperating teacher if it's okay for you to try something different from what he/she does. *Karl, secondary student teacher*

✔ I learned that sometimes the students listened more to how I was talking rather than what I said. I was shocked to see how many listened when I whispered to get their attention. *Tabitha, secondary student teacher*

✔ Write out and practice giving directions. You'll be surprised how hard it is to tell students what they need to know. *Katarina, elementary student teacher*

✔ Try out the technology before class. It's no fun having a roomful of students waiting for you to figure out how the LCD panel works. *Nicholas, secondary student teacher*

Bibliography

Arends, R. I., N. E. Winitzky, and M. D. Tannenbaum. 2001. *Exploring teaching: An introduction to education.* 2nd ed. New York: McGraw-Hill.

Cattermole, J., and N. Robinson. 1985. Effective home/school communication—From the parents' perspective. *Phi Delta Kappan* 67, 2: 48–50.

Cinelli, B., L. J. Bechtel, M. Rose-Culley, and R. Nye. 1995. Critical thinking skills in health and direction. *Journal of Health Education* 26, 2 (March–April): 119–120.

Danielson, C. 1996. *Enhancing professional practice: A framework for teaching.* Alexandria, VA: Association for Supervision and Curriculum Development.

Elder, L., and P. Richard. 1998. The role of socratic questioning on thinking, teaching, and learning. *Clearing House,* 71, 5: 297–301.

Garmston, R., and B. Wellman. 1998. Teacher talk that makes a difference. *Educational Leadership* 55, 7 (April): 30–42.

Guskey, T. R. 1996. Communicating student learning. In *Yearbook,* (pp. 1–187). Alexandria, VA: Association for Supervision and Curriculum Development.

Hoy, W. K. 1987. *Educational administration: Theory research and practice.* New York: Random House, 357.

McNergney, R. F., and J. M. Herbert. 2001. *Foundations of education: The challenge of professional practice.* Boston: Allyn and Bacon.

Orlich, D. C., R. J. Harder, R. C. Callahan, and H. Gibson. 2001. *Teaching strategies: A guide to better instruction.* Lexington, MA: Houghton Mifflin, 245–252.

Sicley, D. 1993. Effective methods of communication: Practical interventions for classroom teachers. *Intervention in School and Clinic* 29, 2 (Nov.): 105–108.

Simiyu, J. 1990. The importance of good communication in schools. *Education Canada* (Winter): 43–45.

Tjeerdsma, B. L. 1997. Enhancing classroom communication between teacher and student. *Journal of Physical Education, Recreation and Dance* 68, 5 (May): 26–33.

Turnbull, H. P., and H. R. Turnbull. 1990. *Families, professionals, and exceptionality: A special partnership.* Columbus, OH: Merrill.

Ysseldyke, J. E., B. Algozzine, and M. L. Thurlow. 1992. *Critical issues in education.* Boston: Houghton Mifflin.

7
Planning Instruction

"The difference, he continues, is to recognize that good teaching cannot be reduced
to technique. Good teaching comes from the identity and integrity of the teacher.
Good teachers join self and subject and students in the fabric of life."
—*Parker J. Palmer*

Standard #7 The teacher plans instruction based upon knowledge of subject matter, students, the community, and curriculum goals.

Performance Indicators: *The teacher . . .*

- Continually seeks advice/information from appropriate resources including feedback, interpreting the information, and modifying plans appropriately. Planned instruction incorporates a creative environment and utilizes varied and motivational strategies and multiple resources for providing comprehensible instruction for all students. Upon reflection, the teacher continuously refines outcome assessment and learning experiences.
- Consistently demonstrates competency in content area(s) to develop student knowledge and performance.

Vignette Heather, a fifth-grade student teacher, planned well-organized, age-appropriate lesson plans. Her problem was she always included more activities than class time allowed. She generally rushed to complete each lesson in its entirety. During one observation, Heather's college supervisor noted that several students were demonstrating overt expressions of frustration. When Heather's supervisor discussed the matter with her, Heather's explanation was that she did not want to run out of material to teach during the class period. In addition, Heather desired to challenge the students in her classroom (Wentz 2001).

Fundamental Principles

Successful teaching is a result of effective planning. Teacher planning has been described as "the thread that weaves the curriculum, or the what of teaching, with the instruction, or how of teaching" (Freiberg and Driscoll 1992, 22). An effective teacher plans learning experiences based on a set of diverse factors, each of which influences the outcome of student learning. First, subject matter is considered. Second, the individual needs of learners are addressed. Third, community needs and resources are a factor in planning lessons. Four, curriculum goals provide direction in making plans (Campbell et al. 1995).

First, reflect on Dewey's ([1904] 1964) statement, as was mentioned in Chapter 1, that "Scholastic knowledge is sometimes regarded as if it were something assumed, method becomes an external attachment to knowledge of subject matter" (160). What he meant by that is teachers must have a thorough knowledge of the composition of the subject being taught as well as an understanding of teaching methods that are unique to that subject. Knowing subject matter and translating that knowledge to the lives of students are key to learning. Planning requires creating an authentic environment for learning when the student is consciously engaged in meaningful activities that promote an active exploration of the environment. Using district, state, or national curriculum standards in designing plans provides the rationale for the choice(s) of instructional strategies and judges what is important for learners to know and achieve at a particular level.

Secondly, planning for the individual needs of students can be a difficult process. Coordinating activities that meet the lesson objectives and respond to varied learners within a specified time frame takes organization and planning. Gathering information concerning achievement levels, language abilities, and student interests helps prepare for variations and adjustments necessary in planning for individual differences among learners (Goethals and Howard 2000).

Instruction has become more student-centered and learning activities more developmentally appropriate. Teachers are expanding the variety of approaches needed to tailor classroom experiences to the needs of individual learners. Writing a well-developed plan for teaching usually begins with a reflection on the needs of the individual learners within the class. Assessing what the learner knows and has demonstrated in previous lessons usually precedes the development of the plan. Taking into account the learning styles of students and using the multiple intelligences enable the teacher to develop a plan with broader perspective. Developing lesson plans for teaching the learners in the class gives direction and focus.

Orlich, et al. (2001) suggest four techniques that effective teachers use in the planning process:

- Planning routines to expedite the daily flow of instruction, making sure students know what is expected, and making arrangements to regulate activities beforehand

- Talking to oneself or using a reflective dialogue about best instructional practices or management techniques to adopt with the class

- Developing interdependent planning levels (long range, unit, and daily), helping to convert long-range goals into daily activities

- Collecting a variety of teaching materials that provide a rich environment for learning

When planning for instruction, teachers may think about classroom management. By establishing clear rules and routines, teachers minimize confusion and maximize instructional time. This aspect of planning is particularly important at the beginning of the year when teachers establish patterns, limits, and expectations that often persist for the remainder of the year (Clark and Dunn 1991).

Teachers may also consider ways to motivate students when thinking about instruction. According to

Jere Brophy (1987), teachers may achieve this goal by: (a) establishing a supportive classroom environment in which students feel comfortable taking intellectual risks, (b) selecting activities that are at the appropriate level of difficulty "that teach some knowledge or skill that is worth learning," and (c) using a variety of motivational strategies (208). Such strategies include characterizing the lesson to be taught in familiar, general terms so students can conceptualize what they will be learning, and explaining goals and objectives for a lesson and their relevance to students' personal lives.

It is difficult to overestimate the importance of planning how to evaluate the relative success of a lesson. When left to chance, evaluation can be haphazard and yield only partial or misleading information. Such feedback may prompt a teacher to make erroneous decisions about content and methods of instruction most meaningful to students. Teachers' day-to-day evaluations of instruction often rely on their perceptions of students' in-class reactions (McNergney and Herbert 2001).

Corno (1987) and Winne (1991) contend that when planning academic lessons, teachers should also include, on a regular basis, activities that will teach students specific and general learning and self-management strategies. This may mean showing students how to take notes from lectures, how to organize their thoughts when writing a paper, or how to monitor and control their concentration during instruction. By providing students with the tools for becoming independent learners, teachers welcome students as "integral, conscious, and rational participants in instructional activities" (Winne 1991, 211). Such skills, in combination with content knowledge, prepare students to continue learning throughout their lifetimes.

Thirdly, planning also requires that an effective teacher be well aware of the community needs and resources. Students are representatives of the community. Any student is a part of the community. Each community is represented by a given set of beliefs and attitudes which should be reflected in planning for the educational needs of students. Community organizations can support the education program by making various resources (e.g., personnel, materials, and equipment) available. Giving students the opportunity to use the community as a "living laboratory" also contributes greatly to overall learning. Other people and resources in the community may contribute to student learning. Developing appropriate relationships with those agencies outside the education setting helps ensure to the provision of services necessary to promote student learning.

Finally, when planning the curriculum, an effective teacher is knowledgeable about the philosophy of the school. Given the philosophy of the school, the teacher integrates the statewide scope and sequence plan for the particular discipline and grade level. Merging the state plan with needs of the school population gives the teacher a baseline from which to begin specific planning. Writing course goals for the year and dividing goals into objectives for units gives the teacher a readily available starting point for writing unit plans (Wentz 2001). When identifying goals and objectives, teachers determine what it is students should learn or be able to do as a result of instruction. Such decisions help teachers clarify their thinking about methods and materials to use during instruction. Objectives are typically influenced by state and local mandates for instruction. They are also shaped by teachers' perceptions of students' needs and abilities before and after instruction (McNergney and Herbert 2001).

Despite all the advice on how best to plan, teachers usually plan instruction in ways that make sense to them. Inexperienced teachers tend to pay more attention to students' interests, both in planning and subsequently in teaching, than to students' performances and instructional involvement. Learning how to be a teacher means in part developing one's identity as a teacher. This identity is shaped by social interaction between the teacher and students, colleagues and staff, parents, administrators, and community members. While in the classroom, teachers need to be reflective of their current practice and be open to adjustments and revisions that become necessary in working with students (Campbell, et al. 1995).

Questions for Reflection

- How does subject matter influence instructional planning?

- Why is planning necessary when meeting the diverse needs of students?

- What community needs and resources affect planning for instruction?

- In what ways does the philosophy of the school set the stage for curriculum planning?

Commentary on Standard #7

JAY B. RASMUSSEN, Ph.D. | Professor of Education and Director of Graduate Programs in Education, Bethel College, St. Paul, Minnesota

Teaching is often viewed by the American public in an overly simplistic manner. Many are convinced that teachers merely stand in the front of the room and spout wisdom, to the delight of students sitting in neat rows and listening with rapt attention. As all teachers quickly find, effective teaching is not this simple.

Teaching is a complex process that involves sophisticated content area knowledge, an understanding of how students learn, significant community interaction, and a clear understanding of long- and short-term curriculum goals. No longer are teachers merely the sage on the stage. At the heart of effective teaching is planning that bridges curriculum goals and student experiences. Planning must be conducted short and long term, must respond to the full range of learner diversity, and must be continually adjusted. Those teachers who consistently engage the learner in appropriate challenges experience success. Effective teachers meter the challenge to the ability level of the student; too much challenge for a student with less ability results in anxiety, too little challenge for a student with high ability results in boredom.

If learner engagement is passive and shallow, then the resulting learning is likely to be superficial. A famous Teton Lakota Indian saying reminds us, "Tell me, and I'll listen. Show me, and I'll understand. Involve me, and I'll learn." The result of skilled planning is a learner able to construct his/her own meaning instead of merely reproducing the teacher's knowledge. By encouraging deep and elaborate encoding of new information, the teacher increases the likelihood of successful decoding and retrieval of information from long-term memory. That information and acquisition of processes used to acquire information can serve students well in the future.

According to Louise Rosenblatt, "The criteria for judging the success of any educational process is its effect on the actual life of the student; its ultimate value depends on its assimilation into the very marrow of personality." Teachers who embody the knowledge, dispositions, and performance of Standard #7 are likely to experience success as measured by impact on student's lives. Teachers who embody all ten INTASC standards are almost guaranteed a successful teaching career.

As we have seen, the *Stand and Deliver* model of instruction represents an incomplete view of teaching and teachers. The images of teachers are clearly changing. Metaphors such as instructional architects, leaders and inventors, problem posers, investigators, coaches, and improvisational artists/performers may be more appropriate.

Planning Instruction Self-Assessment

The teacher plans instruction based upon knowledge of subject matter, students, the community, and curriculum goals.

Knowledge/Performance Indicators

	Yes*	Not Sure	No
1. I understand learning theory, subject matter, curriculum development, and student development and know how to use this knowledge in planning instruction to meet curriculum goals.	2	1	0
2. I plan instruction using contextual considerations that bridge curriculum and student experiences.	2	1	0
3. I plan instructional programs that accommodate individual student learning styles and performance modes.	2	1	0
4. I create short-range and long-range plans that are linked to student needs and performance.	2	1	0
5. I design lessons and activities that operate at multiple levels to meet the developmental and individual needs of students and to help all progress.	2	1	0
6. I implement learning experiences that are appropriate for curriculum goals, relevant to learners, and based on principles of effective instruction including activating student prior knowledge, anticipating preconceptions, encouraging exploration and problem solving, and building new skills on those previously acquired.	2	1	0
7. I evaluate plans in relation to short-range and long-range goals, and systematically adjust plans to meet student needs and enhance learning.	2	1	0

* A "Yes" response indicates that you can describe, document, and cite examples related to your student teaching assignment.

Self-Assessment Summary and Reflection

1. Which Knowledge/Performance Indicators can I currently describe, document, and cite examples?

_____

_____

2. Which Knowledge/Performance Indicators need some work or improvement?

_____

_____

3. What specific actions can I take to enrich my knowledge or skill in this area?

_____

_____

Activity 7.1 Before We Get into Groups . . .

Context Teachers recognize the advantages of group activities, such as acquisition of social and cooperative skills, opportunities for peer teaching, and capitalizing on student interest. But teachers also recognize that groups do not always work effectively. Sometime a student will sit back and let the rest of the group do the work, or there will be a high noise level and too much student movement. It takes good planning to get the most benefits from group work.

Purpose This activity will help you identify areas that need careful planning.

Directions Think of a lesson that you will be teaching in the near future where group work is appropriate or advisable. Answer the questions *before* writing your lesson plan.

1. What is the purpose/objective of your lesson?

   _____

   _____

2. How will working in groups help the students meet your purpose/objective?

   _____

   _____

3. How many times (lessons/class periods) will students work in this group?

   _____

   _____

4. What group size and makeup will work best (e.g., random, interest, ability, mixed)?

   _____

   _____

5. How will students know their groups (e.g., self-selected, teacher reads list, overhead diagram with names and locations)?

   _____

   _____

6. What tasks are the groups to do?

   _____

   _____

7. What directions will you give the students before they move into groups?

   _____

   _____

8. What directions will you give the students after they are in groups?

   _____

   _____

9. How will you present the directions (e.g., orally, list on board, handout, step by step, demonstration)?

_____

_____

10. Where will the groups work? How will the furniture be arranged?

_____

_____

11. How will materials be distributed?

_____

_____

12. What are your expectations for group work (e.g., noise level, attention signal, product, sharing of responsibilities, use of equipment, time limit)?

_____

_____

13. How will you make the students aware of your expectations?

_____

_____

14. What product/process are the groups expected to complete? How will they be evaluated?

_____

_____

Activity 7.2   Oh Right, the Students

Context   Teachers teach many of the same lessons from one year to the next. Secondary teachers, and some elementary teachers, teach the same lesson to different groups of students. Why is it that the lesson works beautifully one time, but not so well the next? An important factor in successful lessons is the students. Teachers must consider the students' interests, abilities, and learning strategies when planning their lessons, and they must tailor each lesson to meet the needs of the students in that class.

Purpose   These questions will help you focus on your students and their learning needs as you plan lessons.

Directions   Think of a lesson you will teach in the future. Answer the following questions.

1. What is your lesson objective?

   _____

   _____

2. How does this objective fit into the curriculum and what the students are currently learning?

   _____

   _____

3. Why is this objective important to the students, and how will you convey that to them?

   _____

   _____

4. How will you find out what the students already know about this objective/topic/skill?

   _____

   _____

5. What do you know about your students' learning styles and experiences?

   _____

   _____

6. What will you do to get the students interested in this topic/skill?

   _____

   _____

7. How will you make the learning meaningful to the students (e.g., real-life examples, connections to their experiences, demonstration, hands-on material)?

   _____

   _____

8. How will the students interact with the topic or skill?

   _____

   _____

9. How will you give feedback to the students about their learning?

_____

_____

10. How will you assess how successful the students were?

_____

_____

11. What are some things that you expect the students to have difficulty with, and how will you help them work through those difficulties?

_____

_____

12. What are the special needs of this group of students or individual students in this group? (e.g., range of ability)?

_____

_____

13. What alternate activities/assignments do you have for students needing them?

_____

_____

14. What will students be able to do as a result of successfully learning in this lesson?

_____

_____

15. How do your answers to questions #1 and #14 compare?

_____

_____

Activity 7.3 Each and Every Time

Context   Lesson plan formats vary greatly from teacher to teacher. This is especially true when the plans of beginning teachers and experienced teachers are compared. Yet each successful plan contains most of the same components.

Purpose   In this activity you will identify those lesson plan components you feel should be included in all of your plans.

Directions   Categorize these common components according to how frequently they should appear in your lesson plans.

E = Every time
U = Usually
O = Occasionally

Under your *U* and *O* answers, give a rationale for your opinion.

_____ Anticipatory set

_____ Alternate assignment

_____ Assessment

_____ Check for understanding

_____ Closure

_____ Curriculum standard

_____ Demonstration

_____ Evaluation

_____ Grade level

_____ Guided practice

_____ Independent practice

_____ Input

_____ Introduction

_____ Learner objective

_____ Level of mastery

_____ Materials

_____ Modeling

_____ Motivation

_____ Post-assessment

_____ Pre-assessment

_____ Procedure

_____ Purpose

_____ Review

_____ Special needs learners

_____ Student diversity

_____ Subject and/or class period

_____ Teacher objective

_____ Time frame (e.g., minutes, periods, days)

_____ Title of lesson

_____ Transitions

Case Study

Lesson planning is important to Christa. It's something that she's good at. She likes to know what she's doing at least a week in advance. She wrote out all the lessens for her unit and showed them to her cooperating teacher a week before she was to start teaching the unit. Her cooperating teacher was pleased with the activities that Christa had planned, but she wasn't sure that the time she had allotted for each of them was adequate.

Sure enough. After just two days of teaching, Christa was behind. The students took much longer to accomplish the group work than she had planned. But they enjoyed the activities and seemed to be learning. However at this rate, she'd never get through the whole unit in the three weeks she had.

- What should Christa do? Should she just plow on and get the students to do the activities faster or should she eliminate some of the activities?

- If Christa eliminated some lessons, how would she meet all the goals of the unit?

- What criteria should she use to decide which lessons to teach?

- Maybe she shouldn't have planned out the whole unit and just planned a few lessons at a time. What would you have done?

- Was there something that her cooperating teacher could have done to help her avoid this situation?

Student-to-Student Tips

✔ Prepare on the weekend for the entire week. Then there will be less for you to do each night to get ready for the next day. *Robin, secondary student teacher*

✔ Get as much done as soon as possible. It really piles up at the end. But don't let yourself be overwhelmed at the beginning. *Scott, elementary student teacher*

✔ Keep ahead. Know a week in advance what you will be doing. *Angelica, elementary student teacher*

✔ Have a folder for each day or subject. *Heidi, elementary student teacher*

✔ Color-coded folders make life so much easier! You can put your gradesheets, lesson plans, and worksheets in them so you know where everything is! *Megan, elementary student teacher*

✔ Plan ahead, but be flexible. Don't do detailed plans a week in advance; have an outline ready for the week. Do your detailed plans day by day. That lets you reflect on your teaching and takes into account how the students did. *Jennifer, elementary student teacher*

✔ Have a backup plan. You always need something extra to do in case there is a schedule change. *Chris, secondary student teacher*

✔ Be as prepared as possible. The students will know it if you aren't and will get off task. *Rosa, secondary student teacher*

✔ Be organized. Prepare as far in advance as possible. It's better to share your plans with your cooperating teacher ahead of time and get suggestions then, rather than only get suggestions and ideas after you've taught. *Maikau, secondary student teacher*

✔ Begin working on your unit early. It's important to view it as a whole unit; what you want students to learn and to do. If you only plan it lesson by lesson you lose a lot. It takes a lot of time to find the resources and materials you need, so start early. *Tom, secondary student teacher*

✔ Think through every detail as you plan your lessons. Be detail-oriented. *Margy, elementary student teacher*

✔ Plan for those things you don't think about, like transitions. *Dean, elementary student teacher*

✔ Be on top of things, every single night. If you're not organized, you're in big trouble. *Brent, elementary student teacher*

✔ Know your schedule. Always be a week ahead in your plans. That way you are ready and can make any changes later as needed. *Marla, elementary student teacher*

Bibliography

Brophy, J. 1987. On motivating students. In *Talks to teachers*, ed. D. C. Berliner and B. V. Rosenshine (pp. 201–245). New York: Random House.

Campbell, D. M., P. B. Cignetti, B. J. Melenyzer, D. H. Nettles, and R. M. Wyman. 1995. *How to develop a professional portfolio*. Neeham, NJ: Allyn and Bacon.

Clark, C. M. and S. Dunn. 1991. Second-generation research on teachers' planning. In *Effective teaching: Current research* (pp. 183–200), ed. H. C. Waxman and H. J. Walberg (pp. 201–245). Berkeley, CA: McCutchan.

Corno, L. 1987. Teaching a self-regulated learning. In *Talks to teachers*, ed. D. C. Berliner and B. V. Rosenshine. (pp. 249–266) New York: Random House.

Dewey, J. [1904] 1964. *John Dewey on education.*, ed. R. Archanbault. Chicago: University of Chicago Press.

Freiberg, H. J., and A. Driscoll. 1992. *Universal teaching strategies*. Boston: Allyn and Bacon.

Goethals, M. S. and R. A. Howard. 2000. *Student teaching: A process approach to reflective practice.* Upper Saddle River, NJ: Prentice-Hall Inc.

McNergney, R. F., and J. M. Herbert. 2001. *Foundations of education: The challenge of professional practice.* Boston: Allyn and Bacon.

Orlich, D., R. Harder, R. Callahan, and H. Gibson. 2001. *Teaching strategies: A guide to better instruction.* Boston: Houghton Mifflin.

Wentz, P. J. 2001. *The student teaching experience: Cases from the classroom.* Upper Saddle River, NJ: Merrill/Prentice-Hall.

Winne, P. H. 1991. Motivation and teaching. In *Effective teaching: Current research*, ed. H. C. Waxman and H. J. Walberg. (pp. 210–230) Berkeley, CA: McCutchan.

8
Assessment and Evaluation

"Assessment is the process of observing, recording, and documenting
the work children do and how they do it, for the purpose of making
sound educational decisions for each individual child."
—*Jardine*

Standard #8 The teacher understands and uses formal and informal assessment strategies to evaluate and ensure the continuous intellectual, social, and physical development of the learner.

Performance Indicators: *The teacher . . .*

- Collects and uses data gathered from a variety of sources. These sources include both traditional and alternative assessment strategies. Furthermore, the teacher can identify and match the students' instructional plans with their cognitive, social, linguistic, cultural, emotional and physical needs.
- Consistently applies appropriate assessment strategies to evaluate and ensure the continuous intellectual, social, physical, and emotional development of the learner.

Vignette Four different preparations in social studies were all in a day's work for Joy, who was student-teaching in Mr. Stahn's classroom. Joy believed the key to effective student learning was to give daily paper-and-pencil quizzes on the material presented the previous day. Realizing that a number of students could benefit from alternative forms of evaluation, Mr. Stahn shared some examples of authentic assessments he has used. In spite of the suggestions, Joy continued to use paper-and-pencil tests (Wentz 2001).

Fundamental Principles

When they are well-devised and implemented, academic standards and tests, and the accountability provisions tied to them, can change the nature of teaching and learning. They can lead to a richer, more challenging curriculum. They can foster conversation and collaboration among teachers within and across schools. They can create a more productive dialogue among teachers and parents. And they can help focus everyone's attention on raising student achievement. When they are poorly devised and implemented, standards, assessments, and accountability can become a distraction and a source of frustration in schools (Gandal and Vranek 2001).

No process is more central to teaching than evaluation, a process that involves collecting information, forming judgments, and making decisions. The purpose of assessment is to assist students, teachers, schools, and parents in recognizing what students have learned and to identify areas in which students need improvement. Properly designed assessment instruments and procedures can improve decision making regarding learner performance. Assessment, therefore, is essential for improvement of the curriculum, of instruction, and of student learning (Goethals and Howard 2000). Only through the assessment of student learning can teachers know if students have met the instructional goals of a unit or lesson. The more diverse the types of instructional goals, the more diverse the approaches to assessment must be (Danielson 1996).

Teachers use a variety of means, some formal and others informal, to determine how much and how well their students are learning. For example, to formally evaluate student learning, most teachers use quizzes, tests, examinations, term papers, lab reports, and homework. These formal evaluation techniques help the teachers evaluate student achievement and assign grades. To evaluate classroom learning informally, teachers also use a variety of techniques. An informal test is a non-standardized test, often teacher-constructed, that is designed to give an approximate index of a student's level of ability or learning style. Informal evaluations permit teachers to make adjustments in their teaching; to slow down or review material in response to questions, confusion, and misunderstandings; or to move on when student performance exceed expectations. Such information enables teachers to: (a) determine what students already know and want to know about topics, (b) plan instruction that is appropriately challenging, (c) motivate student performance, (d) assess progress toward affective and cognitive goals, and (e) communicate progress to others (McNergney and Herbert 2001). Therefore, assessment is frequently defined as any method used to identify academic growth and develop further competencies in assessing student progress. Learning implies that what a student knows is always changing and that we can make judgments about student achievement through comparisons over a period of time (McNergney and Herbert 2001). Assessment may affect decisions about grades, advancement, placement, instructional needs, and curriculum (Dietel, Herman, and Knuth 1991).

As programs for school improvement proliferated in the 1980s, the trend toward assessment of the quality of schools and teachers using standardized tests also grew in influence. Many states now require high school students to perform well on tests of general academic competence as a prerequisite for graduation, and almost all states require local public school districts to test students at some point(s) between grades one and twelve. Traditional assessment has been based on specific information that students acquire. Observations, tests on content, and standardized tests are examples of traditional evaluative measures that provide indicators for gauging academic progress.

Many teachers are uncomfortable with the process of testing and grading students, and most are aware that testing has its limitations. Examples of test limitations include the match (or lack thereof) between what is tested and what is taught, which is termed curriculum alignment; poor test performance due to student fatigue, illness, or anxiety; the relative clarity of test items; and the reliability of the grading process. All these factors can result in student knowledge being underestimated. Surprisingly, formal testing can also overestimate what students understand. The school's requirement, therefore, that permanent grades be assigned is not always welcome (Arends, Winitzky, and Tannenbaum 2001).

Recently, however, there has been a concern that this traditional assessment format reflects little about the depth of knowledge in relation to solving real-life problems (O'Neil 1992; Wiggins 1989). These tests, some educators argue, do not represent activities students typically perform in classrooms, despite their universal presence. Standardized tests do not necessarily measure what should be taught or the levels at which students should perform. The scores students acquire on these tests are estimates of what they know or can do. They are only samples of students' learned behaviors at a particular point in time (McNergney and Herbert 2001). Another concern is that standardized tests cannot be used to closely monitor student progress in the school curriculum throughout the year since they are only administered once or twice a year (Herman 1992). Since the format of standardized tests is primarily multiple choice items, they are better suited to assess factual knowledge than to assess more complex cognitive skills, such as problem solving or creativity. Simply testing an isolated skill or a retained fact does not effectively measure a student's capabilities. To accurately evaluate what a person has learned, an assessment method must examine one's collective abilities. Unfortunately, this fact often gets lost in the competition between students, schools, and districts for high test scores.

New approaches to assessment have tried to address these concerns by focusing on performance samples in which students demonstrate that they can perform a task such as giving a speech, playing an instrument, or writing a story (Campbell et al. 1995). This means assessing students with real-world challenges that require them to apply their relevant skills and knowledge. Learning entails not only what students know but what they can do with what they know; it involves not only knowledge and abilities but values, attitudes, and habits of mind that affect both academic success and performance beyond the classroom. In other words, the assessment would actually measure what we wanted students to be able to do rather than relying on them to choose the correct response on a multiple choice test item. This type of assessment is known as authentic, alternative, or performance assessment (Ryan and Cooper 2000).

The terms alternative assessment, authentic assessment, and performance assessment are often used synonymously, yet have different meanings (Hill and Ruptic 1994):

- *Alternative assessment* usually applies to all assessments different from multiple choice, timed approaches that characterize most standardized and many teacher-made tests. Assessment is authentic when teachers directly examine student performance. They are called alternative because the task assessed involves an improvised or created "alternative" to a real-life problem-solving situation. Alternative assessment is less concerned with students' recognition and recall of facts and more interested in students' abilities to analyze, apply, evaluate, and synthesize what they know in ways that address real-world concerns. Teachers design their own criteria and standards for student work.

- *Authentic assessment* conveys the idea that students are engaged in applying knowledge and skills to real-life situations and problems. The purpose of authentic assessment is intended to help students understand their own work in relation to that of others. In other words, authentic assessments are designed to be criterion-referenced rather than norm-referenced, and to formatively identify strengths as well as weaknesses, but explicitly do not compare students to each other or rank students.

- *Performance assessment* indicates students' progress by demonstrating their understanding and application of knowledge, skills, and attitudes. Performance assessment may include any of the following approaches: (a) open-ended or constructed response items that ask students to respond in their own words; (b) projects or experiments that may take several days or even several weeks to complete; (c) a presentation by one student or by a group of students to demonstrate the skills used in the completion of an activity; or (d) portfolios that consist of a collection of student works showing the student's efforts, progress, and achievements in one or more areas. A portfolio should include a variety of both au-

thentic and alternative assessment samples. More specifically, teachers evaluate items such as learning logs, journals, criterion-referenced tests, observations, peer evaluation and self-evaluations, homework, and group projects.

Another new approach to evaluating student learning is portfolio assessment. A portfolio is a collection of student work that documents the student's effort, progress, or achievement toward a goal or goals. In addition, portfolios generally contain multiple examples of a student's work over a period of time, which gives them the capacity to demonstrate improvements in performance (Hall and Hewitt-Gervais 1999). In order to select materials to reflect their progress, students must examine their work, reflect on what it represents, and assess it relative to the portfolio goal. This self-selection, reflection, and assessment process makes portfolio development an instructional tool. A portfolio is not an assessment until criteria for assessing either the entire collection of materials or the individual aspects of it are identified. A question, therefore, that the teacher needs to consider relates to whether progress toward a goal or improvement will be assessed and, if so, how it will be measured. If the portfolio includes a variety of materials, how will these materials be weighted in the overall assessment? Portfolios take a variety of formats and utilize numerous tools. Electronic portfolios allow collection, organization, and storage of a variety of types of information into an electronic file. Information may represent digital pictures, rubrics from different assignments, digitized video segments, text, graphics, and scanned photographs. Although they are not without controversy, portfolios have been promoted as a means for evaluating higher-order, complex skills and for providing opportunities for student goal setting and self-evaluation of progress (McNeil 1999).

Journals, another form of authentic assessment, allow students to reflect upon and share their thoughts, feelings, impressions, perceptions, and attitudes about their performance, an event, an assignment, or other learning experiences. A journal serves as a means of describing a situation, reacting to that situation, reflecting upon the actions, and using those reflections to learn and to grow. Journal writing may be conducted in class as a unit experience or linked to a specific aspect of instruction through a homework assignment; it may become a habit for students to develop as part of activity participation or be a means of helping students examine their beliefs and attitudes toward a specific topic. Because journals reflect personal feelings, thoughts, and perceptions, they typically are not graded for their content. They can, however, be assessed for completion or by using a set of criteria that guided the journal writing itself. Care must be taken in scoring the student journal because it may tend to stifle reflection, honesty, and the sharing of personal feelings and perceptions.

Danielson (1996) reiterates that authenticity in assessment motivates students and provides teachers with excellent insight into student learning. People recognize the value of judging students' higher-order thinking skills and practical skills. It is designed to be criterion-referenced rather than norm-referenced assessment. Such evaluation identifies strengths and weaknesses, but does not compare or rank students. There are several challenges to using authentic assessment methods such as cost, managing its time-intensive nature, ensuring curricular validity, minimizing evaluator bias, and ensuring that grades are applied consistently among students. Moreover, disagreements over assessment standards will mean that some people do not view such assessments as rigorous (Nuthall 1992).

Scoring criteria are the key to turning assessment tasks into true assessments, rather than just a series of learning experiences or tasks that students perform. A scoring rubric defines the criteria by which a performance or product is judged (Nott, Reeve, and Reeve 1992). Essentially, it consists of levels of performance (criteria) and a list of characteristics describing performance at each level. Rubrics help teachers score students' work more accurately and fairly (ASCD 1994). Rubrics can be used to judge performance for many assessment strategies, including portfolios, journals, and group projects. A rubric is, however, more than an assessment tool; it should also enhance instruction and facilitate learning. If an assigned task is accompanied by a scoring rubric, it provides students with a clear and specific goal. Rubrics make levels of learning public and thus promote good performance by showing that quality work is achievable and expected. In addition, because rubrics contain specific criteria for guiding and evaluating performance, they also provide the language and dimensions for useful and informative feedback.

The following list and description of the different types of rubrics serve as a guide (Pate 1993):

- **The point system:** Points are assigned for certain features of a student's response. Open-ended questions are often scored with this approach because points can reflect partial as well as full credit for a response.

- **Checklists:** A checklist is a list of dimensions, characteristics, or behaviors that are essentially scored as "yes-no" ratings. A checklist can be used to rate the presence or absence of a performance, or it can indicate that a student has effectively completed the steps involved in a task or demonstration. Checklists can be applied to written work (e.g., journals) or observable behavior.

- **Analytical rating scales:** A numerical scale uses numbers or assigns points to a continuum of performance levels. A qualitative scale uses adjectives rather than numbers to characterize student performance. Rating scales describe performance along a continuum so they are more appropriate for discovering the extent to which dimensions were observed or the quality of performance. The strength of analytic rating scales is that they offer diagnostic information to the student about the strengths and weaknesses of their performance on a variety of dimensions so that they can better target the areas of their performance that need to be improved.

- **Focused holistic rating scales:** Rather than assigning separate scores for each important aspect of task performance, focused holistic ratings consider all the criteria simultaneously and result in a single summary rating or grade. This approach may be most appropriate when the purpose is to provide students with an overall index of their performance on a task or product.

- **Holistic:** No specific rating criteria are identified in holistic scoring. Instead, model responses are selected that represent numbers on the scale to be used. Student responses are compared to the model responses and are given a number corresponding to the model response they are most like.

Assessment results have important implications for instruction. The primary aim of assessment is to foster learning of worthwhile academic content for all students. Schools use assessment results in a formative way to determine how well they are meeting instructional goals and how to alter curriculum and instruction so that goals can be better met. But unless the content of assessment (what schools assess) and the format of assessment (how schools assess) match what is taught and how it is taught, the results are meaningless, if not potentially harmful. The same is true if assessment tools are not of high quality. There is also potential for harm when decisions affecting students' futures are being made based on results of assessments made with tools that are not appropriate for the purpose.

Goethals and Howard (2000) recommend several attributes related to assessment as teachers develop their own system. Effective assessment is:

- **Continuous or ongoing:** Daily and weekly assessment of identified teaching goals and assessing the progress of each learner are the first steps toward authentic assessment.
- **Flexible:** Assessment needs to concentrate on the identified areas of weakness or goals for each learner. Effective teachers are always adjusting their instructional activity to meet the needs of individual learners.
- **Cumulative:** A longitudinal approach to assessment puts the results of any one assessment into perspective.
- **Diverse:** Multiple instruments should be used to assess learner progress. There simply is no one right way to assess students.

The selection and use of various assessment instruments involve much reflection and research. The choice of an assessment instrument depends on the evaluative decisions about student learning. Whatever type of assessment is used, each should reflect the following three qualities:

1. The assessment should be as reliable as possible. This means that the assessment should provide dependable, consistent results.
2. The assessment strategies used by the teacher should be valid. In other words, the teacher should make sure that the assessment strategy measures what it claims to measure.
3. The strategies should be fair, impartial, and unbiased (Campbell, et al. 1995).

Assessment and evaluation of student achievement are intended for teachers, students, and parents to identify what students know and what they are learning. Assessment is a major, essential, and integrated part of teaching and learning (Wiggins 1998).

Grading is a requirement of most schools. If grades are intended to communicate to students how they are doing relative to course expectations and serve as a motivator for future participation, then they must be based on learning outcomes and performance which demonstrate that learning. If grades are going to be meaningful and useful to students, the criteria behind them must be explicit and shared with learners before instruction begins. This will allow them to understand the expectations and provide them with the opportunity to set their goals toward achieving them. The grading system must match program outcomes. This suggests that teachers identify the learning outcome categories to be included in the grading system, determine how they will be weighted, and define the criteria that will form the basis for each portion of the grade.

Grading grows from a philosophy of teaching and learning. It reflects what a teacher believes about learning. The following actions reflect this philosophy (Tomlinson 2001):

- Grade for success in the same way that you teach and assess for success. It means the degree of student success must reflect the degree of their growth.
- Grade the student's work on the basis of clearly delineated criteria for quality work on that task. It makes little sense to assign an appropriately challenging task and then grade a student on something else.
- Give students consistent, meaningful feedback that clarifies for them present successes and next learning steps. Using such methods as student self-assessments based on pre-established criteria, teacher–student conferences about specific work, mutual goal setting, and written teacher comments with student responses may be more helpful than assigning a letter or number grade.
- Look for growth patterns over time when assigning grades.
- Find a way to show individual growth and relative standing to students and parents. This can be accomplished by developing report cards that use checklists of escalating competencies that allow for reporting specific progress, combined with notations of where students of similar age generally perform on those checklists. It can also be accomplished by attaching a note to the report card or conducting parent–student conferences. Doing so allows the teacher to explain that the student's grade takes into account both differentiated and common tasks, to show how the grade reflects both, and to interpret what the grade means from the particular student's learning.

Questions for Reflection

- What is the purpose of assessment?

- What have been the concerns with the use of traditional assessment formats?

- Differentiate between alternative, authentic, and performance assessment.

- What are the implications of assessment for instruction?

Commentary on Standard #8

TRACY PELLETT, Ed.D. | Director of Clinical and Field Experiences, College of Education, Minnesota State University, Mankato

Assessment and evaluation have become extremely important in today's age of educational accountability and reform, and are unmistakably interdependent with teaching and learning in the educational process. Evaluation plays an important part in instructional planning and design with the primary purpose of improving instruction. Assessment and evaluation emphasize the importance of learning and demonstrating knowledge and skills. This helps make students accountable for their performance and teachers responsible for student achievement. Meaningful and informative assessment and evaluation are not easy to achieve because of large class sizes, heavy teaching loads, and limited planning time. However, teachers who assess and evaluate regularly (a) know which students have met educational objectives, (b) assign activities that are better matched with student abilities, and (c) are better able to individualize instruction.

Assessment and evaluation are critical at the beginning, during, and at the conclusion of instruction. At the beginning, evaluation provides teachers with information concerning students who have already mastered content. Students who already possess skills can be directed into more challenging activities, while students who lack prerequisite skills can be given help to improve their performance and eventually achieve course objectives. In other words, how can you plan on where students are going without assessing where students have been? During instruction, evaluation can provide students information concerning how they are progressing. In effective teaching, students are prepared for tests in advance with no surprises about what is required. Good evaluation can also serve as a learning activity in itself as it can motivate students, arouse their interest, and require them to apply information in real or simulated conditions. At the conclusion of instruction, evaluation helps teachers check the effectiveness of the teaching process. It helps the teacher and student know whether each student has achieved specific objectives and the progress they made in doing it. Overall, assessment and evaluation are critical in the process of effective teaching. It provides a basis by which teachers and students know where they have been, where they are going, and where they have ended up.

Assessment and Evaluation Self-Assessment

The teacher understands and uses formal and informal assessment strategies to evaluate and ensure the continuous intellectual, social and physical development of the learner.

Knowledge/Performance Indicators	Yes*	Not Sure	No
1. I am able to assess student performance toward achievement of state graduation standards.	2	1	0
2. I understand the characteristics, uses, advantages, and limitations of different types of assessments including criterion-referenced and norm-referenced instruments, traditional standardized tests, performance-based tests, observation systems, and assessments of student work.	2	1	0
3. I understand the purpose of and differences between assessment and evaluation.	2	1	0

4. I understand measurement theory and assessment-related issues, including validity, reliability, bias, and scoring concerns.	2	1	0
5. I select, construct, and use assessment strategies, instruments, and technology appropriate to the learning outcomes being evaluated and to other diagnostic purposes.	2	1	0
6. I use assessment to identify student strengths and promote student growth and to maximize student access to learning opportunities.	2	1	0
7. I use varied and appropriate formal and informal assessment techniques including observation, portfolios of student work, teacher-made tests, performance tasks, projects, student self-assessments, peer assessment, and standardized tests.	2	1	0
8. I use assessment data and other information about student experiences, learning behaviors, needs, and progress to increase knowledge of students, evaluate student progress and performance, and modify teaching and learning strategies.	2	1	0 .
9. I use students' self-assessment activities to help them identify their own strengths and needs and to encourage them to set personal goals for learning.	2	1	0
10. I evaluate the effect of class activities on both individuals and the class as a whole using information gained through observation of classroom interactions, questioning, and analysis of student work.	2	1	0
11. I monitor teaching strategies and behaviors in relation to student success to order to modify plans and instructional approaches to achieve student goals.	2	1	0
12. I establish and maintain student records of work and performance.	2	1	0
13. I responsibly communicate student progress based on appropriate indicators to students, parents or guardians, and other colleagues.	2	1	0

* A "Yes" response indicates that you can describe, document, and cite examples related to your student teaching assignment.

Self-Assessment Summary and Reflection

1. Which Knowledge/Performance Indicators can I currently describe, document, and cite examples?

_____

_____

2. Which Knowledge/Performance Indicators need some work or improvement?

_____

_____

3. What specific actions can I take to enrich my knowledge or skill in this area?

_____

_____

Activity 8.1   *If You Can See It, You Can Evaluate It*

Context   Effective teachers do not wait for a quiz or test to evaluate student learning. They often know the progress of each student before the day's lesson has ended. This gives them an opportunity to adjust their teaching and to increase student understanding. In typical classroom situations, teachers will plan to informally check the progress of each student throughout the lesson. For example, they may ask questions to which students must respond with a thumbs up or thumbs down or they may ask students to number 1–5 on a piece of scratch paper and write the answers to particular questions. Teachers are informally evaluating students when they use individual marker boards, have students clap out a rhythm to poetry, or raise their hands when they've figured out a problem. By monitoring the students' understanding during the lesson, teachers can adjust their instruction accordingly.

There are other classroom situations in which teachers will have a sense only of what the class as a whole understands. This occurs when the teacher requests a unison response from the students or leads large-group discussions with few (or the same) students answering questions. It may also occur when teachers ask, "Does anyone have a question?" before students begin an assignment, or when they respond only to those students who request assistance. Teachers may have an accurate idea of what the class (as a whole) understands but not of what individual students understand. Effective teachers incorporate both approaches to informal evaluation in their planning and teaching.

Purpose   Through this activity, you will identify those strategies that enable the teacher to informally evaluate the progress of individual students in learning a skill or concept.

Directions

- Write *Yes* in the space if the instructional task/activity is designed to check the understanding of each student during that day's lesson.

- Write *No* if the task is not is designed to check the understanding of each individual during that day's lesson.

Scenario 1: _____

In geography class, students are studying climate and each student has two items of clothing, one for hot weather and one for cold weather. When the teacher directs them during the class discussion, students must hold up the item of clothing that would be appropriate for: Australia in May; Suriname in September; Japan in August.

Scenario 2: _____

For the first five minutes of class each day, the students are asked questions in Spanish by their teacher which they have to answer in Spanish. For this activity, the teacher uses index cards with individual student names written on them and randomly calls on students.

Scenario 3: _____

In language arts class students silently read a short story which they will discuss the following day. They are responsible for reading the discussion questions as homework in preparation for the following day's large-group discussion.

Scenario 4: _____

For science, students are reading a section of the chapter and taking notes which they'll hand in the following day. The teacher monitors students for on-task behavior.

Scenario 5: _____

In math class, students are completing problems 1, 3, and 7 as the teacher walks around the room looking at their answers. The teacher initials the papers of those who complete all three problems correctly. Students will complete the rest of the assignment as homework.

Scenario 6: _____

When students walk into their biology class, they notice that the teacher has drawn a large diagram of a flower on the chalkboard. He instructs them to get out a piece of paper, number it 1–10 and identify the flower parts (labeled 1–10). When students finish, they are to compare their answers to a classmate's, and star any questionable answers. During the ensuing discussion, the teacher checks the status of the students' answers and then they hand in this mock quiz.

Activity 8.2 Assessment and Evaluation

Context   Assessment and evaluation practices have always been used by teachers. However, in more recent years, the assessment and evaluation of student progress have been more heavily emphasized. Consequently, there has been considerable discussion and confusion of these terms which are often used interchangeably. Although assessment and evaluation are interrelated, the terms are not synonymous.

Assessment is the process through which teachers gather information about how much and how well their students are learning. Evaluation is making a judgment and placing a value on the information gathered. Thus, teachers gather information about their students' learning through observation, written assignments, questioning, student performance, and tests. Teachers often record assessment information over a period of time. They record days absent, number of books read, number of assignments completed, class participation, standardized test scores, discipline problems, and contact with parents.

Teachers use assessment information for a variety of purposes. The most immediate use is to adjust their teaching to meet the needs of their students. This may entail reteaching a concept/skill in response to student confusion or misunderstandings or moving on more quickly when student performance exceeds expectations.

But what about evaluation? Once teachers have assessed their students, i.e., gathered information, they sometimes make a judgment based on the information and take some action. When teachers make a judgment, then they have evaluated the student(s). Thus, when a teacher notes that a student correctly answered eighteen of twenty questions on an assignment and that the two incorrect answers were related to the same concept, she has assessed the student's knowledge. If she determines that 18/20 warrants a "B" on that assignment, she has evaluated the student's progress. Additionally teachers record evaluation information with grades on: homework, quiz/test grades, presentations and projects, and daily assignments. Both assessment and evaluation are important tools to foster learning of worthwhile academic content for all students as these practices identify for teachers, students, and parents what students know and what they are learning.

Purpose   Through this activity, you will differentiate assessment and evaluation practices.

Directions

- After reading each classroom situation, decide if the teacher is assessing her students *(A)* or evaluating her students *(E)*.

- Write the appropriate letter in the space.

- Star the practices that you would like to try in your classroom.

1. _____ In preparation for a test, the teacher provided an optional review study guide. Before students take the test, those who completed the study guide hand it in to the teacher who makes a note of it in her gradebook.

2. _____ At the beginning of the year, the teacher is given information about students with special needs. She makes a note about each child on her seating chart.

3. _____ The social studies teacher uses a checklist for the project her students are in the midst of completing. Each day several students bring their checklist and project to her. She looks at a student's project and then circles "excellent" and "needs more work" by several items on the checklist and hands it back to the student.

4. _____ In English class, students are used to a routine for checking homework completion. They get out their homework assignment and place it on their desk so the teacher can check it. While they're reading a novel, the teacher checks students' assignments and initials their last answers to document how much they had completed before the assignment is discussed. Later the teacher will note the students who had incomplete assignments.

5. _____ Students have been engaged in group work for about ten minutes when the teacher takes a "status" check. She tells those groups who need more time to raise their hands and all groups raise their hands, so she says that she'll extend their time an extra five minutes.

6. _____ The teacher is curious about her students' learning styles, so she keeps track of student participation during class discussions by putting a checkmark next to a student's name on the seating chart each time that student volunteers an answer.

7. _____ Students receive their unit tests back in math class. Many are happy with their grades but for those who are not, the teacher has provided extra study sessions and an opportunity for a retake.

8. _____ Before students begin their math homework assignment, the teacher assigns them problems 1, 2, and 5 to complete. While students are solving these problems, she walks by the desk of each student to check progress and answer questions. She realizes that most students are confused by problems 2 and 5 so she stops the class, reteaches the concept, and then modifies the homework assignment.

9. _____ Improved reading fluency and enjoyment is the number one schoolwide goal at River Falls Elementary School, so teachers administer a Reading Interest Inventory to their students at the beginning of the school year. Teachers make copies of the completed surveys for their information and return the originals to the reading specialist.

10. _____ The science teacher noticed that many of the same students blurted out answers when she asked simple knowledge questions. She rephrased her questions, making them more open-ended. She noticed when she phrased a question, "Think about yesterday's discussion and write down one idea about. . . ," the blurting stopped and most students participated.

Remember: assessment = gathering information

evaluation = making a judgment *and* taking action

Activity 8.3   Feedback, the Breakfast of Champions

Context   Teachers need to assess and/or evaluate their students' learning while they're teaching so that they can make adjustments in their lessons. Teachers who make these adjustments as a part of their teaching use instructional time better and increase the likelihood that students will successfully meet the learning objectives.

Purpose   This activity will help you plan ways to elicit feedback from your students while you're teaching. This feedback will enable you to adjust your lessons to promote student success.

Directions

- List six concepts or skills that you will be teaching during the next two weeks.
- Write a learning objective for each concept/skill and identify the level of cognition the students will need to demonstrate for each objective.
- For each learning objective, design two ways that students will be able to demonstrate (to you) that they have met it. *The first one has been done for you.*

1. Concept/Skill: *characteristics of effective group members*

   Learning Objective/Level of Cognition:

   Students will describe the qualities of a helpful group member.

   Ways to Assess Student Progress:

   a) *Before the lesson, have students pair up and jot down ideas in answer to this question, "What made someone a helpful member of a team or group that you have been a part of?"*

   b) *Write a list of characteristics on a transparency. Have students give a thumbs up or a thumbs down in response to each one to indicate if the quality describes a helpful group member.*

2. Concept/Skill: _____

   Learning Objective/Level of Cognition:

   _____

   Ways to Assess Student Progress:

   a) _____

   _____

   b) _____

   _____

3. Concept/Skill: _____

   Learning Objective/Level of Cognition:

   _____

   _____

Ways to Assess Student Progress:

a) _____

_____

b) _____

_____

4. Concept/Skill: _____

Learning Objective/Level of Cognition:

_____

_____

Ways to Assess Student Progress:

a) _____

_____

b) _____

_____

5. Concept/Skill: _____

Learning Objective/Level of Cognition:

_____

_____

Ways to Assess Student Progress:

a) _____

_____

b) _____

_____

6. Concept/Skill: _____

Learning Objective/Level of Cognition:

_____

_____

Ways to Assess Student Progress:

a) _____

_____

b) _____

_____

Activity 8.4   Show and Tell

Context   Most of us learn by doing. Take the woman, for example, who learned how to use a miter saw when she was invited to help build a straw bale house. Her eighteen-year-old nephew taught her to saw lengths of board by explaining the process, showing her the technique, and then having her practice. After cutting 100 lengths of board , she knew the rudiments of using a miter saw! The concept of "learning by doing" is explored in Activity 2.3 where you practiced designing active participation tasks by combining overt and covert words/ word phrases.

Engaging students in active participation can serve another important instructional purpose. By having students tell what they know or show what they can do, teachers have the opportunity to informally evaluate each student's understanding of a concept or skill—taking out the guesswork! For example, before a teacher begins a unit on the Civil War, she can evaluate her students' prior knowledge by saying, "Think back to what you know about Abraham Lincoln. Write down two facts you remember." During a lesson, a teacher may check the students' understanding by saying, "Think about causes of the Civil War that we've been discussing today. Write down two that you consider the most important." As students are writing, the teacher can walk around, look at their answers, and evaluate their understanding. Based on their understanding, she can reteach, clarify, or move on. When teachers use active participation tasks for evaluation purposes, they may be evaluating students' prior knowledge or checking their understanding so that they can adjust their teaching.

Purpose   Through this activity, you will differentiate those tasks used by teachers to actively engage their students in learning and those used to informally evaluate students' knowledge.

Directions

- Read each active participation task.

- Place an *A* if the task *actively engages* each student but no evaluation takes place.

- Place an *E* if the task *enables* the teacher to informally evaluate students.

1. _____ "*Remember* a time when you were young and were really scared. *Tell* a classmate about your experience." (Teacher then leads a large-group discussion and lists words or phrases that depict fear.)

2. _____ "*Analyze* the information on page 1 of your study guide. *Highlight* all of the words that suggest this is an excerpt from a diary from the 1940s." (Teacher monitors students' selections by walking around and checking.)

3. _____ "*Consider* the five options written on the whiteboard. *Write* them down in the order of importance according to what you think your parents would choose." (Teacher leads a discussion to reach a consensus on their parents' top two options.)

4. _____ "*Look* at the diagram that I've drawn on the board illustrating the parts of the plant. *Label* the parts on a piece of scratch paper." (Teacher walks around, looking at student answers and then directs students to work with a partner to arrive at the correct answers.)

5. _____ "*Brainstorm* a list of reasons to vote in local and national elections. *Show* your list to your 'row partner.' " (The teacher uses this as a springboard for a discussion on the legal definition of adult responsibilities and rights.)

6. _____ "*Practice* sets of five free throws with a partner. *Provide* feedback to each other on proper technique." (The teacher walks around the gym, observing students who are shooting the basketball and listening to those students who are providing feedback. Based on this, he or she clarifies the proper follow-through technique.)

Case Study

Pao Vang had a wonderful background to teach global geography. Originally from Laos, she had lived in parts of Europe, Asia, and the United States. She incorporated artifacts, personal stories, and a contagious enthusiasm into her daily lessons. She established a collegial relationship with her cooperating teacher, Mr. Stow, as they shared similar background and interests. In fact, Mr. Stow complimented Pao by asking her if he could "take notes" of Pao's instructional activities to add to his teaching files. Of course, Pao was delighted and honored by the request.

Imagine the dismay and concern when many of Pao's students scored very poorly on her unit test even though they had been actively engaged in all of the unit activities. Imagine Mr. Stow's and Pao's surprise and confusion by the test scores. Pao constructed the test applying assessment theory and practice. She showed the test to Mr. Stow who thought the multiple choice, true/false, and fill-in-the-blank questions would accurately evaluate student learning. What could have happened?

- Are Pao's and Mr. Stow's concerns about poor student test scores justified?

- What variables could account for poor test scores on the part of many students who had been actively engaged in the unit activities?

- What should Pao do in response to the poor test scores?

- How might this experience affect his evaluation and assessment choice(s) for the next unit of study?

Student-to-Student Tips

✔ Start saving copies of students' work right away. *Meisha, elementary student teacher*

✔ Plan ahead, but be flexible. I planned a week at a time, but I was also prepared to make changes when the schedule changed or I needed to adjust what I was teaching. *Tim, elementary student teacher*

✔ Make sure you assess students by their ability. Not everyone can accomplish the same things. *Jan, secondary student teacher*

Bibliography

Arends, R. I., N. E. Winitzky, and M. D. Tannenbaum. 2001. *Exploring teaching: An introduction to education.* 2nd ed. New York: McGraw-Hill.

Association for Supervision and Curriculum Development (ASCD). 1994. *Assessing student outcomes: Performance assessment using the Dimension of Learning model.* Alexandria, VA: ASCD.

Campbell, D. M., P. B. Cignetti, B. J. Melenyzer, D. H. Nettles, and R. M. Wyman. 1995. *How to develop a professional portfolio.* Boston: Allyn and Bacon.

Danielson, C. 1996. *Enhancing professional practice: A framework for teaching.* Alexandria, VA: Association for Supervision-Curriculum Development.

Dietal, R. J., J. L. Herman, and R. A. Knuth. 1991. *What does research say about assessment?* Chicago: North Central Regional Educational Laboratory.

Gandal, M., and J. Vranek. 2001. Standards: Here today, here tomorrow. *Educational Leadership* 58, 1 (Sept.): 7–13.

Goethals, M. S., and R. A. Howard. 2000. *Student teaching: A process approach to reflective practice.* Upper Saddle River, NJ: Merrill/Prentice Hall.

Hall, B., and Hewitt-Gervais. 1999. The application of student portfolios in primary/intermediate self-contained/multi-age classroom environments. Paper presented at the annual meeting of the American Educational Research Association, Montreal.

Herman, J. L. 1992. What research tells us about good assessment. *Educational Leadership,* 49 (8), 74–78.

Hill, B., and C. Ruptic. 1994. *Practical aspects of authentic assessment: Putting the pieces together.* Norwood, MA: Christopher-Gordon.

McNeil, L. M. 1999. Local reform initiatives and a national curriculum: Where are the children? In *The hidden consequences of a national curriculum* (pp. 14–17). Washington, DC: American Educational Research Association.

McNergney, R. F., and J. M. Herbert. 2001. *Foundations of education.* Boston: Allyn and Bacon.

Nott, L., C. Reeve, and R. Reeve. 1992. Scoring rubrics: An assessment option. *Science Scope* 15, 6: 44–45.

Nuthall, D. D. 1992. Performance assessment: The message from England. *Educational Leadership* 49, 8 (May): 54–57.

O'Neil, J. 1992. Putting performance assessment to the test. *Educational Leadership* 49, 8 (May): 14–19.

Pate, P. E. 1993. Designing rubrics for authentic assessment. *Middle School Journal* 25, 2: 25–27.

Ryan, K., and J. M. Cooper. 2000. *Those who can teach.* 9th ed. Boston: Houghton Mifflin.

Tomlinson, C. A. 2001. Grading for success. *Educational Leadership* 58, 6 (March): 12–15.

Wente, P. J. 2001. *The student teaching experience: Cases for the classroom.* Upper Saddle River, NJ: Merrill / Prentice Hall.

Wiggins, G. 1989. A true test: Toward more authentic and equitable assessment. *Phi Delta Kappan* 70: 703–714.

———. 1998. *Educative assessment: Designing assessments to inform and improve student performance.* San Francisco: Jossey-Bass.

9

Reflection and Professional Development

"Who dares to teach must never cease to learn."
—*John Cotton Dana*

Standard #9   Teachers are reflective practitioners who continually evaluate the effects of their choices and actions on others (students, parents, and other professionals in the learning community) and who actively seek opportunities to grow professionally.

Performance Indicators: *The teacher . . .*
- Realizes this is the initial stage of a lifelong learning process and that self-reflection is one of the key components of that process. While concentration is, of necessity, inward and personal, the role of colleagues and school-based improvement activities increases as time passes. The teacher's continued professional improvement is characterized by self-reflection, working with immediate colleagues and teammates, and meeting the goals of a personal professional development plan.
- Continually evaluates the effects of choices and actions and actively seeks opportunities to grow professionally.

Vignette   Jared disagreed with the midterm evaluation that Mrs. Gonzales, his college supervisor, had written about him. The two sat down to discuss the matter and determine what could be done. Mrs. Gonzales informed Jared that his lessons were dull and unimaginative; lacking creativity. Jared replied that his cooperating teacher welcomed him to use her lesson plans and need not write his own (Wentz 2001).

Fundamental Principles

A good teacher is one who matches instruction to the needs of students. This teacher spends much time evaluating the implications of one's teaching decisions in the classroom. This is the mark of a reflective practitioner. Such self-reflection leads to greater knowledge about the students, about the subject being taught, and about the act of teaching (Campbell, et al. 1995, 55).

According to the thesaurus of the Educational Resources Information Center (ERIC) database, professional development refers to activities to enhance professional career growth. Such activities may include individual development, continuing education, and in-service education, as well as curriculum writing, peer collaboration, study groups, and peer coaching or mentoring. Hargreaves and Fullan (1992) expand the definition to include "the sum total of formal and informal learning experiences throughout one's career from pre-service teacher education to retirement" (326). Professional development helps teachers not only learn new skills but also develop new insights into pedagogy and their own practice, and explore new or advanced understandings of content and resources. In essence, professional development refers to relevant content, strategies, and organizational supports that ensure the preparation and career-long development of teachers whose competence, expectations, and actions influence the teaching and learning environment. It serves as the bridge between where prospective and experienced teachers are now and where they will need to be to meet the new challenges of guiding all students in achieving higher standards of learning and development (Birman, et al. 2000).

The principles of professional development include but are not limited to:

1. Focusing on individual, collegial, and organizational improvement

2. Focusing on teachers as central to student learning, yet including all other members of the school community

3. Respecting and nurturing the intellectual and leadership capacity of teachers, principals, and others in the school community

4. Enabling teachers to develop further expertise in subject content, teaching strategies, uses of technologies, and other essential elements in teaching to high standards

5. Promoting continuous inquiry

The challenge for all professionals is to select choices that give the most meaning to their professional lives. The following list of professional development possibilities, although unoriginal and far from being comprehensive, shows the wide variety of excellent professional growth opportunities that are available: (1) self-reflection through recall and/or videotaped lessons, (2) observation and discussion with colleagues and/or administration, (3) professional reading, (4) attending workshops, conferences, and conventions, (5) becoming active in the profession at the local, state, or national level, (6) searching the Internet for selected topics of interest, (7) continuing-education coursework, (8) presenting at local, state, regional, or national conferences, and (9) professional writing and research.

Reflection is deemed an important component of the teaching profession. INTASC, NBPTS, and Pathwise (PRAXIS III) formalize the expectations for teaching reflection (Cady 1998). One of the five tenets of the national board certification is the ability to reflect on practice. The tenet states, "Teachers think systematically about their practice and learn from experience." Reflection on one's classroom practices encourages growth. Learning to teach well is a result of reflective practice (Goethals and Howard 2000). As teachers engage in instruction and then reflect on it, the process offers insights into various dimensions of teaching

and learning that can lead to better teaching (Schon 1987). Ross, Bondy, and Kyle (1993) describe characteristics and abilities essential to developing effective reflective techniques. The teacher must:

1. Demonstrate introspection, responsibility, and open-mindedness

2. See things from multiple perspectives

3. Use adequate evidence to support or assess decisions

4. Use educational, ethical, and practical criteria

As teachers engage in reflection, they become more thoughtful about their practice and, consequently, more effective teachers.

Self-reflection also takes place in considering the teacher's relationships with parents and educational professionals. These relationships require the teacher to constantly re-evaluate the effects of his or her decisions on all who are involved with the education of the students (Campbell, et al. 1995). Communication with families involves keeping them informed of events in a class, such as procedures and grading systems, and of the academic and social progress of their children. It may also involve engaging parents in the actual instructional program. Danielson (1996) reminds us that while parents vary enormously in how active a part they can take in their children's learning, most parents care deeply about the progress of their children and appreciate meaningful participation.

Regarding staff development as it relates to in-house observations and discussions, research has identified three structural features that set the context for professional development and three core features that characterize the processes that occur during a professional development experience:

- **Forum:** Was the activity structured as a "reform" activity (study group, teacher network, mentoring relationship, committee or task force, internship, for example)?

- **Duration:** How many hours did participants spend in the activity and over what span of time did the activity take place?

- **Participation:** Did groups of teachers from the same school, department, or grade level participate collectively, or did teachers from different schools participate individually?

- **Content focus:** To what degree did the activity focus on improving and deepening teachers' content knowledge?

- **Active learning:** What opportunities did teachers have to become actively engaged in a meaningful analysis of teaching and learning?

- **Coherence:** Did the professional development activity encourage continued professional communication among teachers and incorporate experiences that are consistent with teachers' goals and aligned with state standards and assessments (Birman, et al. 2000)?

"Continuing development is the mark of a true professional. Committed teachers invest much energy in staying informed and increasing their skills. Content knowledge is one area where teachers can grow and develop professionally" (Danielson 1996, 115). Learning is accomplished when the students are presented with current, up-to-date, relevant information. This can only take place when the teacher is prepared. The greater the skills and knowledge of the teacher, the more the students will benefit. What teachers know and how they present their knowledge to their classes depend on their professional development. In-service education is one means by which the teacher can keep up to date. This kind of education, concerned with activities engaged in by professional teaching personnel, is planned by school or professional organizations and agencies or both. Its purposes are to improve teacher competencies in teaching and to improve the standards of the profession in general. Continuing-education contact hours are another method of providing opportunities for professional growth and development. Activities often take the form of a single meeting or a series of meetings referred to as workshops or institutes.

To keep abreast of current information, teachers must be familiar with a variety of resources. Resources are necessary for developing and maintaining successful programs as well as for staying current in the content. A variety of carefully selected resources maximizes the quality of instruction by making learning experiences more effective and exciting. Furthermore, varied resources facilitate the ways in which students learn. This may include reading professional educational journals. "Most teachers can profit from a focus on the latest work in pedagogical research and its application to classroom practice" (Danielson 1996, 115). "Expanding developments in information technology are yet another vehicle for intense professional development" (Danielson 1996, 115). Teachers have easy access to the Internet, where more and more vendors are providing valuable information for instructional purposes.

Professional organizations offer viable opportunities for professional development. Teachers join these organizations at the local, state, regional, and national levels. Involvement and contribution may include membership, attendance at conferences or conventions, presentations, and/or committee work. In any event, these professional organizations are intended to help practitioners in being as effective as possible at the work site and in finding ways to make learning a more positive experience for students.

Teachers may also find it useful to conduct local research in the classroom to evaluate more directly what works, what does not; what is worth trying again, what may need to be revised/modified/discarded. The results can be shared with colleagues through conference presentations and/or articles.

Because the teaching profession is a dynamic and changing field, teachers cannot rely solely on their past preparation and experiences. Adequate undergraduate and graduate preparation in education alone does not ensure continued competency. The teacher should keep abreast of latest developments in the field. This is essential if teachers are to help students translate what they learn in the classroom to real-life experiences.

Questions for Reflection

- What are several examples of professional growth?

- How would you define a self-reflective practitioner?

- How are in-service and continuing education opportunities similar or dissimilar?

- What types of professional organization involvement are common place for educators?

Commentary on Standard #9

DIANE HOFFBAUER | Ed.D., Director of Curriculum and Instruction, North Slope Borough School District, Barrow, Alaska

Teachers from across the North Slope Borough School District in Alaska gather to learn about a new health curriculum. The teachers in Barrow, the hub of the district, meet in a district classroom and teachers from the seven rural Inupiat villages gather on the compressed video, distance-delivery system. If everything goes right with the satellite, 20 teachers from across 90,000 square miles can learn at the same time about new teaching ideas and materials. Professional development is critical for all teachers, and is an important part of all school districts.

As a new teacher, you will find yourself involved in professional growth from the day you start your first teaching job and are required to learn about a reading curriculum. Early in the year, your principal will talk with you about professional goals and evaluation plans for the year. You will soon see that professional development ranges from traditional models to more current practices using professional portfolios, mentoring, peer coaching, and networking. Becoming active in your local, state, and national education associations will provide you with additional opportunities for on-going professional growth, development, and advancement.

Important keys to continual professional growth include valuing your learning, knowing how you best learn, and establishing habits to ensure your professional growth. Consider how you will meld your educational and life experiences with your practice in the classroom and in school. Determine how you will solve the immediate and long-term dilemmas in your new assignment. Reflect on how your actions will impact your students. Evaluate the methods you will use to determine if your actions were effective or not. Consider how you can become a positive presence in your classroom, school, and community. These questions and others are best answered through thoughtful reflection on your practice, through reading, through relationships and dialogue with colleagues, and by actively seeking out professional development opportunities.

Lack of time to reflect is often the excuse offered by practitioners who are reluctant to take ownership in their professional development. They may tell you they do not have time to think about their practice. Too often educator attitudes mirror a belief that professional development is the responsibility of someone else, when in reality it belongs to you, the teacher.

To become the successful, effective educator we all aspire to be, you must become the habitual reflector. To become a good teacher, you must take time each day to reflect on your practice while sponging feedback from one or more colleagues.

Take fifteen minutes at the end of your day to relax and think about how the day went. Consider what worked and what did not. Think about your feelings throughout your day. Finally, record your impressions. Over time, a pattern will emerge to guide you in setting a course for your professional development. Patterns will emerge, problems and their potential solutions will come clear, and a focus on student learning will continue. Reflection is a critical piece in becoming a skillful teacher.

As you continue with your reflection, you will find a need for dialogue with a colleague you know and trust. You may or may not have excellent supportive colleagues. You may or may not have a principal willing to provide you with an ear and ideas. However, within your school, there is a colleague who would welcome the opportunity to revisit their first year of teaching by collaborating with you.

You must commit to involving others in your professional development for it to occur. Keep in mind that some teachers, whether experienced or not, do not offer help or ask for assistance without invitation, so do not hesitate to ask.

While some schools have established mentoring and/or peer coaching programs, most do not. Demonstrate your commitment to continued learning by stepping out of your classroom and seeking a mirror, a guide, and a trusting colleague with whom to collaborate. Reciprocal classroom observations and dialogue will also be of great benefit.

Beyond reflection and collaboration, you will find yourself facing students with assorted academic and social obstacles to learning. Thoughtful consideration of and planning for the cultural, language, and gender differences of your students further promote learning.

You may choose to conduct an in-class research project or you may want to identify and implement an intervention strategy. In either case, the key is maintaining a focus on student growth and a clear eye on observable data to demonstrate the effectiveness of your intervention. This is a repetitive process of identifying, designing, implementing, and assessing.

As you enter your career, it is to your benefit and ultimately to your students, their parents, and your community for you to become an effective, successful, and engaged teacher. Actively search out people and opportunities to support your needs and wishes. Welcome new ideas, programs, and materials as a way to expand your own thinking and improve your classroom practice. Engage in thoughtful practice, reflect and seek feedback on your practice, observe other teachers, take advantage of staff development opportunities, read, and continue your education. Professional development is the foundation to your success as a teacher and to your sense of accomplishment and professional pride.

Reflection and Professional Development Self-Assessment

The teacher is a reflective practitioner who continually evaluates the effects of his/her choices and actions on others (students, parents, and other professionals in the learning community) and who actively seeks out opportunities to grow professionally.

Knowledge/Performance Indicators	*Yes**	*Not Sure*	*No*
1. I understand the historical and philosophical foundations of education.	2	1	0
2. I understand methods of inquiry, self-assessment, and problem-solving strategies for use in professional self-assessment.	2	1	0
3. I understand the influences of the teacher's behavior on student growth and learning.	2	1	0
4. I know major areas of research on teaching and of resources available for professional development.	2	1	0
5. I understand the role of reflection and self-assessment in continual learning.	2	1	0
6. I understand the value of critical thinking and self-directed learning.	2	1	0
7. I understand professional responsibility and the need to engage in and support appropriate professional practices for self and colleagues.	2	1	0
8. I use classroom observation, information about students, and research as sources for evaluating the outcomes of teaching and learning and as a basis for reflecting on and revising practice.	2	1	0
9. I use professional literature, colleagues, and other resources to support development as both a student and a teacher.	2	1	0
10. I collaboratively use professional colleagues within the school and other professional arenas as supports for reflection, problem solving, and new ideas, actively sharing experiences, and seeking and giving feedback.	2	1	0
11. I understand standards of professional conduct in the state Code of Ethics for _____.	2	1	0
12. I understand the responsibility for obtaining and maintaining licensure, the role of the teacher as a public employee, and the purpose and contributions of educational organizations.	2	1	0

---

* A "Yes" response indicates that you can describe, document, and cite examples related to your student teaching assignment.

Self-Assessment Summary and Reflection

1. Which Knowledge/Performance Indicators can I currently describe, document, and cite examples?

_____

_____

2. Which Knowledge/Performance Indicators need some work or improvement?

_____

_____

3. What specific actions can I take to enrich my knowledge or skill in this area?

_____

_____

Activity 9.1   I Did What?

Context   Teachers know how important it is to reflect on a lesson. They reflect to discover ways to improve their teaching, to make learning more interesting for their students, and to set goals for themselves.

Purpose   This activity will help you focus your reflection time in order to become a more effective teacher.

Directions   Videotape a lesson. View the tape at least twice and then answer the questions.

1. How did you start the class? How much time was spent on attendance, answering questions, etc., before the students were engaged in a learning activity?

   _____

   _____

2. How did you let the students know your objective?

   _____

   _____

3. Were you organized and prepared throughout the lesson? How could an observer tell?

   _____

   _____

4. Were your directions and instructions clear to the students? How do you know?

   _____

   _____

5. In general, were your students on task throughout the lesson? Was there a time when a number of students were off task? What did they do?

   _____

   _____

   What did you do to bring them back on task, and how successful were you?

   _____

   _____

6. What evidence shows that the students were learning?

   _____

   _____

7. Watch a portion of the tape with the sound off. Describe your body language and movement and note whether something is effective or distracting (e.g., hand gestures, pacing, movement around the room).

   _____

   _____

8. Listen carefully to your enunciation and grammar (e.g., gonna, yup, "good/well" usage). Listen also for slang terms, overused words, or casual, nonprofessional language (e.g., ok, you guys, you know). Note those items that you want to improve/change.

   _____

   _____

9. What were the strengths of this lesson?

   _____

   _____

10. What would you do differently if you were to teach this lesson again?

   _____

   _____

Activity 9.2   How Would You Have Handled It?

Context   When students misbehave, teachers have a variety of ways to respond and often must decide on the spot which course of action to take. Afterward, there is time to reflect and evaluate the effectiveness of the response and discover ways to avoid the student misbehavior in the future.

Purpose   Inexperienced teachers can be flustered by unexpected student behaviors and may not know how to respond. This activity will direct your reflection after an incident and allow you to be better prepared in the future.

Directions   Briefly describe a classroom management or discipline incident that happened recently and answer the questions.

1. Describe the student(s) involved and what happened.

_____

_____

2. What was your reaction/response?

_____

_____

3. Did the student break a rule? _____ What was the student's response or explanation for the behavior?

_____

_____

4. Has the student behaved this way before? _____ What interventions have you tried with this student?

_____

_____

5. Did you select an appropriate time or place to discuss the incident with the student? _____
   Were you calm? _____ Unemotional? _____

   What changes would you make in your behavior?

_____

_____

   What pleased you about your behavior?

_____

_____

6. What do you know about the student that helps put the behavior in context (e.g., special needs, new to class, easily frustrated)?

_____

_____

7. Was there a need to involve other adults (e.g., principal, parent, another teacher)?_____ Describe what you need to do as a follow-up.

_____

_____

8. How has this incident affected your feelings toward the student?

_____

_____

9. What are other ways you could have handled this incident?

_____

_____

10. What advice and/or support did your cooperating teacher give you?

_____

_____

Activity 9.3 A.O.K.

Context Cooperating teachers need to evaluate student teachers and often are asked to use a rating scale. The evaluation can be formative (designed to foster improvement and goal setting) or summative (final rating or ranking).

Purpose By knowing what's important to and expected of teachers, you can "grade" yourself on your progress toward the ideal.

Directions Rate yourself with these criteria. You may want to make a copy for your cooperating teacher to complete and then compare results.

A= Area of strength

O= Observable, but inconsistent

K= Keep on working

1. _____ Takes initiative; sees what needs to be done
2. _____ Follows through on responsibilities
3. _____ Is prompt; completes work in timely fashion
4. _____ Spends the time necessary to do the work required
5. _____ Does more than is expected
6. _____ Listens well
7. _____ Asks for and accepts feedback
8. _____ Reflects on own teaching
9. _____ Takes responsibility for own behavior
10. _____ Comfortable working with other adults
11. _____ Works well in team situation
12. _____ Respects confidentiality
13. _____ Is willing to take risks
14. _____ Holds high but realistic expectations for self
15. _____ Dresses, talks, and acts in professional manner
16. _____ Holds high expectations for students
17. _____ Treats all students fairly
18. _____ Shows a respect for all students
19. _____ Sees students as individuals
20. _____ Greets students and treats them courteously
21. _____ Helps each student be successful
22. _____ Interacts with students in a professional manner, not as a pal
23. _____ Models expected behavior for students
24. _____ Relates positively to students
25. _____ Is enthusiastic

26. _____ Uses humor appropriately

27. _____ Acknowledges students' appropriate behavior

28. _____ Understands students' perspective

29. _____ Speaks clearly and with inflection

30. _____ Enjoys students and teaching

Activity 9.4   Dear Diary

Context   Teachers reflect on their teaching. They also keep records of what they do each year—units, successful lessons, things to remember, to-do lists, and a variety of other things that will help them in years to come.

Purpose   What to collect; what to save? "I didn't even think of that!" This activity will help you know what's important to record and save.

Directions: Part 1   In a notebook or journal make daily (or at least three per week) entries. Use the checklist to direct what you *record* and *reflect* on during the week.

1. _____ Lesson or activity that worked—and why

2. _____ Lesson or activity that didn't work, why, and how I can change it

3. _____ Student who was successful or achieved a new skill

4. _____ Student who wasn't successful and what I can do to reteach

5. _____ I learned . . .

6. _____ I was surprised . . .

7. _____ Something my cooperating teacher did that I would like to try

Directions: Part 2   In a notebook or portfolio keep a copy or description of these items.

1. Lesson plans

2. Unit outlines

3. List of meetings, in-services, conferences, and workshops attended

4. List of meetings and conversations with parents

5. Photos and diagrams of room arrangement, displays, student activities

6. Study guides, project expectations, rubrics, and checklists

7. Parent–teacher conference preparation and procedures

8. Daily schedule and yearly calendar

9. Preparation and projects for Open House, Parents' Night, programs and fairs

10. Beginning of year to-do list

11. Equipment, material, and resources available and used

12. School and district policies

13. Procedures and resources for special education and social services referral

14. Documentation of intervention strategies used with individual students

15. Discipline policies and classroom rules

16. Classroom procedures and routines

17. Copies or photos of student work

18. Examples of student health file, cumulative file, and report card

Case Study

Alicia was doing a great job in her student teaching assignment. The students were learning, her cooperating teacher was pleased with her lessons, and her university supervisor gave her positive feedback. Eager to grow and be a better teacher, at one of her conferences with her supervisor Alicia set a goal to give more specific feedback to the students. She was already giving the students many affirmations such as "great job," "good thinking," and "correct answer." Now she wanted to use statements like, "Great answer. You remembered what we learned yesterday." and "I can tell that you used your work time wisely."

Another strategy that Alicia used to reach her goal was to write on a sticky note a personal message to each student. She wrote at least one positive thing about their classroom behavior and cited specific examples. This took a long time, but she was glad that she did it.

- Would you have done the things that Alicia did to reach her goal? Why or why not?
- What other things could she have done?
- Should she continue to write weekly notes to the students? Why or why not?
- Do you think that the students appreciated all the time that Alicia put in to writing the notes? Does it matter if they did or didn't?

Student-to-Student Tips

✔ Enjoy the experience—you've worked hard to get here. *Andrew, secondary student teacher*

✔ Relax and be yourself. Don't be all business. Laugh and show your personality. *Kris, secondary student teacher*

✔ Come in with the expectation that you'll have no free time and your entire commitment is to student teaching. Every minute of your free time is devoted to that. Then when you have some free time you'll be pleasantly surprised. *Ochan, secondary student teacher*

✔ Get lots of sleep. Be prepared for no social life. *Fiona, secondary student teacher*

✔ Enjoy it while you are there. Each day is so special. *Stephanie, elementary student teacher*

✔ Save copies of neat worksheets used by you or your teacher. Write down ideas or take pictures of the things you do. *Alicia, elementary student teacher*

✔ Remember that you'll have good days and bad days, just like a regular teacher. When you have bad days, think about all of the good days you've had and remind yourself that tomorrow is a new day! *Megan, elementary student teacher*

✔ Accentuate your positives instead of worrying about your negatives. *Amy, elementary student teacher*

✔ Journal every day. *Joleen, elementary student teacher*

✔ Take time for yourself. *Holly, elementary student teacher*

✔ Take all your expectations for student teaching and throw them out the window. Go in with an open mind. Don't waste time trying to make everything fit your expectations. Take things as they come. *Teri, elementary student teacher*

✔ Make sure to make each day worthwhile, because it's over too quickly. *Mulki, secondary student teacher*

✔ Organize the material that your cooperating teacher shares with you, but don't do this until you are done teaching. Going through the material then brings back a lot of memories. *Heather, elementary student teacher*

✔ Show initiative. Get to school early and stay until things are done. *Abang, secondary student teacher*

✔ Watch other teachers. Pick up as much as you can while you are still a student. *Erin, elementary student teacher*

✔ Don't be afraid to get constructive criticism. *Sonja, secondary student teacher*

✔ Write down what you do and learn in order to be able to remember and use it again when you have your own class. (This is the idea behind the journal that *your university supervisor* wants you to keep.) *Naomi, secondary student teacher*

✔ Go to every meeting that you can to learn about what is going on in the school. *Paul, secondary student teacher*

✔ Seek out feedback from everyone, not just your cooperating teacher and *university supervisor*. Talk to your grade level teachers, substitutes, the principal, others at lunch. *Tzong, elementary student teacher*

✔ Remember that student teaching is a learning experience. If you have a bad day—and I did—just remember that tomorrow is a new day. *Leah, elementary student teacher*

✔ Start looking for things to put in your portfolio right away. Collect student work from lessons that go well. *Darrin, elementary student teacher*

✔ Be there early and stay late. That gives you time to talk to your teacher and to be more prepared. Plus, it looks more professional. *Nissa, elementary student teacher*

✔ Don't take everything too seriously. If you put too much pressure on yourself, you worry too much. It is manageable, even if it seems overwhelming at first. *Sanji, elementary student teacher*

✔ Keep things in perspective. Smile at yourself. *Dean, elementary student teacher*

Bibliography

Birman, B. F., L. Desimone, A. C. Porter, and M. S. Garet. 2000. Designing professional development that works. *Educational Leadership* (May): 28–33.

Cady, J. 1998. Teaching orientation teaching. *Education* 118, 3: 459–471.

Campbell, D. M., P. B. Cignetti, B. J. Melenyzer, D. H. Nettles, and R. M. Wyman. 1995. *How to develop a professional portfolio.* Boston: Allyn and Bacon.

Danielson, C. 1996. *Enhancing professional practice: A framework for teaching.* Alexandria, VA: Association for Supervision—Curriculum Development.

Goethels, M. S., and R. A. Howard. 2000. *Student teaching: A process approach to reflective practice.* Columbus, OH: Merrill/Prentice Hall.

Hargreaves, A., and M. G. Fullan. 1992. *Understanding teacher development.* New York: Teachers College Press.

Ross, D. D., E. Bondy, and S. W. Kyle. 1993. *Reflective teaching for student improvement: Elementary curriculum and methods.* New York: Macmillan.

Schon, D. 1987. *Educating the reflective practitioner.* San Francisco: Jossey-Bass.

Wentz, P. J. 2001. *The student teaching experience: Cases from the classroom.* Upper Saddle River, NJ: Merrill/Prentice-Hall.

10

Collaboration, Ethics,
and Relationships

"A teacher affects eternity; no one can tell where his/her influence stops."
—*Henry Adams*

Standard #10 The teacher fosters relationships with school colleagues, parents, and agencies in the larger community to support students' learning and well-being.

Performance Indicators: *The teacher . . .*
- Communicates and works cooperatively with families and colleagues to improve the educational experiences at the school.
- Establishes and maintains strong working relationships with parents and members of the school community to support student learning.

Vignette Brant was student teaching in Mr. Suby's 11th-grade English class. For reasons Brant can only guess at, Mr. Suby was demonstrating hostile behavior towards Megan, one of the best students in the 11th-grade class. Besides regular ridicule, Mr. Suby has given Megan very low marks on writing assignments and term papers that Brant frankly thinks are "A" work. As a result, Megan is running a low "C" in English, which has been her best subject. This could mean she will not qualify for the school's National Honors Society. Brant tries to talk with Mr. Suby about the situation, but after telling Brant about a teacher's right and responsibility he threatens to turn in a less then honest student teaching evaluation if Brant continues to "meddle in the affair."

Fundamental Principles

Effective teachers engage in a variety of experiences within and beyond the school that promote a spirit of collaboration, collegiality, and personal growth. They work in cooperative teams, endorse collegial efforts, and seek opportunities to work with parents and the community at large. These teachers recognize the importance of sharing experiences and ideas (Campbell, et al. 1995, 59).

Creating the school community and establishing a healthy climate (one in which teachers, students, and staff come together to learn and to teach) require co-operation and collaboration (Goethals and Howard 2000). A good case has been made for greater collaboration among professionals at schools and between schools and community agencies (Adelman and Taylor 1998; Lawson and Briar-Lawson 1997; Stoner 1995; White and Wehlage 1995). One aim of such collaboration is to develop efficient and effective working relationships that can enhance learning in the educational setting. Teachers join the efforts of others in addressing students' needs and school-related problems (Zabel and Zabel 1996). Within this working relationship that Goethals and Howard (2000) label as collaboration and teamwork, they recommend asking the following questions:

- Is the teacher a team player?
- Is the teacher willing to participate actively in the formation of a dynamic community?
- Is there recognition and respect for each other's competence?
- Is diversity celebrated among the community members, individually and collectively?
- Do members interact with each other to communicate pragmatic concerns and identify common problems?
- Are conflicts resolved through a critical examination process that promotes a wise and decisive course of action?

Being fully cognizant of expectations the teacher holds for oneself (and other colleagues) is an important starting point for reflecting on collaboration and teamwork.

Good collaborators, according to Pugach and Johnson (1995), are willing to invest the time and energy necessary to improve their own professional practice. Improving collaborative skills leads to a sense of collegiality, creating a climate for successful student achievement.

Effective teachers realize the importance of interpersonal skills, communication skills, joint problem solving, decision-making strategies, and conflict resolution strategies in working with others. These skills are necessary to collaborate and work with others to more effectively provide the most productive learning climate for all students.

Howard, Williams, Port, and Lepper (1997) describe factors necessary for successful collaboration:

- Trust (trust grows only after members learn to validate each other's contributions)
- Face-to-face interaction (motivation and skills seem to develop best when the process is structured in a way that facilitates communication and provides support and direction)
- Interpersonal skills on the part of all team members (establish clear agendas and have regular contact)
- Voluntary collaboration (a privilege rather than an obligation)
- Equity among participants (designate a leader and make a record of plans and assignments for follow-up and review)

Collaboration extends beyond the school community. Partnership programs between schools and families/communities are becoming more and more common. Schools are embracing the idea and are encouraging more family/community involvement. The research confirms that when families and communities work together with schools, students do better in school (Epstein 1996; Haynes and Emmons 1997; Henderson and Berla 1995). Parents influence their children's academic achievement by exposing them to intellectually stimulating experiences, directly teaching them, monitoring homework, and communicating with the school. The importance of building partnerships in education is becoming more widely recognized, as young people must be educated to a higher standard than ever before. Families want to support their children's learning more effectively, to work with teachers, and to have a greater choice of schools (Kelley-Laine 1998). Parents also strengthen ties by volunteering at the school, attending conferences, requesting information, and participating in school governance (Eccles and Harold 1996).

Reasons parents look to be involved in school functions include (Kelley-Laine 1998):

- **Student achievement:** Parents wish to improve their children's performance and want to find out how best to do so.
- **Parental education:** The need to support a child's learning compels some parents to attend classes that cover aspects of the curriculum, or provide information on good parenting, or offer joint literacy activities.
- **Communication:** Parents want to find out more about their children's progress, to find out what happens each day in school, and seek to increase the school's openness.
- **Influence:** Parents wish to influence the curriculum, or to transmit family values and cultures in the school.
- **Support for the school:** Parents recognize that schools often need funds and teachers are overburdened. They may offer to help by fundraising or assisting in other ways.
- **Support from the school:** Parents sometimes need individual help and advice during a family crisis, or they may be interested in attending lectures or workshops on problems that challenge all families (e.g., drug abuse, health issues, the difficulties of adolescence, parenting issues, etc.).

The larger and more diverse a school is, the less likely parents are to be involved. As students are assigned to multiple teachers for various classes, and as teachers teach large numbers of students in staggered classes, close teacher–student relationships are unlikely to develop. Teachers do not get to know their students well. And teachers are unlikely to encourage parental involvement because they find the idea impractical. In these situations, teachers tend to focus on the strongest and weakest students because they seem to require the most attention. The parents of the students of average achievement, then, may be among those least likely to be linked closely to schools (Dornbusch and Glasgow 1996).

Positive connections between home and school also may be influenced by social networks and social class. The social networks to which parents belong, which may be influenced by their linguistic and ethnic backgrounds, can affect their attitudes and beliefs about schools. Some research suggests that middle- and upper-class parents are more likely to think of education as a joint responsibility of school and home, while parents of lower socioeconomic status are more likely to view education as the teacher's job (Lareau 1996). As children grow older, their parents become less likely to be involved in school activities (Alexander and Entwisle 1996).

Parents are important resources for meeting the mission and goals of schools. Site-based decision making engages parents and teachers working together in planning school improvement. How do parents become more involved as active partners in a collaborative relationship between home and school? Communication is the key; whether that method be direct, personal, informative, and/or interactive. For effective communication to occur between teachers and parents, input from both is essential. Parents need a method of communication that regularly provides them with information regarding homework, classwork, and classroom behavior (Giannetti and Sagarese 1998). Comer (1984) discusses the emotional support that children need in order to learn, indicating that such an environment of support is optimally created when families and school personnel cooperate. Rich, Mattox, and VanDien (1979) point to the improvements in student attendance and behavior and in parent–teacher relations that happen as a result of parental involvement. Bennett (1986) cites the benefits to parents themselves as they gain greater confidence and expertise in helping their children succeed academically. Epstein (1996) has been one of the principal researchers on the important topic of parental involvement and its effects on student achievement, parental attitudes, and education practices. She identified five categories of parent involvement in the education of their children: (1) providing for children's basic needs, (2) communicating with school staff, (3) volunteering or providing assistance at their child's school, (4) supporting and participating in learning activities with their children at home, and (5) participating in governance and advocacy activities.

There appears to be a positive relationship between parent involvement in education and the progress that students make in academics and in their attitudes toward learning. Parent involvement takes many forms and can occur at home, in the school, and in the community. School personnel have an obligation to reach out to all families so that all students may benefit. Because modern communities are increasingly diverse in their social, cultural, and linguistic composition, flexibility and multiple approaches for reaching out are needed to ensure that no one is excluded. Schools seeking parental participation and input need to recognize parents as the primary educators of their children and be both flexible and innovative in reaching out to the diverse community. For example, such practices as evening or early morning conferences, childcare during meetings, parent education classes, personal contact with families, and learning activities for families to use at home are effective strategies which enable families to become involved in their children's education.

Collaboration within a community is also a key issue. Schools must work with all aspects of the community to ensure that students and their families have access to needed health and social services as well as academic services. Schools and teachers need to be sensitive to racial, ethnic, and economic differences, as well as language and literacy obstacles; lack of sensitivity can inhibit communication and collaboration. Effective teachers learn how to successfully use churches, civic, and community-based organizations as resources and as ways of motivating and encouraging positive growth in students (Campbell, et al. 1995). As an illustration, school health services function to support the process of education and ensure that children are healthy enough to participate in the educational process. Most schools operate under the philosophy that the parent is the primary provider of health services. School health services should play a supplemental role to the parent. Most often the school nurse is the key person for these services. For example, health services provided by some schools and communities to their students would include: immunizations, vision and hearing screening, speech therapy, postural screening, management of asthmatics, etc. School health services were never intended to replace the existing health care delivery system of the community. They are, however, often the best location for providing collaborative services by other community agencies. When the school does not have the resources necessary to meet the health needs of students, it is imperative to identify appropriate prevention, detective, and treatment services provided by community agencies.

Health observation is an important part of the school health appraisal. The classroom teacher makes daily informal observations of the student. Every teacher should carefully observe his/her students for possible departures from normal health. Abnormal health conditions should be obvious to the teacher, because frequent prior observations have provided a base line for comparing day-to-day changes. Therefore, the first line of school health services should be preliminary evaluation by classroom teachers. Teachers are not professional health workers, but they should be able to detect possible health problems and make a referral according to school policies. In some districts, the teacher makes the referral to the school administration, in more cases to the school nurse; but in other instances, the teacher may contact the parent directly or community resource agency that is partnered with the school district. Teachers, in accordance with school policy, should make every effort to assist students in need and their parents in taking advantage of community resources.

Developing appropriate relationships with colleagues, parents, and the community is a significant segment of teaching. The quality of the interactions between the teacher and those involved with learning programs affects the success of the teacher (Goethals and Howard 2000).

Questions for Reflection

- In what ways can schools and communities collaborate for improving educational experiences?

- Why are trust and interpersonal skills necessary for effective collaboration?

- How are parents important in supporting student learning?

Commentary on Standard #10

Kathleen M. Rourke, Ph.D., R.N., CHES | Graduate College of Interdisciplinary Arts and Sciences, The Union Institute and University

Collaboration, ethics and relationships, to me, are the fundamentals of teaching. The majority of individuals who choose to teach will say they do so and continue to do so because of the relationships they enjoy with their students. Yet an essential element to excellence in teaching is to move beyond that basic level, on to the universe for the student and the community in which they live. This is often forgotten in the rush to meet goals in proficiency and standardized testing. This is unfortunate as each student is a compilation of relationships for which collaboration is the vehicle to maximizing each student's potential. The day 911 is such a poignant example of how collaboration, ethics, and relationships can be enlisted for the betterment of the student and the community. My own story for 911 offers a good example of how a teacher can use their relationship with a child's parents to improve academic performance and perhaps classroom behavior. During this fall period, I was working in a community close to a crash site. My children remained in the Midwest and were troubled by my not being home and so physically close to such a tragic event. This played out in my son's classroom behavior and ability to concentrate. Yet when availed of an opportunity to find out more from me about events and relationships that might interact with his ability to learn, the teacher asked nothing of us, the parents, as to what if anything might be troubling this ten-year-old and chose to focus instead on the outcome, which was his poor classroom behavior. After four months of difficulty in handling him in class and the resultant poor academic performance, I insisted the school officials know more about my son's relationships, and I unfortunately was the individual that insisted that school officials maintain a better collaborative relationship with us, the parents. The results of this improved understanding of my son's relationships with loved ones in tragic times and a plan to work collaboratively with the parents, paid off with an improvement in his behavior and illustrated the pointless loss of four months of constructive academic work had relationships and collaboration been considered from the outset by the teacher.

Therefore, I am thrilled to read a pre-professional text that encourages student teachers to reach beyond their didactic lesson plans and a quest for excellence in proficiency exam and encourage these young student teachers to understand the multiplicity of relationships that make up each student and their will to learn. As a professor, I have always found that a better understanding of relationships that make up the whole and efforts to collaborate with individuals, groups and communities not only enhances the outcome of my efforts but makes those efforts much more enjoyable and fulfilling in the process.

Collaboration, Ethics, and Relationships Self-Assessment

The teacher fosters relationships with school colleagues, parents, and agencies in the larger community to support students' learning and well-being.

Knowledge/Performance Indicators	*Yes**	*Not Sure*	*No*
1. I understand schools as organizations within the larger community context and understand the operations of the relevant aspects of the systems within which the teacher works.	2	1	0
2. I understand how factors in a student's environment outside of school, including family circumstances, community environments, health and economic conditions, may influence student life and learning.	2	1	0
3. I understand student rights and teacher responsibilities to equal education, appropriate education for students with disabilities, confidentiality, privacy, appropriate treatment of students, and reporting in situations of known or suspected abuse or neglect.	2	1	0
4. I understand the concept of addressing the needs of the whole learner.	2	1	0
5. I understand the influence of use and misuse of tobacco, alcohol, drugs, and other chemicals on student life and learning.	2	1	0
6. I understand data practices.	2	1	0
7. I collaborate with other professionals to improve the overall learning environment for students.	2	1	0
8. I collaborate in activities designed to make the entire school a productive learning environment.	2	1	0
9. I consult with parents, counselors, teachers of other classes and activities within the school, and professionals in other community agencies to link student environments.	2	1	0
10. I identify and use community resources to foster student learning.	2	1	0
11. I establish productive relationships with parents and guardians in support of student learning and well-being.	2	1	0
12. I understand mandatory reporting laws and rules.	2	1	0

* A "Yes" response indicates that you can describe, document, and cite examples related to your student teaching assignment.

Self-Assessment Summary and Reflection

1. Which Knowledge/Performance Indicators can I currently describe, document, and cite examples?

   _____

   _____

2. Which Knowledge/Performance Indicators need some work or improvement?

   _____

   _____

3. What specific actions can I take to enrich my knowledge or skill in this area?

   _____

   _____

Activity 10.1   First Days in the Classroom

Context   Teachers value initiative—in their students, in their colleagues, and in student teachers. It's important for student teachers to be involved in the classroom from the very beginning since it helps the students view them as an integral part of their classroom. It also helps student teachers feel connected, and helps cooperating teachers realize that they have responsible, involved colleagues with whom to work.

Purpose   This activity allows you to identify ways to be involved in the classroom and be of help to your cooperating teacher and students. Of course you'll need to do a lot of observing, but you can observe while you do. Teachers must be skilled at doing more than one thing at a time, so here's your chance to start.

Directions

- Plan your first week in the classroom by putting:

   0 before the activities that you will do before the first day

   1 before the activities that you will do the first day

   2 before the activities that you will do the second day and continue on through day 5.

- Check off each item as you complete it.

1. _____ Be clear on expectations and times for arriving at school, eating lunch, leaving school, prep time, breaks, etc.

2. _____ Be familiar with the classroom and school rules and guidelines.

3. _____ Copy, collate, staple, cut materials, prepare transparencies, set up equipment, etc.

4. _____ Correct students' work and/or record scores.

5. _____ Exchange contact information with your cooperating teacher (phone number, e-mail address, preferred method of notifying if absent, etc.)

6. _____ Get a copy of the school's calendar and scheduled events.

7. _____ Give your cooperating teacher a copy of your student teaching calendar and discuss requirements.

8. _____ Know emergency procedures (fire, evacuation, etc.).

9. _____ Learn the names of students in each class (if students exchange classes).

10. _____ Learn the names of your homeroom students.

11. _____ Learn where supplies are kept and how they are distributed.

12. _____ Locate the teacher workroom, copy machine, mailboxes, main office, nurse's office, media center, and lounge.

13. _____ Make a seating chart for your homeroom class.

14. _____ Make seating charts for each class (if students exchange classes).

15. _____ Meet (and observe if appropriate) other adults who work with your students.

16. _____ Organize your desk/table and know where to store personal items.

17. _____ Plan a way to introduce yourself to the students (bio bag, bulletin board, get-acquainted activity, etc.).

18. _____ Prepare make-up work for absent students.

19. _____ Schedule a planning time with your cooperating teacher.

20. _____ Supervise students in the halls or on the playground.

21. _____ Take attendance/lunch count or help/supervise student who does.

22. _____ Teach part of a lesson (introduction, directions, demonstration), give a spelling test, or work with a small group of students.

23. _____ Understand the procedures/expectations for working with paraprofessionals.

24. _____ Work with students (one on one, small groups, monitoring, etc.)

25. _____ Write an introduction letter to the parents.

11
Documentation and Evidence

"What we see depends mainly on what we look for."
—John Lubbock

Reflection is an extremely important component in the documentation of teaching performance. The reflective stage involves the assessment, analysis, and judgment of your specific teaching experiences. And then, most importantly, you must be able to apply your reflective evaluation to future teaching situations. Experience and effort will often improve your reflection skills.

Words of wisdom for teachers:

"If you don't learn from your mistakes, there's no sense making them."—unknown

"If the going is real easy, beware, you may be headed downhill."—unknown

"Seeing yourself as you want to be is the key to personal growth."—unknown

Successful teachers possess a wide range of knowledge and skills. Specifically:

1. They know their subject matter
2. They understand how children learn and develop
3. They understand how students learn differently
4. They know how to deliver efficient and effective lessons to a variety of learners
5. They know how to make the environment conducive to learning
6. They are excellent communicators
7. They are expert planners
8. They know how to assess and evaluate teaching and learning

9. They know how to reflect on teaching and learning
10. They strive for excellence through staff development, collaboration, and professionalism

Introduction

The previous ten chapters of this textbook have been aligned with, and devoted to, each of these attributes of successful teaching and learning.

During the student teaching experience, student teachers are often required to demonstrate their competence in a variety of ways.

Many colleges and universities recommend (or require) their student teachers to document and produce evidence of their teaching and learning knowledge, skills, abilities, competence, and professionalism. Multiple methods of documentation are recommended. One of the common ways evidence is gathered by student teachers is by direct observation and feedback by the cooperating teacher, university supervisor, and/or other teaching professionals. In addition to direct observations, self-assessment and reflection "evidence forms" are often used.

The purpose of this chapter is to provide samples of evidence forms. Several of these sample forms are written in the context of self-assessments.

You may use these evidence forms to assess and evaluate your teaching and learning progress. Many student teachers also find it advantageous to ask a fellow student teacher, cooperating teacher, or university supervisor to observe their teaching and complete the evidence form. Then, using the same evidence form, compare your self-evaluation information with the observer's information. In addition to these forms, your college or university may have other specific evidence forms developed for this purpose.

Evidence forms are designed to help the student teacher focus on specific elements of teaching and learning. Evidence forms may prove to be valuable information. For example, a cooperating teacher or university supervisor may ask you about your contact with your students' parents. If you were using Evidence Form 11.23 (found in this chapter), you would be able to quickly and easily document the parent and family contacts you have made. Or, if you were asked to document your technology skills, Evidence Form 11.19 may be useful. There are 23 sample evidence forms in this chapter.

After the selected evidence forms in this chapter are used, it is recommended that they be filed in a notebook or other location by teaching category, standard, or domain.

One way to organize your evidence forms is by the categories of this textbook as they pertain primarily to:

- Subject matter
- Student learning
- Diverse learners
- Instructional strategies
- Learning environment
- Communication
- Planning instruction
- Assessment and evaluation
- Reflection and professional development
- Collaboration, ethics, and relationships

You will notice some of the evidence forms could appropriately be placed in more than one of the above categories. In such cases, you may duplicate your evidence and put it in multiple categories or, if you prefer, place it only in the most helpful category.

Several of these completed evidence forms may be appropriate for inclusion in your professional or academic portfolio.

Index of Chapter Evidence Forms:

Note: These evidence forms have been adapted from the "Teacher as Professional" packet, Minnesota State University, Mankato.

Final thoughts:

"If you feel you have no faults . . . there's another one."—*unknown*

"The biggest room in the world, is the room for improvement."—*unknown*

Evidence Form 11.1   Lesson Plan Analysis

Name _____   Date _____

Purpose   This checklist may be helpful when preparing for discussions of written lesson plans.

Scale:

2 = Yes
1 = Somewhat
0 = No
NA = Not Applicable

1. _____   Is (are) the objective(s) clearly stated? Does it have clear meaning?

2. _____   Is the objective important enough to spend the allotted time on it?

3. _____   Does the objective match the curriculum to be taught?

4. _____   Does the introductory approach to the lesson show awareness of the interests and concerns of students? Does it relate to prior lessons or current happenings?

5. _____   Did you select the most appropriate teaching procedures?

6. _____   Did you review information students should have learned previously?

7. _____   Are the main points to be learned and remembered clearly identified?

8. _____   Will the lesson help students see relationships to other learning?

9. _____   Did you present information in more than one mode?

10. _____   Do you connect the lesson to the experiences of students from various backgrounds?

11. _____   Are examples provided when appropriate?

12. _____   Have you taken advantage of opportunities to enhance multicultural understanding?

13. _____   Is the lesson procedure likely to stimulate divergent thinking?

14. _____   Does the lesson include active involvement of the students?

15. _____   Does the lesson stress processes as well as recall of information?

16. _____   Is the grouping of students for activities likely to work?

17. _____   Will the activity help the students accomplish the objective?

18. _____   Do the directions for activities seem thoroughly considered? Likely to work?

19. _____   Do the activities seem like they will be "fun" to do?

20. _____   Do the activities allow for any humor or playfulness?

21. _____   Will task management skills be practiced during the activities of the lesson?

22. _____   Does the activity allow for individual differences in ability?

23. _____ Do you have realistic estimates of the time needed for each part of the lesson?

24. _____ Have you allotted time for procedures to wrap up and clean up after the activity?

25. _____ Have you gathered and organized all of the materials you will need?

26. _____ Is the necessary equipment on hand and working?

27. _____ Is the assignment appropriate for reinforcing the lesson objective ?

28. _____ Is the assignment appropriate for independent work? Does the time needed to complete the assignment seem realistic?

29. _____ Will you know if the students have learned the objective? (How?)

30. _____ Have you thought about how you might alter the lesson if your time is shortened? (What is "Plan B"?)

31. _____ Will "Plan B" accomplish the objective also?

Evidence Form 11.2   Teaching through Activities

Name _____   Date _____

Purpose   Answer these questions if you teach courses such as physical education, computer technology, media, the arts, or any class in which students learn through activities.

1. What was your teaching/learning objective? What was actually accomplished during this class period?

   _____

   _____

2. Were you well organized at the beginning of class? For example, was the equipment ready, directions for students established, and little time lost getting started?

   _____

   _____

3. How did the students know where they were to be and what to do as class began?

   _____

   _____

4. What new information was introduced during the class, and how did you do that?

   _____

   _____

5. Was there a clear time schedule for beginning, changing phases of the activity, and cleaning up?

   _____

   _____

6. How did you spend your time? Were you available to help many students during the class?

   _____

   _____

7. Were you repeating to individuals information they should have learned in a group?

   _____

   _____

   _____

8. Were you clearing up misunderstanding, showing new techniques, encouraging individuals and groups?

   _____

   _____

   _____

9. How much of your time was spent in discipline issues?

_____

_____

10. How do you think the students would describe your role in the classroom?

_____

_____

11. Do you usually interact more positively with some students than with others? Why? How can you move toward greater equity?

_____

_____

12. Were the materials and equipment under control (organized at the beginning, available for use, and reorganized at the end)?

_____

_____

13. Were all of the students thoroughly engaged and on-task throughout the class? If not, who was idle or wasting time? How could this be improved?

_____

_____

14. Were safety rules and precautions observed by everyone during the class?

_____

_____

15. What will you do differently next time you conduct this lesson?

_____

_____

Evidence Form 11.3   *Giving Directions*

Name _____ Date _____

Purpose   Giving directions to a large group is often more difficult than anticipated. It is an important classroom skill. Use this checklist to think through all the directions you will need to give before you start. Then, following your class, reflect using this checklist:

Scale:

2 = Yes
1 = Somewhat
0 = No
NA = Not Applicable

1. _____ I had the attention of the class while directions were being given.

2. _____ I told the class clearly and succinctly what they were to do.

3. _____ I made sure the class knew what they were supposed to learn from the activity (unless they were to discover it for themselves).

4. _____ I gave the directions in sequential order.

5. _____ I showed the directions related to actual materials the students would be using.

6. _____ I used a visual aid to help students follow a sequence of steps.

7. _____ If alternatives were permitted, I made the choices clear.

8. _____ I showed an example of a successful product (if appropriate).

9. _____ I cautioned the class about probable pitfalls, but did not overemphasize them.

10. _____ I refrained from over-directing. I did not make decisions that the students could and should be making for themselves.

11. _____ I was clear about the consequences of good work, e.g., grade, transition to next activity, etc.

12. _____ I allowed time for students to ask questions about the directions.

13. _____ I showed flexibility in changing directives that—when re-evaluated under student questioning—clearly would not work.

14. _____ I showed that the assignment had been thought through very carefully—few changes were needed.

15. _____ I did not allow anyone to start until the process of giving directions was over.

16. _____ If a directive was omitted or added later, I found a way to inform all students; I did not yell at them as they were leaving the room.

Evidence Form 11.4   Group Work

Name _____ Date _____

Purpose   Giving class and student directions is often more complex than you might think. Check yourself before and after having your students work in groups.

1. From the directions given to students, do you know what the lesson objective is? (Why are they doing this? Is it clear why working together today is a good idea? Is there something about this lesson that will be better because students share their ideas?)

   _____

   _____

2. Are the size and makeup of the groups workable and appropriate for the lesson?

   _____

   _____

3. From the directions given to students, what are the groups supposed to do? (Write the directions as you told them to students. Would you know exactly how to go about doing the work?)

   _____

   _____

4. Do the students, in fact, know what they are supposed to be doing? (Ask three students, from different groups, what they are supposed to do. Have they convinced you that they know? Does their understanding match yours?)

   _____

   _____

5. What is the end product? What will students produce to show results of their work? Does it fit the objective of the lesson? (Is the description of the end product clear? Describe it here.)

   _____

   _____

6. Do the students seem to know how to go about working collaboratively? (Are you seeing intense, task-oriented behaviors? What dysfunctional behavior do you see?)

   _____

   _____

7. How well does the physical environment support collaborative work? (Can the students see each other? Can they easily share visual materials? Can all the members of the group easily work on the task? Are materials readily available?)

   _____

   _____

   _____

8. Is the noise level of the classroom conducive to/indicative of collaborative work? (Are the students free to talk to each other? Can they hear each other? Do the students seem to be exercising self-discipline regarding noise control?)

_____

_____

9. Is there a clear evaluation plan for this activity? Did they have time to finish? (What will be evaluated? How? Self-evaluation? Peer evaluation? Teacher observation? Product evaluation? Notes to be checked by the teacher? Other . . . ?)

_____

_____

10. Is there a clear signal about when to stop working or to listen for further directions? (timer, bell?)

_____

_____

Evidence Form 11.5   *Maintaining and Enforcing Classroom Rules*

Name _____   Date _____

Purpose   Use this checklist to help you prepare for, or reflect on, a situation involving student discipline.

Scale:

2   =   Yes
1   =   Somewhat
0   =   No
NA =   Not Applicable

1. _____ I expressed disapproval in a convincing manner, but did not show uncontrolled anger.

2. _____ I respected the dignity of the student throughout the encounter.

3. _____ I told the student what rule had been violated.

4. _____ I reprimanded the student privately or with as little public display as possible.

5. _____ I allowed the student time to explain his/her actions.

6. _____ I actually listened to the student's explanation.

7. _____ I maintained an adult role; did not try to be a "buddy" of the student.

8. _____ I did not use aggression to fight aggression.

9. _____ I stuck to this incident; did not "pile up" all previous behaviors of the student.

10. _____ I separated the behavior involved in the violation from an understandable emotional reaction of the student to being accused.

11. _____ I showed concern and caring for the student.

12. _____ I followed preannounced guidelines; did not make up a "last minute" punishment.

13. _____ I made the severity of the punishment fit the importance of the violation.

14. _____ I explained how to show acceptable behavior in the future and made future approval a real, available possibility for the student.

15. _____ I did not use threats of future consequences that would be hard to follow through.

16. _____ I made an effort to solve the problem without excluding the student.

17. _____ I did not seem to be "picking on" the student, if the student had former offenses.

18. _____ I did not seem to be playing favorites, if the student was a "good student."

19. _____ I provided for individual differences without being unfair to others.

20. _____ If warranted, I accepted responsibility for structuring a future situation differently so that the violation would be less likely to occur.

21. _____ I sought assistance from other adult(s) of the school in a timely and appropriate manner.

22. _____ I involved parents in a timely and appropriate manner, if the situation warranted.

23. _____ I provided choices for the student.

Evidence Form 11.6   The Little Things I Do

Name _____   Date _____

Purpose   Take a look at little things today. Are you aware of how you communicate with the students and your peers? You may want to listen to yourself on an audiotape or ask for feedback. Remember, nobody's perfect!

Directions   Check (✔) the statements that are true. Then complete the open-ended prompt associated with each statement.

1. _____   Sometimes my voice is too loud or too soft for the occasion. The situation I need to watch for is . . .

    _____

    _____

2. _____   I tend to overuse expressions, such as "OK," "all right," or "you know." My favorite expression is . . .

    _____

    _____

3. _____   I need to use standard English, rather than "em" for "them" or "gonna" for "going to." The words I need work on are . . .

    _____

    _____

4. _____   I need to avoid slang, such as "you guys" or "grab your books." My pet slang expression is . . .

    _____

    _____

5. _____   I have a physical mannerism that may be annoying because I use it too much. I keep doing this:

    _____

    _____

6. _____   I tend to overuse "I" and "me" when it should be "we" and "us." The last time I did this was when . . .

    _____

    _____

7. _____   I need to say "please," "thank you," and/or "excuse me" more often. One time I omitted this was when . . .

    _____

    _____

8. _____ I need to use people's names more often when greeting/talking with them. I know I should have done that when . . .

_____

_____

9. _____ I need to move around more/less in my classroom. My personal rut is . . .

_____

_____

10. _____ I need to address both sides of the room/front as well as back. I tend to speak more to . . .

_____

_____

11. _____ I need to get students' attention without shouting at them. The last time I needed a strategy was . . .

_____

_____

12. _____ I need to look at people more directly when talking with them. I could have done this better when . . .

_____

_____

13. _____ I need to use body language to show I am an active listener. I could have done this better when . . .

_____

_____

14. _____ When challenged, I should learn to repeat to myself what I think has been said before reacting or replying to the challenge. This strategy would have helped me when . . .

_____

_____

15. _____ When students want me to help too much, I need to respond with a question rather than telling them the answer they should find. This strategy would have helped me when . . .

_____

_____

16. _____ I need to control my frustration and/or anger better than I do. The last time I "lost it" was . . .

_____

_____

17. _____ I need to laugh (later) at frustrating situations; I take it all too seriously. For example . . .

_____

_____

Evidence Form 11.7   Setting Classroom Rules and Behavior Expectations

Name _____   Date _____

Purpose   Use this form to help determine and implement your classroom rules and behavior expectations.

1. What are the rules of your classroom? Put yourself in the place of a student and write the rules you think students should know.

   _____

   _____

   Still more rules? Do you have too many? Which ones can be combined or eliminated?

   _____

   _____

2. How did you go about establishing these rules?

   _____

3. How do students find out what the rules are?

   _____

4. Are you using a system of rewards in your classroom? _____ If so, consider . . .

   a. Does the reward itself send the right message to the student? Example: What messages about diet and dental care are you sending if you use candy as a reward?

   b. Are there enough different occasions for rewards so that all students might have an opportunity to get one?

   c. Are all students held to the same standard to get a reward? Should they be?

   d. Is the reward system effective? Is it getting the behavior you want? Does the system get in your way?

   e. Are there frequent issues among students regarding fairness?

   f. Is the reward itself too important, i.e., the goal rather than a tool to recognize success?

5. What are the consequences when students break a rule?

   _____

   a. Do the students know up front what the consequences are likely to be?

   b. Do you make threats you don't intend to keep?

   c. Are you consistent in applying the consequences?

   d. Are all students held to the same standard? Should they be?

   e. Do the consequences fit the seriousness of the violation?

6. How do you think the students view you, e.g., heavy-handed, fair, nice?

   _____

Evidence Form 11.8   Sample Student Work

Name _____   Date _____

Purpose   Use this form to help gather and document a range of student work under your direction.

Instructional Concept/Topic: _____

Directions

- Attach directions or an assignment that engages students in learning about the concept or topic cited above. Examples are a worksheet, homework or class assignment, project guidelines, or a problem.

- Provide several samples of student work on this assignment. They should reflect the full range of student ability in your class and include feedback you provided to the students on their papers/projects.

- Write a brief commentary about the assignment, answering the following questions:

1. What is the context of the assignment in terms of students' prior knowledge and the other topics they have been studying?

   _____

   _____

2. What do the samples of student work tell you about the students' level of understanding?

   _____

   _____

3. How does the assignment help students develop their understanding?

   _____

   _____

4. What do you plan to do next with these students?

   _____

   _____

Note   Consider including some of these student works in your professional portfolio.

Evidence Form 11.9   Teaching Facts and Concepts

Name _____   Date _____

Purpose   Use these questions and guidelines when you plan to present a considerable amount of new information.

1. List the specific concepts, vocabulary, and/or events "covered" during this lesson. Is your list realistic?

   _____

   _____

2. On your list, mark the items that students must remember and will be tested on.

   _____

   _____

3. If only two or three things can actually be remembered (by some students), what should they be? Mark them on your list.

   _____

   _____

4. How will you indicate to students which material they "absolutely must know"?

   _____

   _____

5. What method will you use to organize your presentation, e.g., outline, flow chart, time line, map, concept web, vocabulary list?

   _____

   _____

6. What modes of presentation will you use to appeal to different learning styles?

   _____

   _____

7. What examples of "fascinating information" will you include to "give life to" the material?

   _____

   _____

8. What student questions do you anticipate? What will you be able to tell about their degree of involvement from their questions, e.g., thinking about the information, sidetracking you, expressing concern about grades?

   _____

   _____

9. How will you help students rehearse and remember the information in future lessons?

_____

_____

10. Will you tell students where and how they can learn more about this topic?

_____

_____

11. Will you connect the new information to what these students already know? How?

_____

_____

12. What bias will you express in presenting this material? Will you be fair? Accurate? Will you clearly identify your opinion (as different from the facts)?

_____

_____

13. What sources will you use in preparing the lesson? Are they biased? What other sources would balance your background?

_____

_____

14. How and when will you find out what students have learned?

_____

_____

15. What can you do to make students more responsible for their own learning?

_____

_____

Evidence Form 11.10   Conducting a Whole-Class Discussion

Name _____ Date _____

Purpose   Consider these guidelines when you are planning for whole-class discussion of a topic. After class, reflect on your skills by marking this checklist. You may want to ask your cooperating teacher or university supervisor to observe you and complete this checklist also. Then compare.

Scale:

2   =   Yes

1   =   Somewhat

0   =   No

NA =   Not Applicable

1. _____ I thoroughly knew the subject we were discussing.

2. _____ I had prepared the students with sufficient background for the discussion.

3. _____ I had materials ready to distribute and/or use.

4. _____ I asked a lot of questions that stimulated thinking.

5. _____ I expected a response from every member of the class at least once.

6. _____ I directed my attention to all parts of the classroom.

7. _____ I moved about the room, making contact with students I often avoid.

8. _____ I gave encouragement and support to students as they responded.

9. _____ I was careful not to inhibit participation by embarrassing students.

10. _____ I used wait time effectively in eliciting responses.

11. _____ When responses were wrong, I validated the response but made sure the errors were eventually corrected.

12. _____ I was able to turn an error into a positive learning experience for the class.

13. _____ When responses were wrong or a student did not respond, I used follow-through questions to guide the student's thinking.

14. _____ I brought a sense of humor to class today, but I was businesslike when appropriate.

15. _____ I really listened to student responses and engaged them in meaningful dialogue.

16. _____ I let every student speak until he/she was finished (within reason, of course).

17. _____ I encouraged students to answer questions raised by peers; not all conversation flowed through me.

18. _____ I permitted students to disagree with my opinions.

19. _____ I encouraged students to extend and clarify their answers.

20. _____ The class discussion resulted in students learning the objective for the lesson, but may also have included learning not anticipated in the plan.

Evidence Form 11.11   *Organizing Classroom Stuff*

Name _____   Date _____

Purpose   Are you an organized person? Most teachers want to be organized but don't always take the time required. Consider each item and determine the best possible resolution. Then, check it off the following list. You don't have to rearrange everything in the classroom. Just know why things are where they are.

1. _____ Does the arrangement of the student desks or tables support instruction?

2. _____ When students work together, can they see and hear each other? Have you considered other patterns, e.g., partners, rows, triads, large horseshoe shape, circle, centers?

3. _____ Does each student have a personal space where things can be kept? Is there a system for keeping these spaces neat and orderly?

4. _____ Is the teacher's desk in the best possible location?

5. _____ Is the work table in the best possible location? Near materials? Noise level OK?

6. _____ Is it possible to move around the room easily? Can you easily reach each student to provide assistance?

7. _____ Where are the materials stored?

    a. _____ Can students easily access those they need to have?

    b. _____ Are teacher materials kept in a separate and safe place?

    c. _____ Are there tests or records in your room that should be secured? Are they?

    d. _____ Are the storage areas neat and orderly? If not, what could be done?

    e. _____ Are bookcases filled with materials you use? Are they orderly?

8. _____ Are there "mailboxes" or some means of giving messages and papers back to students?

9. _____ Where is the pencil sharpener in the room? Can students access it easily?

10. _____ Where is (are) the computer(s)? Is this the best place?

11. _____ Are the drawers in your file cabinet organized in a logical and usable way?

12. _____ Look around the room as though you were seeing it for the first time:

    a. _____ Does the appearance of this room match the image you want to convey?

    b. _____ Are the surfaces of files or bookcases kept clean and orderly?

    c. _____ Is the room attractive? Is it colorful? Is there a touch of humor?

    d. _____ Is student work displayed? Is this attractive enough to feel like a reward?

    e. _____ Does your room show your awareness of diversity?

    f. _____ Are bulletin boards up-to-date and purposeful?

    g. _____ Is there evidence of enrichment activities?

13. _____ Are reminders posted about ideas you want students to follow? Such as:

a. _____ Treating other with respect and rules for routine behaviors

b. _____ Criteria for the arrangement of information on papers, etc.

c. _____ Safety rules or how to get help if needed

d. _____ Fire drill and emergency routes

e. _____ Duties for the day or week

f. _____ School announcements

Evidence Form 11.12   *The Successful Teacher*

Name _____   Date _____

Purpose   Successful teachers have many common attitudes and traits. Getting to be a successful teacher is a long-term idea; you'll grow with experience. But it is time to start now. Use this checklist and talk with your co-operating teacher and university supervisor to identify some specific goals—and make a plan.

Scale:

2 = Yes
1 = Somewhat
0 = No
NA = Not Applicable

Professionalism

1. _____ I take initiative to do what needs to be done.

2. _____ I invest enough time to do a thorough job.

3. _____ I seek and accept feedback.

4. _____ I make time available to share reflections and feedback.

5. _____ I seek help in a timely manner.

6. _____ I use confidential information ethically.

7. _____ I refrain from making hasty judgments.

8. _____ I work well with colleagues in team situations.

9. _____ I listen to colleagues.

10. _____ I express appreciation for help received from colleagues or students.

11. _____ I have high but realistic expectations for self.

12. _____ I am willing to take risks within the limits of good judgment.

13. _____ I show appropriate energy and vitality.

14. _____ I present myself in a professional manner.

15. _____ I show respect for and loyalty to my cooperating teacher.

16. _____ I attend and participate in all scheduled meetings.

Relationship with Students

17. _____ I have high expectations for students.

18. _____ I convince students that I can help them learn the objectives.

19. _____ I treat students fairly, impartially, and courteously.

20. _____ I set an good example physically, mentally, and emotionally.

21. _____ I model good citizenship regarding policies and rules.

22. _____ I show respect for individuals when differences emerge.

23. _____ I encourage students to do their best and be proud of their work.

24. _____ I give positive, accurate feedback to students.

25. _____ I can see matters from a student's point of view.

Communication Skills

26. _____ I appear confident and poised.

27. _____ I have appropriate physical appearance and grooming.

28. _____ I have a pleasant, warm, enthusiastic manner.

29. _____ I use effective and appropriate verbal and nonverbal language.

30. _____ I show a sense of humor.

31. _____ I listen to students.

32. _____ I speak clearly, audibly, and with adequate inflection.

33. _____ I avoid distracting mannerisms.

Evidence Form 11.13   *Picture This!*

Name _____ Date _____

Purpose   Use videotape to become your own coach. Check to see if your school has any special guidelines regarding videotaping. Many schools permit lesson videotaping if only the teacher, not the students, is being videotaped. After you videotape a large segment of your lesson, answer the following questions. Make a plan for improvement. Then, tape another lesson. When you finally have a tape to be proud of, consider including it in your portfolio when you apply for a job.

Scale:

2   =   Yes
1   =   Somewhat
0   =   No
NA =   Not Applicable

1. Did you start the lesson promptly without spending too much time getting organized, taking attendance, or handling individual concerns?

    _____

2. Did you clearly introduce the day's objective(s) at the beginning of the lesson?

    _____

3. Did you appear to be prepared and organized for the day's work?

    _____

4. Did the students understand your directions and begin working without wasting time?

    _____

5. Did you change activities smoothly and frequently enough to prevent boredom and fatigue? How much time was spent in transitions?

    _____

6. What evidence does the tape include to show students were learning? What shows that some were not understanding or paying attention? Why did this happen?

    _____

7. Did you know the answers to students' questions? If you didn't, what did you do?

    _____

8. Did you usually repeat what someone said to you? If so, why? Were there occasions when you should have repeated a question or comment?

    _____

9. If something funny happened or a student made the others laugh, how did you react? Was your reaction appropriate?

    _____

10. What image did you project to your students during the lesson?

_____

11. Did you get seriously sidetracked during your lesson? How much time was spent? Would you want that to happen next time you teach the lesson? Why?

_____

12. What did students probably learn from this lesson that was not included in your plan?

_____

13. If you had been a student in your class today, would you have been interested and involved in the work? Why?

_____

14. If anyone challenged you or disagreed with you, describe your body language and your verbal reaction. Were they appropriate?

_____

15. Did you show impatience with anyone? What prompted this, and how did you show it?

_____

16. Did a few students dominate the discussion or absorb most of your attention? Why? How could you work toward greater equity?

_____

17. Did you model courtesy and good manners, e.g., "please," "thank you," "I'm sorry"?

_____

18. Did you have control of your body movements, e.g., nervous habits, pacing?

_____

19. Examine your use of language during the lesson: Did you use standard English rather than slang? Did you put "ing" endings on your words? Did you use correct expressions, e.g., "want to" not "wanna" or "no" not "nope"? Did you overuse some expressions, e.g., "right," "all right," "like," or "you know"? Did you overuse "I" and "me" when you could have said "we" or "us"?

_____

20. At what points were you proud of your work during this lesson?

_____

21. What will you try to improve before the next taped session?

_____

Evidence Form 11.14   Looking Back

Name _____   Date _____

Purpose   Looking back and reflecting on a specific lesson is one way to determine the lesson's effectiveness.

Directions   Attach a recent lesson plan and answer the following questions.

1. As I reflect on the attached lesson, to what extent were students productively engaged?

    _____

    _____

2. Did the students learn what I intended? Were my instructional goals met? How do I know, or how and when will I know?

    _____

    _____

3. What did I omit in my lesson plan that should have been there?

    _____

    _____

4. Did I alter my goals or instructional plan as I taught the lesson? Why?

    _____

    _____

5. If I had the opportunity to teach this lesson again to this same group of students, what would I do differently? Why?

    _____

    _____

Evidence Form 11.15   *Your Students Did a Great Job!*

Name _____   Date _____

Purpose   How did you tell your students they did extraordinary work? Consider these guidelines when you want to tell your students they have done well.

Which Way Did I Do It?

<u>This way</u> . . .   or   <u>This way</u> . . .

This way . . .	This way . . .
_____ Recognize effort or success at difficult tasks	_____ Give praise indiscriminately without regard for effort or accomplishment
_____ Tell a student what he/she did well	_____ Give positive comments based on how the student "always is"
_____ Help the student appreciate his/her strengths and improvement	_____ Compare the student to others and promote competition
_____ Link success to hard work and determination	_____ Link success to good luck or the deeds of others
_____ Promote pride in a job done well	_____ Promote dependence on external rewards as conditions of further effort
_____ Show sensitivity to effect of adult praise on student's peer relationships	_____ Embarrass student in front of peers
_____ Communicate sincere appreciation for good work	_____ Avoid praising student to prevent inflated ego

Evidence Form 11.16   *Do I Care about My Students?*

Name _____   Date _____

Purpose   Good teaching is a matter of the heart as well as the head. Students respond to teachers who show they care about them. How do you show that you care? Use this checklist to assess yourself.

Scale:

2 = Yes

1 = Somewhat

0 = No

NA = Not Applicable

1. ———   Do I show enthusiasm for working with the students?

2. ———   Do we all have a laugh together now and then—but not at the expense of anyone?

3. ———   Am I willing to laugh at myself and allow students to laugh with me?

4. ———   Do I show respect for every student, regardless of gender, ability, or social status?

5. ———   Do I approach and visit with students about matters outside the lessons?

6. ———   Do I greet the students with a smile and a word of personal warmth each day?

7. ———   Do I tell the group that they have done a good job (when it is merited)?

8. ———   Do I let individual students know that I appreciate their hard work and perseverance?

9. ———   Do I privately thank students for going beyond what is strictly their share of work?

10. ———   Do I show a broad-minded attitude toward differences in student beliefs and values?

11. ———   Can the students trust that I will keep private matters confidential?

12. ———   Do I show empathy when a student is struggling?

13. ———   Am I considerate of students' feelings, even when they seem immature?

14. ———   Do I know some positive, unique qualities or interests about every student?

15. ———   Do I remember and follow up on matters students share with me?

16. ———   Do the students seem to feel comfortable asking for help?

17. ———   Do I listen carefully to both sides of the story when there is a disagreement?

18. ———   Am I loyal to the cooperating teacher and school administrators?

19. ———   Do I set a good example in every way, every day?

20. ———   Do I treat all students fairly? Do I avoid favoritism? Do I pay attention to everyone?

21. ———   Do I give the students more than one chance to earn my trust and respect?

22. ———   Do I treat serious matters in a businesslike manner? Avoid threats?

23. —— Am I aware of what the members of the class are doing at all times?

24. —— Do I admit that I was wrong ?

25. —— Do I admit that I do not know something?

26. —— Do I consistently avoid acting like a "buddy"?

27. —— Have I handled student crushes tactfully, but firmly discouraged them?

28. —— Do I allow decisions to be made democratically whenever possible?

29. —— Am I careful not to embarrass students when praising them or correcting them?

30. —— Do I notice and provide support to the students who need guidance to succeed socially? Academically?

31. —— Do I firmly prevent students from treating each other rudely and insensitively?

32. —— Do I really listen to students' responses, not rehearse my next comment?

Evidence Form 11.17   Planning a Single Lesson

Name _____   Date _____

Purpose   There are many things to consider as you plan a lesson. Use these questions to help you create and organize a single lesson plan.

1. Briefly describe the students in this class, including those with special needs.

    _____

    _____

2. What are your goals for the lesson? What do you want the students to learn?

    _____

    _____

3. Why are these goals suitable for this group of students? What is the relevance between content and student?

    _____

    _____

4. How do these goals support the district's curriculum, state frameworks, and content standards?

    _____

    _____

5. How do these goals relate to national curriculum goals or standards in the discipline?

    _____

    _____

6. How do you plan to engage students in the content? What will you do? What will the students do? What are the time estimates?

    _____

    _____

7. What difficulties do students typically experience in this area, and how do you plan to anticipate and deal with these difficulties?

    _____

    _____

8. What instructional materials or other resources, if any, will you use?

    _____

    _____

    _____

9. How do you plan to assess student achievement of the goals? What procedures will you use?

_____

_____

10. How do you plan to make use of the results of the assessment(s)?

_____

_____

Evidence Form 11.18   Teaching 1, 2, 3, etc.

Name _____   Date _____

Purpose   Teaching a process can be a complex task. The process may involve learning such things as a routine, procedure, specialized method, prescribed manner, or a unique style. Use these questions to help plan the teaching of a new process.

1. What is the process? What is its purpose? What is the end result?

    _____

    _____

2. Who, in the real world of adults, does this process? Have you checked with such a person to be sure this is the way this process is done?

    _____

    _____

3. List the steps of the process sequentially or in a flow chart.

    _____

    _____

4. Mark the steps where students are likely to have the most trouble doing the assignment.

    _____

    _____

5. Exactly which skills/knowledge seem to distinguish the "B" grades from the "C" grades?

    _____

    _____

6. Which part(s) of the process involve higher-level thinking skills? (Check your listing of the steps to find those that are not concrete. The answers to #4, 5, and 6 may refer to the same step, but this is not always the case.)

    _____

    _____

7. What help can you give the students to structure the thinking process (e.g., framework, strategies, good examples and non-examples)?

    _____

    _____

Evidence Form 11.19   Technology Skills Inventory

Name _____   Date _____

Purpose   As a student teacher, you may be asked to use equipment with which you have no experience. Here are some common technology expectations of many teachers. Use this checklist to determine your technology skills and confidence.

Scale:

3   =   I can do this easily

2   =   I may need a refresher

1   =   I have not done this

1. _____   I can produce an attractive classroom assignment on the computer.

2. _____   I can use information from a CD-ROM.

3. _____   I can send and retrieve e-mail messages.

4. _____   I can use the Internet to download software.

5. _____   I can use the Internet to download resource articles from professional education journals related to classroom curriculum.

6. _____   I can use the Internet to download a lesson plans from various websites.

7. _____   I can use the Internet to download a picture from a website.

8. _____   I can use the Internet to download standards, assessments, performance packages, and other materials from our State Department of Education.

9. _____   I can teach students how to work on the computer.

10. _____   I can use and teach students a word-processing program.

11. _____   I can use and teach students how to use a spreadsheet.

12. _____   I can use and teach students how to use a graphics program.

13. _____   I can use and teach students how to run spell-check.

14. _____   I can use and teach students how to dial onto the Internet.

15. _____   I can use and teach students how to join an Internet discussion group.

16. _____   I can use and teach students how to find sites on the Web.

17. _____   I can use and teach students how to use a computer dictionary and thesaurus.

18. _____   I can recommend a useful computer game activity to fit needs and interests of my students.

19. _____   I can operate/run a calculator.

20. _____   I can project a computer screen on a large classroom screen.

21. _____ I can operate the following equipment:

  _____ video camera
  _____ VCR and the television equipment in the classroom
  _____ school phones, including transferring calls
  _____ overhead projector
  _____ screen
  _____ filmstrip projector
  _____ audiotape recorder
  _____ movie projector
  _____ videodisc machine
  _____ laminating machine
  _____ copy machine

22. _____ I can create attractive overhead transparencies, either on the computer or by hand.

23. _____ I can select software to enhance classroom activities or provide alternative learning.

24. _____ I can operate the electronic card catalog in the media center.

25. _____ I can send faxes.

What three technology skills would you like to improve?

1. _____
2. _____
3. _____

Write a plan, with timelines, for improving each skill.

1. _____

_____

2. _____

_____

3. _____

_____

Evidence Form 11.20   Conflicts, Problems, and Troubles

Name _____   Date _____

Purpose   Conflicts and problems are inevitable in a classroom. How you handle the first few may lessen the frequency and/or the severity of future problems. After it is over and you have time to reflect, think through the incident. Consider the following questions.

1. Did you keep cool?

   _____

   _____

2. What did the student do—specifically?

   _____

   _____

3. Are you certain the student knew that his or her behavior would break a rule? How would the student have known? How would the student have known the probable consequences?

   _____

   _____

4. Is this a pattern of behavior? For this particular student? For many other students?

   _____

   _____

5. Did the student hurt someone physically? Emotionally? Did you deal with safety first?

   _____

   _____

6. How did the incident begin?

   _____

   _____

7. Were others involved? Who else was held responsible for this incident?

   _____

   _____

   _____

8. Did you contribute to or escalate the misconduct?

   _____

   _____

   _____

9. Is this the first time you have had to discipline this student? Does the student seem to be involved repeatedly in disruption? Does that affect your interpretation of the seriousness of this incident? Should it?

_____

_____

10. Does the student have special needs? Do other adults need to be involved? Parents?

_____

_____

11. How did you feel about this student before this incident? How do you feel now?

_____

_____

12. What should happen as a result of today's incident?

_____

_____

13. What have you learned from this incident that will help you in the future?

_____

_____

Name _____   Date _____

Purpose   A way to survive the complexity of having a lot of people in a classroom together is the establishment of routines for you and for the students. Have you established a method to accomplish these regular functions smoothly and with minimum effort? Check yourself!

Scale:

2   =   Yes
1   =   Somewhat
0   =   No
NA =   Not Applicable

1. _____   Taking and reporting daily attendance

2. _____   Tardy/late students

3. _____   Parent notes regarding the work of individual students

4. _____   Sign-out list and/or passes for individuals to leave the room to go to:

   _____   restroom, water fountain, locker, or coat rack
   _____   media center
   _____   office
   _____   errand involving another room in the school
   _____   nurse

5. _____   Using the pencil sharpener or getting supplies

6. _____   Assigning jobs and chores on a rotation basis

7. _____   Providing make-up work for those returning from absence/late work

8. _____   Taking the count for lunch and/or milk money

9. _____   Fire and emergency drills

10. _____   Moving through hallways as a group (elementary)

11. _____   What to do when a visitor comes to the classroom door

12. _____   When/how to answer the classroom phone or e-mail

13. _____   How to get help from the teacher

14. _____   Getting permission to talk to another student

15. _____   What to do when work is completed early

16. _____   Preparing to go home, e.g., order of dismissal for bus and walking students

17. _____   Collecting/returning homework

18. _____   Letting students know how they did on a graded activity

19. _____ Phone calls, i.e., time when calls will be returned, parent contacts

20. _____ Beginning-of-the-day ceremony or plans (elementary)

21. _____ School announcements and information received during the day from office

22. _____ Management of portfolios, journals, or other ongoing collections of student work

23. _____ Taking work or textbooks home to share with parents

24. _____ Returning and checking in documents signed by parents

25. _____ Checking out books from the classroom library

26. _____ Signing up for special activities, e.g., using a computer for independent work

27. _____ Getting the students' attention

28. _____ Changing from one regularly scheduled activity to another

29. _____ Orienting a new student to the class

Name _____ Date _____

Purpose   Use this form to record and document out-of-classroom meetings and activities in which you have participated.

When	**Where**	**Who**	**Why**	**Outcomes**
Day/date/time	*Location*	*Participants*	*Purpose of meeting*	*Resolutions/reaction/ consequence/result/reflection*

Evidence Form 11.23   Parent and Family Contact Log

Name _____   Date _____

Purpose   Use this form to help track and document parent/family contacts.

Date	Person contacted	Means of contact	Purpose	Outcomes

12
Beyond Student Teaching

Introduction

As your student teaching experience draws nearer to a successful completion, you may be thinking about all the events that take place immediately following your student teaching assignment. Common concerns focus on graduation, achieving state teaching certification, examining options, and beginning the job search process. However, if at all possible, before jumping into a high-energy job search, take some time off to celebrate the successful completion of your student teaching assignment—perhaps a mini-vacation or a special night out.

Closing up a student teaching assignment sparks many emotions. Feelings of happiness and sadness are often intermixed. Saying good-bye to students, cooperating teachers, university supervisors, and others who have been supportive during your experience is often difficult. Some student teachers give a classroom gift to the students—a special book, a plant, flowers, or classroom supplies. Some student teachers choose to give a small gift of appreciation to their cooperating teacher. This could be flowers, a book, a gift certificate for a restaurant or retail store, or special event tickets such as a concert or play. Perhaps your cooperating teacher would like a memento from your university.

The purpose of this chapter is to provide you with some hints, details, wisdom, and advice on how to effectively move from your professional preparation to professional practice.

Finding a Teaching Position

The sky is the limit—well, maybe not the sky, but certainly the world.

Spring and summer are the typical times when many school districts can most accurately predict their next year's budget and teaching needs. This is the time when most school districts conduct their interviews and offer contracts. However, there are many other reasons that suddenly create teacher positions during the school year. Some of the more common situations that create mid-year openings are retirement, resignation, medical concerns, pregnancy, family leave, personal leave, military leave, and death. For these situations, it is advisable to keep tabs on your most desirable school districts throughout the entire school year.

Examining and determining your priorities are important first steps in helping you prioritize, organize, and implement an efficient and effective search for a teaching position. See Activity 12.1, Finding A Teaching Position. Below are some useful sources of information and job leads.

Campus career development, services, or placement office. Never overlook the value of the placement office! Students are often surprised to find out about the wide variety of services provided by this office. Take the time to find out the many ways this office can assist you in your job search. If you are searching for a teaching job in another state, ask your university office to recommend and possibly connect you with another university office in the your desired area. Some campuses conduct their own job fairs.

University supervisor. Your university supervisor often has a good pulse of the job market. Many university supervisors work with a variety of school districts and learn about potential job openings. In addition, university supervisors frequently communicate about teaching openings with their colleagues in other districts, even other universities.

Cooperating teacher. Cooperating teachers typically have been in the district for several years. They know the people, places, and shortcuts to gather information. They also know some of the potential openings before they become officially announced. Having a head start on a potential teaching position can be quite an advantage.

Other education professionals.   Administrators, teachers, counselors, and other educational professionals can offer an extraordinary insight to a job search. Do not hesitate to tap their wisdom.

Education job fairs.   Generally your campus career development, services, or placement office will have information regarding educational job fairs in the area. They may also be able to help you locate job fairs in other states as well. Job fairs can be hectic and overwhelming at times. Before walking in the door, have a plan. The way to approach a job fair is essentially the way you would prepare for an interview.

Try to obtain a listing of the school districts that will be represented. Learn and study some basic information about the school districts that interest you most. Bring your notes with you—it's easy to confuse one school district with another.

- Plan your attire—dress the way you would for an interview and remember to bring any grooming items you may need.
- Bring plenty of résumés.
- Don't bring a "ton" of materials—keep all of your materials neatly organized in a briefcase or similar bag.
- Practice, practice, practice answering typical interview questions. See Activity 12.4, "Answering Interview Questions."
- It's a good idea not to go to your highest priority school district first; go practice on a couple of lower priority districts so that you will be better prepared and less nervous by the time you get to your most important sites.

Complete your Job Fair Record Form (see Appendix C). Complete as much as possible at the job fair, during lunch time or other break.

Remember the purpose of a job fair from the school district perspective is to determine a pool of the best candidates for the available positions.

Newspaper ads.   In many cities, the Sunday newspaper often has a listing of open teaching positions for that geographical area as well as distant cities, states, and even international openings.

Family and friends.   Spreading the word that you are researching and searching teaching opportunities can be very productive. Your family and friends who share your teaching desires with their families and friends can be the beginning of a expansive network.

Internet searches.   The Internet is a powerful tool that enables you to learn about school districts and teaching opportunities near and far. Most student teachers are competent in using the Internet. If you are not, ask a teacher or friend to assist you. Your campus career development, services, or placement office staff are, most likely, very proficient in using the Internet and can quickly show you how to use it.

Use the Internet to contact:

- Individual school districts
- Individual public and private schools
- College and university campus career development, services, or placement offices
- State Departments of Education
- State Teacher Certification Offices (see Appendix B)
- United States Department of Education, for links to several helpful sites

Consider viewing the USA and International School Web Site Registry at http://web66.coled.umn.edu/schools.html. This site allows you to focus on any of six geographical menu items. They are Australia, Canada, Europe, Japan, USA, and World. For example the USA site shows a map of the United States. Clicking on any state reveals a list of, and link to, all the registered school district web sites in that state.

This site also has special categories including: Arts, Charter, Gifted and Talented, Handicap, International, Math, Montessori, On-Line, Parochial, Private, Science, and Historical and Statistical Information.

Many new (and experienced) teachers consider teaching in an international school. Teaching in an international school can provide unique adventures, experiences, and travel opportunities. Hundreds of schools all over the world, from Argentina to Zimbabwe, offer teaching possibilities. For additional information See Appendix F for a listing of specific international school websites and organizations.

Portfolios

What is a portfolio? A portfolio is a planned and organized collection of information that describes and documents an individual's experiences, knowledge, skill, achievements, competence, and ability. Portfolios are not only used by individuals seeking professional employment. Portfolios are often used to assess and evaluate student performance in elementary, middle, high school, and higher education.

Why do I need a portfolio? A portfolio is one way that teacher candidates can assess themselves and share their teaching strength and potential in a tangible, observable manner. The goal is to prepare a professional portfolio that will meet the needs of potential employers. Some candidates state on their résumés that they have a "Professional Portfolio" available for review.

How do I start a portfolio? Portfolio development provides the opportunity and generates the need for reflection. As you begin the process, constantly remind yourself of the purpose of the portfolio—to assist you in convincing potential employers that you are the best person for the position you are seeking. Consider using some of the evidence forms in Chapter 11.

How do I organize a portfolio? There are many ways to organize a portfolio. Some are organized chronologically. Many teacher candidates choose to organize their portfolios by teaching functions, tasks, or skills. One organizational pattern is achieved by using the ten INTASC Standards of this textbook. Whichever pattern you choose, be sure it is one that is easy to understand and access.

What do I put into the portfolio? You can't put everything in your portfolio. You do not want your portfolio to be cumbersome. It should be a comfortable size and easy to use. So, how do you select what is in and what is out? As mentioned previously, the primary purpose of the portfolio, in this context, is to help you get a teaching job. Include information and materials that reflect your very best teaching and learning abilities. Your portfolio should be considered dynamic—changing to your needs and the anticipated needs of the audience. Depending on the situation, you may choose to add or subtract information. Here are some common areas, based on the INTASC Standards, that you should consider for portfolio entries. Select items that clearly demonstrate and document your understanding and abilities in these areas:

- Subject matter
- Student learning
- Diverse learners
- Instructional strategies
- Learning environment
- Communication
- Planning instruction
- Assessment and evaluation
- Reflection and professional development
- Collaboration, ethics, and relationships

Suggestions of portfolio items include:

- Letters of appreciation from teachers, parents, and students
- Honors, awards, and scholarships
- Memberships/positions in professional organizations
- Memberships on teams and clubs
- Lesson plans
- Significant materials from university courses
- Information about class routines, management, and discipline
- Samples of student work (delete names)
- Photographs
- Information about ways you use technology in teaching and learning

What is the best means for sharing my portfolio items? Many portfolios are primarily in hard copy format. However, many candidates are now including more diverse ways to share their portfolios—either in their entirety or selected portions. These include photographs, video tapes, slides, cassette tapes, CDs, computer programs, and displays.

How do I know if I have the best items in my portfolio? Ask other education professionals to review your portfolio. Classroom teachers, student teaching supervisors, cooperating teachers, administrators, and personnel directors can provide excellent feedback on your portfolio.

How can I use my portfolio? Practice, practice, and practice using your portfolio. Know what information is where! Keep your table of contents accurate. Be sure that all information and photographs are labeled clearly and properly. Practice integrating your portfolio into your answers for common interview questions. To avoid an embarrassing situation, make sure your portfolio is assembled securely. You don't want your materials scattered on the floor during an interview.

Do I need a copy of my portfolio?   You should strongly consider having a backup copy of your portfolio. Prepare for the unfortunate case when a portfolio is lost. In some instances, potential employers may ask you to leave your portfolio for several days so that it can be more closely examined. This would obviously be of concern for you if you had another interview with another school district scheduled the following day.

A final portfolio thought.   You are the author of your portfolio; treat the portfolio as a research project. Document and credit all information that is not your own work. This may include information / materials from your cooperating teacher, other teachers, university supervisor, textbooks, or the internet. If you are using student work, be sure to delete names.

For further information, see *How to develop a professional portfolio: A manual for teachers*, 1997, by D. M. Campbell. Boston: Allyn & Bacon.

Résumés

Your professional résumé is very personal. It represents a summary of your most important teaching and learning experiences and accomplishments. Your résumé is one of the most important elements connecting professional preparation to professional practice. Everyone wants the perfect résumé. There is no one style that fits everyone. Many young people finishing their student teaching view writing a résumé as an overwhelmingly difficult task. The information in this section and in Activity 12.2, "Your Résumé," will help you write a professional résumé.

Starting to write a résumé is often awkward. You may consider just copying one you have seen. But soon you will realize that only you can write your résumé because you are the expert on you!

Before you start writing your résumé, remember that it is not an autobiography or essay. It is, as mentioned previously, a summary of the many experiences and accomplishments you have achieved that are related to teaching and learning.

There are two basic résumé formats. One is a chronological résumé that is organized, as the name implies, in chronological or sequential order. The other basic format is a functional résumé. Functional résumés focus on skills, attributes, and achievements aligned with the desired position.

The good news is that you don't have to choose one format or the other. Many student teachers write impressive and effective résumés by combining elements of both the chronological and functional résumés.

Generally, the first step is to understand the language and nature of your profession and discipline. Each profession has its own language. And each profession dictates its own résumé uniqueness. The résumés of those seeking positions in law, medicine, business, education, and social services will require a variety of language and design.

Even within the field of education, language may vary. For example, in some states or local school districts, the term used to describe the student learning may be goals, outcomes, objectives, competencies, expectations, or standards. Therefore, it's a good idea to review the language used by the state or school in which your are applying.

There are several resources to assist in résumé writing. They include:

1. Your campus career development, services, or placement office
2. Countless résumé books in libraries and book stores
3. The Internet offers an abundant number of résumé resources; for example, www.studentcenter.com or www.careerlab.com
4. Several software programs

The primary purpose of your résumé is to promote *you*! If you research varying résumé formats, you will perhaps see dozens of possible résumé categories. Many student teachers, writing their first résumés, find these four résumé categories helpful.

Teaching (career) objective.   This section identifies the teaching area you are pursuing. Unless you truly mean it, don't restrict yourself by using limiting words such as "urban" or "fifth grade." Many schools welcome and look for candidates that can assist with extra curriculum activities, such as athletics, academic clubs, music, art, or cheerleading. A concluding statement indicating your willingness to assist in extra curricular activities could have a big payoff.

Education (academic background). Include the institution and dates of your professional preparation. List all areas of licensure. Don't forget endorsements and coaching/other certifications

Student teaching. Obviously, candidates completing their student teaching do not have much, if any, customary teaching experience. Provide the location, course/level, other assignments, and dates. Also emphasize your pertinent skills and responsibilities using action words such as organized, managed, created, developed, designed, prepared, or assessed.

Memberships and honors. List professional memberships such as the Minnesota Student Educators Association as well as other memberships such as the jazz band. Also include honors, achievements, and leadership positions such as captain of the tennis team or treasurer of the campus science club.

Other possible categories:
- Related experiences
- Practicum/Internship experiences
- Special training/workshops
- Travel abroad
- Part-time work
- Volunteer experiences
- Leisure activities/hobbies
- Scholarships
- Teaching strengths/skills (include fluency in languages other than English)
- Computer/technology skills

Final résumé suggestions:
- Ask friends and education professionals to review your résumé.
- Proofread—over and over again. Your résumé must be error-free.
- Be consistent in format and font.
- Use white space thoughtfully—no dense blocks of text.
- Print on high-quality, standard-size paper from a high-quality printer.
- White or near white paper is perfectly acceptable—often preferred.
- Generally, one page is sufficient for a first-year teaching résumé.

See Activity 12.2, "Your Résumé."

Cover Letters

Always, always, always send a cover letter with your résumé. Writing a cover letter is easier than writing and preparing your résumé. However, just because it is easier to write does not mean that you shouldn't think carefully about the organization and content of the cover letter. Don't let a poorly written cover letter be the reason that your résumé is never reviewed.

As with résumés, there are ample resources to assist you with your cover letters. Many of the resources for cover letters are the same as for résumés.

The primary purpose of your cover letter is to provoke an interest in your résumé, application materials, and ultimately an interview.

Many first-time cover-letter writers struggle with the opening lines. Be straightforward. Common introductions include clearly stating the purpose of the cover letter and including the specific teaching position you are seeking. It may be appropriate to let the reader know how you found out about the teaching position.

Since the cover letter should not exceed one page, don't waste time and space getting to the main body and purpose of the cover letter. Try looking at your cover letter from the reader's perspective. Immediately start with your best information—the qualifications, knowledge, skills, and experiences that you believe make you the best candidate for the position. Consider aligning the elements of your cover letter to the qualifications/expectations listed in the position posting.

See Activity 12.3, "Cover Letters," for additional information and support in preparing a cover letter.

Teacher Application Forms

Nearly all school districts have specific application requirements. For a candidate to be considered, he/she must have submitted all required forms and documents. These commonly include (1) applicant's letter of interest, (2) résumé, (3) completed school district application, and (4) photocopy of working credential file (college/university transcripts and letters of reference).

Completing a teacher application form for the first time can be exciting, complicated, and confusing all at the same time. An incomplete application may delay or eliminate you from a position.

Obtaining, completing, and sending all application materials are the first steps. The next step, which is often overlooked, is to contact the school district a few days later to confirm that all the required application materials have been received. You can also send the materials using a mail service that provides a confirmation of delivery, in which case you will receive confirmation that the materials you sent were received. This process, however, does not confirm that you sent *all* of the required materials.

Some school districts allow for some or all of their required materials to be obtained, completed, and submitted electronically.

As a general rule, the larger the school district, the longer the process takes. Larger schools districts may require completed applications several weeks, even months prior to the interview process. For this reason, it is advisable to find out the application time schedules for your targeted school districts early! It can be very discouraging to find out that you missed an application deadline.

See Activity 12.5, "Completing a School District Teacher Application," to help you better understand the components in a typical school district teacher application form.

Consider using the Application/Interview Tracking Form found in Appendix D to assist you with keeping an accurate record of your progress.

Interviews

Preparing for your first professional interview often produces a variety of emotions and feelings. With proper preparation, you can enter your interview with less mystery and more self assurance and confidence.

What is the purpose of the interview?   This seems like an obvious question—and it is—from your perspective. Your purpose is to secure a teaching position. Consider for a moment the purpose of the interview from the school district's interviewing team's perspective. Their task is to determine the best candidate for the available position. If they asked "easy" questions to all candidates which could be answered without difficulty, the interviewing team would have a difficult time ranking, or prioritizing, the candidates. The purpose of the interview from the team's perspective is to separate the candidates according to their criteria. To do this, they will probably ask many difficult and open-ended questions.

How is the interview conducted?   There is no one way that interviews are conducted. School districts typically establish their own interviewing policies, procedures, and guidelines. However, there tend to be many common elements in the interview. Frequently, the interview team will take turns (predetermined) asking you questions.

How many people are in the interview and who are they? There may be anywhere from five to fifteen individuals involved on the interview team. These typically include teachers and administrators. Sometimes students and parents are on the interview team. The teachers may or may not be from your specific discipline.

How should I prepare for the interview?   Here are several key elements in preparing for a successful interview:

- Attend an interview seminar offered by your university supervisor or the campus career development, services, or placement office.

- Conduct an extensive self-assessment. Examine your teaching abilities—the things you do well and the things that may need some improvement. Be honest with yourself. Learn and practice the action terms that describe your abilities such as organized, motivating, planner, communicator, collaborator. You may have used some of these words on your résumé.

- Research the school, the position, and the interviewing process. What is the size and diversity of the school? How are classes scheduled? (It would be embarrassing if one of the interview questions focused on your opinion of their alternating block schedule and you had no idea what they were referring to.) Many school districts have websites with sufficient information about their schools. How has the school performed in extracurricular activities such as athletics, music, or art? What is the school district particularly proud off? Try to find out who will be on the interview team. Some interviews involve testing—such as open-ended opinion questions, paper/pencil tests, or hands-on tests of computer skills.

- Plan for your first impression. Don't wait until the last moment to determine your attire for the interview. Attire should be suit or dress and jacket. (The authors have seen men and women candidates in nice suits and dresses wearing tennis shoes! Don't!). Regardless of your gender, take it very easy on the fragrances and jewelry. Remember, you are trying to fit the school's image of a professional teacher.

- Plan your route and parking. Don't plan to be to the interview on time, plan to be there early! Drive the route you plan to take ahead of time. Do it at a time and on a day that is similar to your interview time. For example, you would probably not want to do your practice route on a holiday. Be sure to check on parking. Some locations may require parking permits. Finally, what's your plan if you have car trouble or the parking lot is full?
- Ask a knowledgeable person to conduct a simulated or practice interview with you.
- Remember to bring all of your materials—portfolio, notebook for writing, and a new pen.

I'm at the interview, what's next?   When you arrive the interview location, it's a good idea to visit the rest room and give yourself a final check. Did your hair get blown out of place? Did your shoes get dusty walking across the parking lot? Did a bird flying overhead leave a present on your shoulder? Empty your bladder even if you don't feel you have to—you will not want to excuse yourself mid-interview. After a few deep breaths report to the interview location and introduce yourself. Most candidates don't need to be reminded to be courteous and smile to the office staff. The interviewer will take the lead.

Be sure that your very first impressions—appearance, body language, gestures, and voice—are professional and confident. Most interviews start with a greeting and introductions. If the interview team is not wearing name tags, it might be advisable to write their names in your notebook. The lead interviewer will explain the interview process. Typically, after you have the opportunity to make some introductory remarks, the interview team will ask you questions. Give your responses to the entire team, using eye contact—not specifically to the person who asked the question. Listen carefully to the questions and ask for clarification if you don't understand the question.

Can I ask the interview team questions?   Absolutely yes! Do so! Nearly all interviews allow for candidate questions. Two or three questions are generally appropriate—not a list of 20 questions. Candidate questions might focus on the use of textbooks, class size, opportunities for extracurricular assignments, field trips, available technology, re-

porting student progress, or when will this hiring decision be made.

What are the questions that I will be asked?   In some cases, the candidate is given the list of questions before the interview; in many cases the questions are not known until they are asked. Although the exact question is not known, there tends to be some similarity among teacher interview questions. Here are some examples:

1. Why do you want to be a teacher?
2. Why do you want to be a teacher in our district/school?
3. How are the national standards in your discipline organized?
4. Which of our state standards in your discipline have you taught?
5. Describe your style of teaching.
6. How would you deal with the fast/slow learners in your classes?
7. What are your teaching strengths?
8. What was your biggest teaching concern/problem during student teaching?
9. What is your procedure for handling disruptive students?
10. What are some steps in, or criteria for, creating effective assignments?
11. How would you accommodate one or two ESL students in your class?
12. How will your students describe you as a teacher?
13. What extracurricular activities can you lead or supervise?

See Activity 12.4, "Answering Interview Questions."

What do I do after the interview?   If you are like many candidates, immediately following the interview, you will perhaps think of all the things you *should* have said, but didn't say during the interview. Don't dwell on it. Use the wisdom from this interview to prepare for the next interview. Yes, the next interview. Most candidates go through several interviews before securing a job. In many cases, based on the interview, you may eliminate the district if it isn't a good fit for you. Regardless, the best practice is to send a thank you note. The thank you note can also serve as another way to accent (briefly) your special teaching talent or desire to be in the district. Even if you are not the best candidate for that position, your courtesy will be remembered for future positions or your name may be shared for another position in a neighboring school district. Sometimes districts are unable to make immediate hiring decisions due to budget or other unknowns. However, if you don't hear back from the district in two to three weeks, call and inquire about your status! On the other hand, continual calling can be irritating and counterproductive in your job search. Finally, keep an interview tracking form so you can trace you interviewing progress. See the Application/Interview Tracking Form, Appendix D.

Professional Organizations

Prior to your student teaching experience, during your professional preparation courses, you were perhaps introduced to the professional organization(s) aligned with your teaching endeavors. Professional organizations provide the member with direct and indirect support and resources. Members receive periodic journals, information, and opportunities to attend local/state/national seminars, workshops, conferences, and conventions. Many of the national professional organizations have state affiliations providing state-related information through publications and workshops. See Appendix A for a list of many professional organizations.

State Certification Offices

Most teacher preparation colleges and universities provide their student teachers with extensive information regarding teacher certification and licensure. However, for numerous reasons, many student teachers desire to obtain certification and licensure to teach in another state. Teacher certification is required in all 50 states. Some states share the same certification requirements allowing an individual with certification from one state to be automatically certified in another state. Because state requirements change occasionally, it is recommended that you contact the state certification offices to confirm requirements. See Appendix B for a list of state certification contact numbers.

Internet

Most teachers are continually seeking resources and materials that will lead to improved teaching and learning effectiveness. The Internet has opened communication doors for education professionals and organizations to share resources, materials, and assistance to teachers and students. Many sites contain lesson plans, strategies, individual and classroom activities, and performance assessment and evaluation instruments. They can help teachers plan individual lessons or entire units. Several selected websites are listed in Appendix G.

Activity 12.1   *Finding a Teaching Position*

Context   Teaching positions come in all shapes, sizes, and places. Prioritizing your teaching desires is a difficult, but necessary, task.

Purpose   This activity will help you prioritize, organize, and implement an efficient and effective search for a teaching position.

Directions   Rank (1, 2, 3, etc) each of the items within each of the categories that follow. A ranking score of "1" represents the most desirable item in the category.

School type

_____ public school

_____ private school

_____ religious school

_____ other

School Location

_____ international school—Department of Defense Dependents Schools (DoDDs)

_____ international school—American International Schools

_____ United States rural

_____ United States suburban

_____ United States urban

_____ other

Students

_____ culturally diverse students

_____ culturally analogous students

_____ learning diverse students

_____ learning analogous students

_____ other

School Size

_____ less than 100 students per grade

_____ between 100–500 students per grade

_____ more than 500 students per grade

_____ other

Teaching Assignment

_____ teach several grades/courses

_____ teach single grade/courses

_____ opportunities to supervise extracurricular activities (e.g., music, athletics, arts, academics)

_____ other

Benefits

_____ salary

_____ job security

_____ benefits (medical, dental)

_____ teaching schedule

_____ vacations

_____ other

Miscellaneous

_____ newer school building

_____ younger/newer staff

_____ older/experienced staff

_____ administrative disposition

_____ budget for teaching supplies, books, materials

_____ staff development (in/out of district) opportunities

_____ potential/current spouse employment

_____ mentorship programs

_____ conducive to personal/professional goals and aspirations

_____ other

Summary   Consider the information from all seven categories. Write the five most important to you. You may have more than one from a single category and none from another category.

1. _____

2. _____

3. _____

4. _____

5. _____

Activity 12.2   Your Résumé

Context   For many, the most difficult part of writing a résumé is getting started. Focusing on the connection of self-promotion and your job search will enable you to select the most relevant résumé items.

Purpose   This activity will help you identify the basic experiences, skills, and accomplishments that will form the foundation of your résumé.

Directions   Fill in the blanks associated with each item. When you are completed, evaluate each response. Is it conducive to the job you are seeking? You will quickly see that not all responses are equally important.

Name _____

Address _____

Telephone _____

E-mail _____

College/University _____

Degree(s)/Date _____

Major(s) and GPA _____

License(s)/Certifications _____

Teaching Objective _____

_____

_____

_____

_____

Student Teaching Location _____

_____

Responsibilities (use action words) _____

_____

_____

_____

Practicum Experience Location _____

_____

Responsibilities (use action words) _____

_____

_____

Honors and Awards _____

_____

_____

Extracurricular Interests _____

_____

_____

Teaching Strengths/Skills/Abilities _____

_____

_____

Activity 12.3   Cover Letters

Context   Planning to write your first cover letter can elicit a mixture of anxious and enthusiastic feelings. You are excited about the prospects of a new job and career. At the same time, you may feel anxious or worry about your ability to write a clear and concise cover letter.

Purpose   Getting started is often the most difficult part of writing a cover letter. This activity will help you get your cover letter started and organized.

Directions   Assume you are applying for a position in the school in which you are currently student teaching (or in one similar to it). Complete the following to provide you with a cover letter foundation.

Part 1   Complete these possible introductory cover-letter sentences.

1. I am writing to _____

_____

2. Please consider me _____

_____

3. I would like to _____

_____

4. Please accept _____

_____

5. I am interested in this position because _____

_____

Part 2   Complete these main idea sentences.

1. My credentials and qualifications are _____

_____

2. I have significant preparation and knowledge in _____

_____

3. The skills I will bring to this teaching position are _____

_____

4. I have had several experiences that foster my candidacy for this teaching position. They include

_____

_____

_____

5. Attitude, spirit, and demeanor are key elements among successful teachers. The dispositions that I bring to this teaching position are

_____

6. In summary, my strongest abilities that I bring to this teaching position are

_____

_____

Part 3   Complete these closing sentences.

1. I would welcome the opportunity to _____

_____

2. I look forward to _____

_____

3. Please contact me _____

_____

Part 4   Putting it all together.

On another piece of paper, take your best answers from Parts 1, 2, and 3 and compose a draft of your cover letter. You may want to use or combine several answers from each part.

Part 5   Check the checklist. Asses your cover letter.

Yes	No	
_____	_____	I consistently used professional language.
_____	_____	I included my address and date.
_____	_____	I included my qualifications and relevant skills and experiences
_____	_____	I checked and rechecked to make sure it is free of errors.
_____	_____	I will use single space within a paragraph and double space between paragraphs.
_____	_____	I will use only one side of the page.
_____	_____	I will use the same quality paper as my résumé.
_____	_____	I mentioned that my résumé is enclosed.
_____	_____	I will ask for feedback from my campus career development, services staff, cooperating teacher, and university supervisor.
_____	_____	In the closing, I remembered to type my name and sign my letter.
_____	_____	I will use a quality printer to print my cover letter.
_____	_____	I will consider using a large envelope so that my cover letter and résumé need no folding.

Activity 12.4   Answering Interview Questions

Context   Many beginning teachers report that one of the most agonizing considerations in preparing for an interview is trying to predict and be prepared for possible interview questions.

Purpose   Although you may not know exact questions in advance, there is frequently strong similarity among common teacher interview questions. Here is your chance to think about and write down some thoughts about how you might answer these questions.

Directions   In the space provided, write down some key words, thoughts, and/or phrases that will provide insight and direction to your answer.

1. Why do you want to be a teacher? _____

_____

2. Why do you want to be a teacher in our district/school? _____

_____

3. How are the national standards in your discipline organized? _____

_____

4. Which of our state standards in your discipline have you taught? _____

_____

5. Describe your style of teaching. _____

_____

6. How would you deal with the fast/slow learners in your classes? _____

_____

7. What are your greatest teaching strengths? _____

_____

8. What was your biggest teaching concern or problem during student teaching? _____

_____

9. What is your procedure for handling disruptive students? _____

_____

10. What are some steps in, or criteria for, creating effective lesson plans and assignments? _____

_____

11. How would you accommodate one or two ESL students in your class? _____

_____

12. How will your students describe you as a teacher? _____

_____

13. What extracurricular activities can you lead or supervise? _____

_____

14. What are your professional goals? _____

_____

15. How would your students, during your student teaching, have described you as their teacher?

_____

16. How would you individualize your teaching? _____

_____

17. A student may refuse to do the homework you assign. What will you do? _____

_____

18. You will bring a great deal to teaching. Describe what you will *not* bring to teaching. _____

_____

19. How will you assess and evaluate students? _____

_____

20. How will you "grade" students? _____

_____

In the space below, add additional questions suggested by your cooperating teacher or university supervisor.

Activity 12.5   Completing a School District Teacher Application Form

Context   Completing a teacher application form for the first time can be exciting, complicated, and confusing all at the same time. An incomplete application may delay or eliminate a strong candidate for a position.

Purpose   The goal of this activity is to provide you with the opportunity to practice completing a teacher application form. This practice will, hopefully, reduce your stress (and errors) and increase your confidence when you decide to complete your first "real" teacher application form.

Directions   Provide complete and accurate information in each of the teacher application sections listed.

Hypothetical Public Schools, Ima Town, USA
Teacher Application Form

Section 1   Applicant Identification

Last Name _____

First, Middle Name _____

Present Address _____

_____

Telephone Number _____

Permanent Address _____

_____

_____

Section 2   Teacher Application For:

_____ Kindergarten   _____ Secondary 7–8

_____ Elementary 1–4   _____ Secondary 9–12

_____ Intermediate 5–6   _____ Special Education

_____ other: _____

Section 3   Licensure

1. License Area	Full/Part-Time	State	Exp. Date
_____	_____	_____	_____
_____	_____	_____	_____
_____	_____	_____	_____
_____	_____	_____	_____

2. Undergraduate *overall* grade point average (Based on 4.0 scale) : _____

Section 4 Professional References *(Do not list personal references)*

1. Current Supervisor: _____

2. List professionals in the field of education who have firsthand knowledge of your qualifications for a position—superintendents, principals, professors, K–12 teachers.

Name	Title/Position	Address	Telephone
_____	_____	_____	_____
	_____		
_____	_____	_____	_____
	_____		
_____	_____	_____	_____
	_____		

3. May we contact your present employer?

   Yes _____   No _____

   If no, when may we contact your present employer? _____

Section 5 Co-Curricular Activities

1. Do you have experience as a participant, advisor, director, or coach in co-curricular activities?

   Yes _____   No _____

   If yes, be specific as to activities: _____

2. Do you hold any special licenses or certifications related to co-curricular activities?

   Yes _____   No _____

   If yes, describe: _____

3. If employed, would you be interested in working in co-curricular areas?

   Yes _____   No _____

   If yes, be specific as to activities: _____

Section 6 Termination/Felony Record

1. Have you ever been terminated from employment or resigned, by request of the employer or by mutual consent, for cause of alleged misconduct, alleged unsatisfactory performance, or alleged improper or illegal acts?

   Yes _____   No _____

   If yes: Employer/Location _____

   Name/Title of Supervisor _____

2. Have you ever been convicted of a felony or lesser charge, in which the conviction was not annulled or expunged according to law?

Yes _____   No _____

Comments (if any): _____

_____

_____

3. Have you ever been convicted of a misdemeanor charge for which no jail sentence was imposed?

Yes _____   No _____

Comments (if any): _____

_____

_____

Section 7   Education

1. List graduate and undergraduate degrees.

College/University	Location	Major	Minor	Degree
_____	_____	_____	_____	_____
_____	_____	_____	_____	_____
_____	_____	_____	_____	_____
_____	_____	_____	_____	_____

2. How many graduate credits have you completed beyond the date of your last and highest conferred degree? Quarter _____ and/or Semester _____

3. Do you anticipate completing requirements for a degree within the next six (6) months?

Yes _____   No _____

If yes, Degree _____

Section 8   Student Teaching Experience

Subject(s) / Level(s)   _____

School / Location   _____

Supervising Teacher(s)   _____

Section 9   Full-Time Teaching Experience

How many years, each being a full academic year at full-time employment, have you been working under a regular teacher contract appointment?

	Years	Location	Subject/Level
Public K–12 School:	_____	_____	_____
Private School:	_____	_____	_____
College University:	_____	_____	_____

Section 10   Related Experience

What training or experience have you had, other than teaching, that enhances your qualifications as an applicant for a teaching position in this school district?

_____

_____

_____

_____

_____

_____

Section 11   Employment History

1. Start with your current or most recent position. Do not list positions you had more than (5) years ago.

When	Employer/Location	Position
_____	_____	_____
_____	_____	_____
_____	_____	_____
_____	_____	_____

2. Are you presently under an employment contract? Yes _____   No _____

   If yes, contract expiration date: _____

3. Are you tenured in a school district in this state? Yes _____   No _____

   School District _____ Years ____

4. Are you presently on voluntary or involuntary leave (layoff) from a position? Yes _____ No _____

   School District _____

Section 12   Personal Statement

Write in essay form a statement which expresses your belief in yourself as a teacher. Write carefully, as your style, content, written expression and organization will be used to evaluate you as a candidate for employment in this school district. Please limit your statement to the space available.

_____

_____

_____

_____

_____

_____

_____

_____

_____

_____

_____

_____

_____

_____

_____

_____

_____

_____

Section 13   Confirmation

Please read carefully and sign only if you fully understand and agree with the statement as written:

I hereby affirm that the information provided on this application is true and complete to the best of my knowledge. I understand that falsified information or significant omission on either the application or during an interview may disqualify me from further employment consideration and shall, at the discretion of this school district, provide cause for immediate discharge. I authorize this school district to seek verification of my qualifications as reasonably necessary to arrive at an employment decision. I hereby authorize professional references, my current employer or previous employers and/or organizations, to provide any and all information regarding my employment, as well as other information, personal or otherwise, that may or may not be on record. I release this school district and such employers, companies, and persons from all liabilities and damages whatsoever that may arise from requesting or providing such information.

Signature: _____ Date: _____

Section 14   Completed Application Packet

No applicant will be considered until the application file is complete:

_____ Applicant's letter of interest

_____ Résumé

_____ Completed school district application

_____ Photocopy of working credential file (college/university, transcripts, and letters of reference)

A
Professional Organizations

American Alliance for Health, Physical Education, Recreation and Dance (AAHPERD) consists of six national and district associations with the research consortium:

> American Association for Active Lifestyles and Fitness (AAALF)
>
> American Association for Health Education (AAHE)
>
> American Association for Leisure and Recreation (AALR)
>
> National Association for Girls and Women in Sport (NAGWS)
>
> National Association for Sport and Physical Education (NASPE)
>
> National Dance Association (NDA)

1900 Association Drive
Reston, VA 22091
www.aahperd.org

American Association for the Advancement of Science (AAAS)
1200 New York Avenue NW
Washington, DC 20005
www.aaas.org

American Council on Teaching of Foreign Languages (ACTFL)
6 Executive Plaza
Yonkers, NY 10701-6801
www.actfl.org

Association for Supervision and Curriculum Development (ASCD)
1250 N Pitt Street
Alexandria, VA 22314-1453
Journal: *Educational Leadership*
www.ascd.org

Association of Childhood Education International (ACEI)
11141 Georgia Avenue, Suite 200
Wheaton, MD 20902
Journal: *Childhood Education*
www.udel.edu/bateman/acei/

Council for Exceptional Children (CEC)
1920 Association Drive
Reston, VA 22091
Journal: *Exceptional Children and Teaching Exceptional Children*
www.cec.sped.org

International Reading Association (IRA)
800 Barksdale Road
P.O. Box 8139
Newark, DE 199714-8139
Journal: *Reading Teacher*
www.reading.org

International Technology Education Association (ITEA)
1914 Association Drive, Suite 201
Reston, VA 22091-1539
www.itea.org

Music Teachers National Association (MTNA)
441 Vine Street, Suite 505
Cincinnati, OH 45202-2814
www.mtna.org

National Association for Gifted Children (NAGC)
1707 L Street NW
Suite 550
Washington, DC 10036
www.nagc.org

National Association for the Education of Young Children (NAEYC)
1509 16th Street NW
Washington, DC 20036
Journal: *Young Children*
www.naeyc.org.

National Council for the Social Studies (NCSS)
NCSS Headquarters Office
3501 Newark Street NW
Washington, DC 20016
Journal: *Social Education*
www.ncss.org

National Council of Teachers of English (NCTE)
1111 Kenyon Road
Urbana, IL 61801
Journal: *English Journal, Primary Voices, Voices From the Middle*
www.ncte.org

National Council of Teachers of Mathematics (NCTM)
1906 Association Drive
Reston, VA 22091-1593
Journals: *Arithmetic Teacher* and *Mathematics Teacher*
www.nctm.org

National Council on Economic Education (NCEE)
1140 Avenue of the Americas
New York, NY 10036
www.nationalcouncil.org or *www.ncee.net*

National Middle School Association (NMSA)
2600 Corporate Exchange Drive, #370
Columbus, OH 43231
Journal: *National Middle School Journal*
www.nmsa.org

National Science Teachers Association (NSTA)
1840 Wilson Boulevard
Arlington, VA 22201-3000
Journal: *The Science Teacher* and *Science and Children*
www.nsta.org

School Science and Mathematics Association
Bloomsburg University
400 East Second Street
Bloomsburg, PA 17815-1301
www.ssma.org

Teacher Organizations: American Federation of Teachers (AFT)
555 New Jersey Avenue NW
Washington, DC 20001
Journals: *American Educator* and *American Teacher*
www.aft.org

National Education Association (NEA)
1201 16th Street NW
Washington, DC 20036
Journals: *Today's Education* and *NEA Reporter*
www.nea.org

B
State Certification Offices

Alabama
Teacher Education and Certification
State Department of Education
P.O. Box 302101
Montgomery, AL 36130-2101
334-242-9977

Alaska
Certification Analyst
Department of Education
801 West 10th Street, Suite 200
Juneau, AK 99901-1994
907-465-2831

Arizona
Teacher Certification Unit-70016
P.O. Box 6490
Phoenix, AZ 85005-6490
602-542-4367

Arkansas
Teacher Education & Licensure
State Department of Education
4 State Capitol Mall
Little Rock, AR 72201-1071
501-682-4149

California
Commission on Teacher Credentialing
Box 944270
Sacramento, CA 94244-7000
916-445-7254

Colorado
Educator Licensing State Department of Education
201 E Colfax Avenue
Denver, CO 80203
303-866-6628

Connecticut
Bureau of Certification and Professional
Development
State Department of Education, Box 2219
Hartford, CT 06145-2219
860-566-5201

Delaware
Teacher Certification Department of Public
Instruction
P.O. Box 1402
Dover, DE 19903
302-739-4686

District of Columbia
Teacher Education and Certification Branch
Logan Administration Building
215 G Street NE, Room 101A
Washington, DC 20002
202-724-4246

Florida
Bureau of Teacher Certification
Florida Education Center
325 W Gaines, Room 201
Tallahassee, FL 32399-0400
904-488-2317

Georgia
Professional Standards Commission
Certification Section
1454 Twin Towers East
Atlanta, GA 30334
404-657-9000

Hawaii
State of Hawaii
Department of Education
Office of Personnel Services

P.O. Box 2360
Honolulu, HI 96804

Idaho
Certification Division
State Department of Education
P.O. Box 83720
Boise, ID 83720-0027
208-332-6680

Illinois
Illinois State Board of Education
Certification & Placement Section
100 N First Street
Springfield, IL 62777-0001
217-782-4321

Indiana
Indiana Professional Standards Board
Teacher Licensing
251 East Ohio Street, Suite 201
Indianapolis, IN 46204-2133
317-232-9010

Iowa
Board of Educational Examiners
Grimes State Office Building
Des Moines, IA 50319-0147
515-281-3245

Kansas
Certification Specialist
Kansas State Department of Education
Kansas State Education Building
120 SE 10th Avenue
Topeka, KS 66612-1182
913-296-2288

Kentucky
Kentucky Department of Education
Division of Certification
1024 Capital Center Drive
Frankfort, KY 40601
502-573-4606

Louisiana
Louisiana Department of Education
Teacher Certification, Room 700
P.O. Box 94064
Baton Rouge, LA 70804-9064
504-342-3490

Maine
Division of Certification and Placement
Department of Education
State House Station 23

Augusta, ME 04333
207-287-5944

Maryland
Division of Certification 18100
State Department of Education
200 West Baltimore Street
Baltimore, MD 21201
410-767-0412

Massachusetts
Massachusetts Department of Education
Office of Teacher Certification and Credentialling
350 Main Street
Malden, MA 02148
617-388-3300

Michigan
Office of Professional Services and Certification Services
Michigan Department of Education
P.O. Box 3008
Lansing, MI 48909
517-373-3310

Minnesota
Teacher Licensing
State Department of Children, Families and Learning
1500 Highway 36 West
Roseville, MN 55113-4266
651-582-8691

Mississippi
Teacher Certification
State Department of Education
Box 771
Jackson, MS 39205-0771
601-359-3483

Missouri
Teacher Certification
Department of Elementary and Secondary Education
P.O. Box 480
Jefferson City, MO 65102
573-751-3486

Montana
Teacher Certification
Office of Public Instruction
P.O. Box 202501
Helena, MT 59620-2501
406-444-3150

Nebraska
Teacher Certification
State Department of Education
301 Centennial Mall South
Box 94987
Lincoln, NE 68509-4987
800-371-4642

Nevada
Licensure and Certification
Nevada Department of Education
700 East 5th Street
Carson City, NV 89701
702-687-3115

New Hampshire
Bureau of Credentialing
State Department of Education
101 Pleasant Street
Concord, NH 03301
603-271-2407

New Jersey
Office of Licensing and Academic Credentials
CN 503
Trenton, NJ 08625-0503
609-292-2070

New Mexico
Director
Professional Licensure Unit
Education Building
300 Don Gaspar
Santa Fe, NM 87501-2786
505-827-6587

New York
Office of Teaching
University of the State of New York
State Education Department
Albany, NY 12230
518-4740-3901/2/3/4

Buffalo Board of Education
City Hall
65 Niagara Square
Buffalo, NY 14202
716-842-4646

North Carolina
North Carolina Department of Public Instruction
Licensure Section
301 N Wilmington Street
Raleigh, NC 27601-2825
919-733-4125

North Dakota
Education Standards and Practice Board
Teacher Certification
600 E Boulevard Avenue
Bismark, ND 58505-0440
701-328-2264

Ohio
Teacher Education and Certification
State Department of Education
65 S Front Street, Room 1009
Columbus, OH 43215-4183
614-466-3593

Oklahoma
Professional Standards
State Department of Education
2500 N Lincoln Boulevard, Room 211
Oklahoma City, OK 73105-4599
405-521-3337

Oregon
Teacher Standards and Practices Commission
Public Service Building
255 Capitol Street NE, Suite 105
Salem, OR 97310-1332
503-378-3586

Pennsylvania
Bureau of Certification
Department of Education
333 Market Street
Harrisburg, PA 17126-0333
717-787-2967

Rhode Island
Office of Teacher Certification
State Department of Education
Shepard Building
255 Westminster Street
Providence, RI 02903-3400
401-277-4600

South Carolina
Teacher Licensure
State Department of Education
1015 Rutledge Building
1429 Senate Street
Columbia, SC 29201
803-774-8466

South Dakota
Teacher Education and Certification
Division of Education
700 Governors Drive
Pierre, SD 57501-2291
605-773-3553

Tennessee
Office of Teacher Licensing
State Department of Education
5th Floor, Andrew Johnson Tower
710 James Robertson Parkway
Nashville, TN 37243-0377
615-741-1644

Texas
State Board for Educator Certification
1001 Trinity
Austin, TX 78701
512-469-3001

Utah
Certification and Personnel Development Section
State Board of Education
250 E 500 South Street
P.O. Box 144200
Salt Lake City, UT 84114
801-538-7740

Vermont
Licensing Office
Department of Education
120 State Street
Montpelier, VT 05620-2501
802-828-2501

Virginia
Office of Professional Licensure
Department of Education
P.O. Box 2120
Richmond, VA 23216-2120
804-225-2022

Washington
Office of Professional Education
Teacher Education, Licensing and State Board of Education
Old Capitol Building
P.O. Box 47206
Olympia, WA 98504-7206
206-753-6773

West Virginia
State Department of Education
Building 6, Room 337
1900 Kanawha Boulevard E
Charleston, WV 25305-0330
800-982-2378

Wisconsin
Teacher Education, Licensing and Placement
Box 7841
Madison, WI 53707-7841
608-266-1027

Wyoming
2300 Capitol Avenue
Hathaway Building, 2nd Floor
Cheyenne, WY 82002
307-777-6248

C

Job Fair Record Form

School/District/ Contact Person/ Address/Telephone	Received or requested an application	1–3 days: Send a thank-you note	1–7 days: Send all necessary application materials	1–2 weeks: Call to confirm receipt of all application materials	Other information and notes

School/District/ Contact Person/ Address/Telephone	Received or requested an application	1–3 days: Send a thank-you note	1–7 days: Send all necessary application materials	1–2 weeks: Call to confirm receipt of all application materials	Other information and notes

D
Application/Interview Tracking Form

School/District	Date application requested	Date application completed	Date cover letter and résumé sent	Interview date/time/location	Date interview thank-you note sent	Date follow-up phone call made	Contact person/phone number	Other information

School/District	Date application requested	Date application completed	Date cover letter and résumé sent	Interview date/time/ location	Date interview thank-you note sent	Date follow-up phone call made	Contact person/ phone number	Other information

E
Education Resources

Association for Childhood Education International (ACEI)
11501 Georgia Avenue, Suite 315
Wheaton, MD 20902
Phone: (201) 942–2443 or (800) 423–3563
Fax: (301) 942–3012
Contact: Marilyn Gardner, Director of Conferences & Marketing
E-mail: acei@aol.com
www.udel.edu/bateman/acei

Center for Applied Linguistics (CAL)
4646 40th Street NW
Washington, DC 20016–1859
Phone: (202) 362–0700
Fax: (202) 362–3740
E-mail: info@cal.org
www.cal.org

Center for Research on Education, Diversity, and Excellence
University of California at Santa Cruz
1156 High Street
Santa Cruz, CA 95064
Phone: (408) 459–3500
Fax: (408) 459–3502
E-mail: crede@cats.uscs.edu
www.crede.ucsc.edu

Council for Exceptional Children (CEC)
1920 Association Drive
Reston, VA 20191–1589
Phone: (703) 264–9446
Fax: (803) 264–9494
E-mail: service@cec.sped.org
www.cec.sped.org

Culturally and Linguistically Appropriate Services (CLAS)
Early Childhood Research Institute
Children's Research Center
University of Illinois
51 Gerty Drive
Champaign, IL 61820–7498
Phone: (800) 583–4135
Contact: Ron Banks
E-mail: clas@ericps.crc.uiuc.edu
www.clas.uiuc.edu

National Association of Bilingual Education (NABE)
1220 L Street NW, Suite 605
Washington, DC 20006–4818
Phone: (202) 898–1829
Fax: (202) 789–2866
E-mail: nabe@nabe.org
www.nabe.org

National Association for Multicultural Education (NAME)
1511 K Street NW, Suite 430
Washington, DC 20005
Phone: (202) 628–6263
Fax: (202) 628–6264
Contact: Jill Moss Greenberg, National Coordinator
E-mail: nameorg@erols.com
www.nameorg.org

National Association for the Education of Young Children
1509 16th Street
Washington, DC 20036–1426
Phone: (202) 232–8777 or (800) 424–2460
Fax: (202) 328–1846
Contact: Pat Spahr, Information Services Director
E-mail: pubaV@naeyc.org
www.naeyc.org

National Black Child Development Institute
1023 15th Street NW, Suite 600
Washington, DC 20005
Phone: (202) 387–1281
Fax: (202) 234–1738
E-mail: moreinfo@nbcdi.org
www.nbcdi.org

National Clearinghouse for Bilingual Education (NCBE) Links
The George Washington University
2011 Eye Street NW, Suite 200
Washington, DC 20006
Phone: (202) 467–0867
Fax: (202) 467–4283
Contact: Andrea Todd, Research Associate
E-mail: askncbe@ncbe.gwu.edu
www.ncbe.gwu.edu/links/bies/

National Early Childhood Technical Assistance System
500 NationsBank Plaza
137 E Franklin Street
Chapel Hill, NC 275144–3628
Phone: (919) 962–2001
Fax: (919) 966–7463
E-mail: nectas@unc.edu
www.nectas.unc.edu

National Information Center for Children and Youth with Disabilities
P.O. Box 1492
Washington, DC 20013–1492
Phone: (800) 695–0285 or (202) 884–8200
Fax: (202) 884–8441
E-mail: nichy@aed.org
www.nichcy.org

Office of Special Education
University of Virginia
Curry School of Education
www.curry.edschool.virginia.edu/go/specialed

Parent Advocacy Coalition for Educational Rights Center
4826 Chicago Avenue S
Minneapolis, MN 55417–1098
Phone: (612) 827–2966
Fax: (612) 827–3065
Contact: Paula F. Goldberg, Executive Director
E-mail: pacer@pacer.org
www.pacer.org

F
International Job Search

The Educational Resources Information Center (ERIC)
www.ericae.net

U.S. Department of State, Family Liaison Office, Educational Services
www.state.gov/www/flo/education.html

U.S. Department of Education
www.ed.gov

Association for the Advancement of International Education
www.aaie.org

Department of Defense Schools
www.odedodea.edu

International Schools Services (ISS)
www.ISS.edu

ED-U-LINK Services
www.edulink.com

Near East South Asia Council of Overseas Schools (NESA)
www.nesa.com

The Mediterranean Association of International Schools (MAIS)
www.mais-web.org

European Council of International Schools (ECIS)
www.ecis.org

East Asia Regional Council of Overseas Schools (EARCOS)
www.earcos.org

Central and Eastern European Schools Association (CEESA)
www.ceesa.org

Association of American Schools in South America (AASSA)
info@aassa.com

Association of American Schools of Central America, Columbia, Caribbean and Mexico (Tri-Association)
webmaster@tri-association.org

G
Educational Web Sites

A Guide to Maximizing Learning in Small Groups
*www.cs.ukc.ac.uk/national/CSDN/edu_resources/
small_group_learning.html*

A Model for Case Analysis and Problem Solving
web.cba.neu.edu/~ewertheim/introd/cases.html

Atlapedia Online
www.atlapedia.com/index.html

Alternative Assessment in Practice Database
www.cse.ucla.edu/CRESST/Sample/AAIP. PDF

American Association of University Women
www.aauw.org/texthome.html

American Historical Association
www.theaha.org/

Ask ERIC
ericir.syr.edu/

Ask ERIC Lesson Plans
ericir.syr.edu/Virtual/Lessons/

Assessment and Evaluation of the Internet
eric-ba024.umd.edu/nintbodO.htm

Authentic Assessment
www.nwrel.org/assessment/toolkit98/a2303.pdfl

Balch Institute for Ethnic Studies
www.balchinstitute.org/

Best Practices for Creative Teachers
www.leading-learning.co.nz/

Booklet Helps Parents Help Kids Learn Math
www.ed.gov/pubs/parents/Math/

Center for Civic Education
www.civiced.org

Center for Civic Education
www.sscnet.ucla.edu/nchs

Center for Migration Studies
www.cmsny.org/

Center for the Prevention of School Violence
www.ncsu.edu/cpsv/

CHCP Golden Legacy Curriculum
www.dnai.com/~rutledge/CHCP_legacy2.html

Classroom Connect
www.classroom.com/

Classroom Materials
www.historychannel.com/class/teach/teach.html

ClassroomDirect.com
www.classroomdirect.com/

CNN Newsroom
lc.byuh.edu/CNN_N/CNN_N.html

Constructivist Project Design Guide
jawbone.clarkston. webnet, edu/pages/construct.html

Council of Chief State School Officers (CCSSO)
www.ccsso.org/seamenu.html

County Outline Maps
www.lib.utexas.edu/maps/county_outline.html

Creative and Critical Thinking
*curry.edschool.virgina.edu/curry/class/Museums/
Teacher_Line/creativethinking.html*

**Cross-Age Tutoring (Different from previous
address)**
eric.uoregon.edu/publications/digests/digest079.html

Crossroads: A K-16 American History Curriculum
ericir.syr.edu/Virtual/Lessons/crossroads/

**Department of Education: What's New on DOE®s
Web?**
http://www.ed.gov/News/

Discovery Channel School
www.school.discovery.com/

Education Resource Organizations Directory
www.ed.gov/Programs/EROD/

Education Week
www.edweek.org/

Education World
www.education-world.com/

Educational Extension Systems
www.simcoe.igs.net/homathtutor/ess.html

Envirolink
www.envirolink.org/

Equity Online
www.edc.org/WomensEquity/

ERIC Clearinghouse for Social Studies
www.indiana.edu/-ssdc/eric_chess.html

ERIC Clearinghouse on Assessment and Evaluation
www.ericae.net/majn.html

ESL Cafe
www.eslcafe.com

Federal Resources for Educational Excellence
www.ed.gov/free/

For Teachers Only
www.forteachersonly.com/

Franklin Institute Education Directory
sln.fi.edu/tfi/hotlists/hotlists.html

Geographic Resources for Teachers
www.geocities.com/RainForest/1894/

Geography
eduplace.com/ss/

Geography Education Standards Projects
www.prb.org/Content/NavigationMenu/PRB/ Educators/Teaching_Standards.htm

George Mason University Library
library.gmu.edu/

Gifted Students
www.kidsource.com/kidsource/pages/ed.gifted.html

Gifted Students -archive of articles
www.edweek.org/context/topics/issuespage.cfm?id=33

Gifted Students with disabilities, exceptional students
www.cec.sped.org/

Great Globe Gallery
www.fpsol.com/gems/geography.html

History Buff Home Page
www.historybuff.com

Horus' Web Links to History Resources
ucr.edu/h-gig/horuslinks.html

How Far Is It?
www.indo.com/distance/

How Stuff Works
www.howstuffworks.com/index.htm

Internet Resources for Students of Afro-American History
www.libraries.rutgers.edu/rul/rr/gateway/research guides/history/afrores.shtml

Invention Dimension
web.mit.edu/invent/

J.L. Hammett Co.
www.hammett.com/

K-12 Curriculum Software of Social Studies
www.execpc.com/~dboals/k-12a.html#k-12% SOFTWARE

Language Development Strategies
www.lalc.kl2.ca.us/laep/smart/Sunrise/lang.html

Learn2.com
www.learn2.com/

Learning Disabilities
www.ld.org/index.html

Learning Disabilities "Tips for Teachers"
www.ld.org/info/tips/teacher_index.cfm

Learning Disabilities Resources
www.ldresources.com

Learning Disabilities Strategies
www.ldonline.org

Lesson Plans Library
ali.apple.com/edres/techleam/lessonmenu.shtml

Let's Learn
www.lets-learn.com

Library of Congress of American Memory
lcwebwebboook.loc.gov/ammen/

Map Machine
www.nationalgeographic.com/resources/ngo/maps/

Mapmaker, Mapmaker, Make Me A Map
www.education-world.com/awards/past/r0996-17.shtml

Mathematics
www.mathforum.orgl

Mathematics
www.nctm.org/standards2000/status-timeline.html

Mathematics
*http://www.nctm.org/about/frequently.requested/nctm.faq
    .version1.html*

Mathematics
*www.standards-
    e.nctm.org/1.0/normal/standards/frntTab.html*

Mid-continent Regional Educational Library
www.mcrel.org

Multiple Intelligences
www.edwebproject.org/

Multiple Intelligences
www.ascd.org

Multiple Intelligences
www.ascd.org/readingroom/edlead/9709/checkley.html

National Archives of American History
www.thehistorynet.com/THNarchives/American History

National Center for History in the Schools
www.sscnet.ucla.edu/nchs/

National Clearinghouse for Bilingual Education
www.ncbe.gwu.edu/

National Council on Economic Education
http://www.ncee.net/

National Council for History Education
www.history.org/nche/main.html

National Council for the Social Studies
www.ncss.org/online/home.html

National Council on Geographic Education
www.2.oneonta.edu/~baumanpr/ncge/rstf.htm/

National Library of Education
www.ed.gov/NLE/

**National Science Teachers Association (NSTA)
    resources**
www.nsta.org/recommends

**NEPTUNES WEB of Oceanography Plans for
    Social Studies**
*www.cnmoc.navy.mil/educate/neptune/lesson/
    social/social.html*

PBS TeacherSource
www.pbs.org/teachersource/

Performance Assessment Clearinghouse
arc.missouri.edu/pa/

Performance Assessment Homepage
www.parcinfo.org/

Performance Assessment Internet Resources
*www.geocities.com/EnchantedForest/3457/
    performance/Pba.htm*

Performance Assessment Resources Page
www.members.aol.com/arcalif/

Puzzles
www.freepuzzles.com

School Works Social Studies
socialstudies.com/

Science Fair Central
www.school.discovery.com/sciencefaircentral

Scientific Learning
www.scientificlearning.com/

Scientific Learning
www.brainconnection.com

Seeing, Hearing, and Smelling the World
www.hhmi.org/senses/

Social Studies
*social studies.com/c/@E5CJv4Nl.dEqc/Pages/
    communityworks.html*

Social Studies Education Network
busboy.sped.ukans.edu/-soess/index.html

Social Studies Sources
www.education.indiana.edu/-socialst/

Standards-related materials
www.icsr.org/standards-discuss/0063.html

Steps to Designing Performance Assessments
www.oswego.edu/~mdavis2/assessment.htm

Teacher Motivation
www.dailyapples.com

Teacher's Treasure Trove
http://thetrove.com/

Teachers Helping Teachers
*www.edu-orchard.net/PROFESS/MANDEL/
    mandell1.html*

**Teachers of English to Speakers of other
    Languages**
www.tesol.edu

Teaching ideas and materials for inquiry
www.researchpaper.com

Teaching ideas and materials for inquiry
www.hccs.cc.tx.us/system/Library/Center/lobby.html

Teaching ideas and materials for inquiry
www.nap.edu/html/inquiry_addendum/ch8.html

Teaching ideas and materials for inquiry
www.enc.org/topics/inquiry

Teaching ideas and materials for inquiry
www.nap.edu/html/inquiry_addendum/ch5.html

Teaching Strategies and Cooperative Learning
www.ku.edu/~cte/resources/teachingtips/cooperative.html

Teaching Thinking Skills
www.nwrel.org/scpd/sirs/6/cuI l.html

Technology
www.aarp.org/comptech/

Technology and Learning Online
www.techlearning.com/

The Annenberg/CPB exhibits
www.learner.org/exhibits/

The Exploratorium
www.exploratorium.edu

The JASON Project
www.jasonproject.org/

The Lab
www.abc.net.au/science

The Smithsonian Institution
www.si.edu/

The Teacher Group
www.groups.yahoo. com/group/abta

The Why Files
www.whyfiles.org

Thought and Language
www.msu.edu/~atl/

U.S. Geological Survey
www.usgs.gov/

U.S. Mint H.I.P. Pocket Change
www.usmint.gov

UNICEF USA
www.unicefusa.org/infoactiv/educat.html

Upper Midwest Women's History Center
*www.library.wisc.edu/libraries/WomensStudies/
midwhist.htm*

US Bureau of the Census
www/census.gov/

Welcome to ESL Net
www.esl.net/

Women in Science
www.kings.edu/womens_history/emscience.html

Women's Studies
www.academicinfo. net/women.html

Women's Studies
*www.library.upenn.edu/resources/interdiscipline/gender/
women/women.html*

Women's Studies of Primarily US
www.lib.vt.edu/subjects/wome/

Index

DATE DUE

PRINTED IN U.S.A.

GAYLORD